Psychology in Family and Child Law

Psychology in Family and Child Law

C L van Rooyen

B Mahendra

Family Law

Published by Family Law
A publishing imprint of Jordan Publishing Limited
21 St Thomas Street
Bristol BS1 6JS

Reprinted December 2008

British Library Cataloguing-in-Publication Data

A catalogue record for this book is available from the British Library.

ISBN 978 1 84661 067 7

Typeset by Letterpart Ltd, Reigate, Surrey

Printed in Great Britain by CPI Antony Rowe, Chippenham, Wiltshire

INTRODUCTION

It is by now well appreciated that family and child law play an increasingly important part in society. The need for expert assessments in the course of family and child care proceedings grows apace. One of the numerous types of experts involved in these proceedings is the psychologist who is called upon to assess both adult and child parties. A companion volume to this book, *Adult Psychiatry in Family and Child Law*, was published in 2006. Like its congener, the present work has been prompted by the perceived need to bridge the gap – in knowledge as well as in attitudes – that still appears to exist between the family and child law practitioner on the one hand and the psychological expert on the other.

Psychology deals with behaviour, the term used in its widest sense. As such, virtually all aspects of the behaviour involving the spouse, partner, parent and child become susceptible to psychological study and analysis. An individual grows through several phases to reach adult life. Aspects of behaviour – both normal and abnormal – may lead to difficulties which might come to be identified in the course of family and child care proceedings. To help the non-expert practitioner gain an appreciation of both normal and abnormal behaviour patterns the first part of the book is dedicated to a study of those aspects of growth and development during childhood and adolescence that are relevant in these proceedings. The second part of the book deals with the psychological issues concerning children and adolescents. The final part considers those aspects of adult behaviour which are relevant in these proceedings. It is inevitable that there will be overlap between what engages the psychologist and what interests the psychiatrist (a medically qualified expert dealing with the clinical aspects of abnormal behaviour), and this book attempts to reflect that shared interest.

A couple of points need to be stressed in regard to psychological assessments undertaken in the course of family and child care proceedings. Firstly, unless a psychological evaluation has been expressly undertaken in respect of some specific behaviour (eg marital relationships, parenting etc), it is not appropriate to try to extend psychological findings made on general examination, without doing more, to specific situations. Thus, it is wrong to take a finding of, say, learning disabilities as diagnosed in one or more of the parties and to conclude that such a diagnosis, in itself, impairs in some way the capabilities necessary to be a competent spouse, partner or parent. There are varying degrees of learning disabilities and many who suffer from this disorder are found in practice to be perfectly capable of being adequate spouses, partners or parents. Conversely, individuals possessed of normal intellectual attributes may well be found wanting when their capacity to function as adequate spouses, partners or parents is evaluated. Once a diagnosis is made, further analysis and assessment is usually needed in order to answer questions arising in regard to any suspicion that a particular function in the individual concerned has been compromised. To do anything else is to engage in the exercise of prejudice.

Secondly, it is common to find the results of psychological assessments given in the form of numerical measures where quantitative tests or ratings have been used in the evaluations carried out. It is of the greatest importance for these test results to be used in conjunction with the findings on clinical evaluation. The test scores are capable of yielding false positive and negative results and major errors in assessment may follow the blind acceptance of these scores, which occasionally happens as lay persons appear to be bewitched by the magic of numbers. The situation is analogous to that found in clinical medicine where laboratory test results have validity only against the background of clinical findings. If test results are used in isolation there is risk of being led into error, occasionally even into disaster.

A further point may also be usefully made. For the sake of completeness the full range of psychological therapies has been considered in this book, even if only in outline. It is not often appreciated by those involved in these proceedings that any form of psychological therapy requires time to prove its effectiveness. It is a matter of judgment to decide if a therapy deemed appropriate for any condition is capable of being effectively deployed within the timescales normally envisaged within these proceedings. It is a matter also of common sense to attempt to factor in delays that are inevitable these days when resources are short and waiting times long. It is also not always appreciated that with most psychological therapies the potentialities of the individual called upon to follow some recommended treatment needs also to be considered. Not all individuals referred for psychological treatment are found suitable to follow a particular treatment even if that were in general terms appropriate for the condition in question. Some individuals will drop out of a treatment regime. Some others may not benefit. It is to mislead the court if these factors are not taken into consideration in making a recommendation for treatment or when giving a prognosis.

There has been no attempt made to produce yet another textbook of psychology. Several standard works already exist for study by those specialising in this field and for consultation by any interested person. Rather, in this book, an attempt has been made to provide a readable and yet reasonably comprehensive outline of the salient features of psychological issues for lawyers and other professionals involved in family and child law practice. Our experience suggests that there is a clear need for a source of basic psychological information to be readily available to those professionals who are not expert in psychology. Fairly substantial detail is therefore made available in respect of the common psychological problems but the emphasis has not been on detail but – being mindful that this work is directed primarily at a non-expert readership – on understanding.

Family and, in particular, child proceedings attract a wide range of professionals who each contribute their particular expertise. These professionals include judges, lawyers, social workers and those assessing parenting skills and children's guardians. Medical professionals such as paediatricians, adult psychiatrists and child and adolescent psychiatrists are also commonly involved. It is hoped these professionals will find this work of use to them in their activities in the field of family and child law.

C L van Rooyen
B Mahendra
September 2007

CONTENTS

GLOSSARY

Addiction The state of being both physically and psychologically dependent on a substance.

Adjustment disorder A psychiatric disorder marked by inappropriate or inadequate responses to a change in life circumstances. Depression following retirement from work is an example of an adjustment disorder. A type of condition with emotional or behavioural symptoms that occurs in response to identifiable stress in a person's life.

Affective disorder (also called mood disorder) A category of mental health problems that includes a disturbance in mood, usually profound sadness or apathy, euphoria or irritability, such as is found in the disorder depressive illness.

Affective flattening A loss or lack of emotional expressiveness. It is sometimes called blunted or restricted affect.

Agoraphobia A Greek word that literally means 'fear of the marketplace'. This anxiety disorder is characterised by a fear of open, public places or of being in crowds. Agoraphobics often experience panic attacks in a place or situation from which escape may be difficult or embarrassing.

Amnesic disorder (also called amnesia) A brain disorder marked by memory impairment.

Anger The experience of intense annoyance that inspires hostile and aggressive thoughts and actions.

Anorexia nervosa (also called anorexia) An eating disorder characterised by low body weight, a distorted body image, an extreme aversion to food and an intense fear of gaining weight.

Antidepressants Medication that treats depression as well as other psychiatric disorders.

Antisocial personality A personality characterised by attitudes and behaviours at odds with society's customs and moral standards, including engaging in illegal acts.

Antisocial personality disorder A disorder characterised by a disregard for the feelings, property, authority and respect of others, for an individual's own personal gain. This behaviour may include violent or aggressive and destructive actions toward other people without a sense of remorse or guilt.

Anxiety A feeling of unease and fear of impending danger characterised by physical symptoms such as a rapid heart rate, sweating, trembling and feelings of stress. In contrast to fear, the danger or threat in anxiety is imagined, not real.

Anxiety disorders Conditions characterised by high levels of anxiety. Currently five different anxiety disorders are recognised: generalised anxiety disorder, obsessive-compulsive disorder, panic disorder, post traumatic stress disorder and social phobia.

Apnoea A cessation of breathing.

Attention-deficit disorder (ADD) and attention-deficit/hyperactivity disorder (ADHD) A behaviour disorder, usually first diagnosed in childhood, that is characterised by inattention, impulsivity and, in some cases, hyperactivity.

Autistic disorder (also called autism) A neurological and developmental disorder that usually appears during the first 3 years of life. A child with autism appears to live in his/her own world, demonstrating little interest in others and a lack of social awareness. The focus of an autistic child is a consistent routine and includes also an interest in repeating odd and peculiar behaviours. Autistic children often have problems in communication, avoid eye contact and show limited attachment to others.

Automatic thoughts Thoughts that automatically come to mind when a particular situation occurs. Cognitive behavioural therapy seeks to challenge automatic thoughts.

Avoidant personality disorder People with avoidant personality disorder avoid situations with any potential for conflict or rejection and are disturbed by their own social isolation, withdrawal and inability to form close interpersonal relationships.

Behavioural therapy A form of psychotherapy that focuses on modifying observable problematic behaviours by manipulating the individual's environment.

Binge eating disorder A disorder that resembles bulimia nervosa and is characterised by episodes of excessive overeating (or bingeing). It differs from bulimia because sufferers do not purge their bodies of the excess food via such means as vomiting, laxative abuse or diuretic abuse.

Bipolar disorder A mood disorder (formerly called manic-depressive disorder) that is characterised by episodes of major depression and mania.

Borderline personality disorder People with this disorder present instability in their perceptions of themselves, and have difficulty maintaining stable relationships. Moods may also be inconsistent, but never neutral – their sense of reality is always seen in 'black and white'. Adults with borderline personality disorder often seek care through the manipulation of others, frequently leaving them feeling empty, angry and abandoned, which may lead to desperate and impulsive behaviour.

Brief psychotic disorder An acute, short-term episode of psychosis lasting no longer than 1 month. This disorder may occur in response to a stressful event.

Bulimia nervosa (also called bulimia) A condition characterised by binge eating followed by extreme measures to undo the binge (often by inducing vomiting).

Burnout An emotional condition, marked by tiredness, loss of interest, or frustration, that interferes with job performance. Burnout is usually regarded as the result of prolonged stress.

Child and adolescent psychiatrist A psychiatrist who specialises in the evaluation, diagnosis and treatment of mental disorders in children and adolescents.

Child psychotherapy, clinical psychology and psychiatry are well established disciplines using psychotherapy to address children's severe mental health and personality difficulties.

Chronic A term used to describe long-term persistence. In some mental health disorders, chronic is specified as persisting for 6 months or longer.

Clinical depression When depression is serious enough to require treatment it is called clinical depression. When the symptoms are more severe, an individual is said to be suffering from major depression. This condition may tend to be episodic in nature.

Cognitive-behavioural therapy A method of treating psychiatric disorders based on the idea that the way we think about the world and ourselves (our cognitions) affects our emotions and behaviour.

Cognitive disorders The class of disorders consisting of significant impairment of cognition or memory that represents a marked deterioration from a previous level of functioning.

Cognitive restructuring The process of replacing maladaptive thought patterns with constructive thoughts and beliefs.

Cognitive therapy A method of treating psychiatric disorders that focuses on revising a person's thinking, perceptions, attitudes and beliefs. A psychotherapy technique designed to help people change their attitudes, and patterns of thinking.

Compensation A process of psychologically counterbalancing perceived weaknesses by emphasising strength in other areas. This is considered a defence mechanism.

Compulsion An uncontrollable, repetitive and unwanted urge to perform an act. A compulsive act is a defence against unacceptable ideas and desires, and failure to perform the act leads to anxiety.

Compulsive gambling disorder An impulse control disorder in which an individual cannot resist gambling despite repeated losses.

Compulsive overeating A tendency toward bingeing on large amounts of food, followed by experiencing extreme guilt.

Cyclothymia A mood disorder of at least 2 years' duration viewed as a mild variant of bipolar disorder. Cyclothymia is characterised by numerous periods of mild depressive symptoms not sufficient in duration or severity to meet the criteria for major depression interspersed with periods of hypomania.

Dependence A state in which a person requires a steady concentration in the body of a particular substance to avoid experiencing withdrawal symptoms.

Depersonalisation A dissociative symptom in which the patient feels that his or her body is unreal, is changing, or is dissolving.

Derealisation A dissociative symptom in which the external environment is perceived as unreal.

Detoxification A process whereby an addict is withdrawn from a substance.

Dissociation A reaction to trauma in which the mind splits off certain aspects of the trauma from conscious awareness. Dissociation can affect the patient's memory, sense of reality, and sense of identity.

Delirium An acute but temporary disturbance of consciousness marked by confusion, difficulty paying attention, delusions, hallucinations, or restlessness. Delirium may be caused by drug intoxication, high fever resulting from infection, head trauma, brain tumours, kidney or liver failure, or various metabolic disturbances. A condition in which changes in cognition, including a disturbance in consciousness, occur over a relatively short period of time.

Delusional disorder Individuals with delusional disorder suffer from long-term, complex delusions that fall into one of six categories: persecutory, grandiose, jealousy, erotomanic, somatic, or mixed.

Delusions An unshakeable belief in something untrue which cannot be explained by religious or cultural factors. These irrational beliefs defy normal reasoning and remain firm even when overwhelming proof is presented to refute them. Beliefs such as delusions of grandeur that are thought to be true by the person having them, but where these beliefs are wrong. Individuals with delusions cannot be convinced that their beliefs are incorrect.

Dementia A group of mental disorders involving a general loss of intellectual abilities, including memory, judgment and abstract thinking. Dementias may be associated with poor impulse control and personality changes.

Denial The refusal to accept reality and to act as if a painful event, thought or feeling did not exist.

Dependent personality disorder Individuals with this disorder rely heavily on others for validation and fulfilment of basic needs. They often lack self-confidence, have difficulty making decisions and are unable to properly care for themselves.

Depression A mood disturbance characterised by feelings of sadness, loneliness, despair, low self-esteem, worthlessness, withdrawal from social interaction, and sleep and eating disturbances.

Diagnosis The determination by a health care professional of the cause of a person's problems, usually by identifying both the disease process and the agent responsible.

Dyslexia A reading disorder. A child with dyslexia reads below the expected level given his/her age, school grade and intelligence.

Dysthymia (also known as dysthymic disorder) A mood disorder characterised by chronic mildly depressed or irritable mood often accompanied by a loss of interest or pleasure in normal activities that is present most of the time for at least 2 years. Many individuals with dysthymia experience major depressive episodes at times.

Eating disorders Disorders characterised by abnormal eating behaviours and a distorted body image.

Electroconvulsive therapy Therapy for mood disorders that involves passing electrical current through the brain in order to create a brief convulsion. A treatment method usually reserved for very severe or psychotic depression or manic states that are not responsive to treatment by medication. A low-voltage alternating electric current is sent to the brain on an anaesthetised patient to induce a convulsion or seizure, which has a therapeutic effect.

Endorphins Chemicals in the brain that influence moods and the experience of pain.

Factitious disorders Conditions in which physical and/or psychological symptoms are fabricated in order to place an individual in the role of a patient or sick person in need of help.

Free association A technique used in psychoanalysis in which the patient allows thoughts and feelings to emerge without trying to organise or censor them.

Ganser's syndrome An unusual factitious disorder characterised by dissociative symptoms and absurd answers given to direct questions.

Generalised anxiety disorder (GAD) A psychiatric condition in which the main symptoms are chronic worry and fear that seems to have no real cause. There may be many associated physical reactions, such as trembling, jitteriness, sweating, lightheadedness and irritability.

Hallucinations False or distorted sensory experiences that appear to be real perceptions to the person experiencing them. A strong perception of an event or object when no such situation is present may occur in any of the senses (ie visual, auditory, gustatory, olfactory or tactile).

Histrionic personality disorder People with this disorder are overly conscious of their appearance, are constantly seeking attention, exaggerate emotions and often behave dramatically.

Hostility The disposition to inflict harm on another person and/or the actual infliction of harm, either physically or emotionally.

Hypomania An episode of illness that resembles mania, but is less intense and less disabling. Hypomania is characterised by a euphoric mood, unrealistic optimism, increased speech and activity, and a decreased need for sleep.

Intoxication The desired mental, physical, or emotional state produced by a substance.

Identity Self-knowledge about one's characteristics or personality. A sense of self.

Impulse-control disorders Disorders characterised by the inability to inhibit impulses that may be harmful to oneself or others.

Insomnia Difficulty falling asleep or staying asleep when one has the opportunity to be sleeping.

Intermittent explosive disorder A personality disorder in which an individual is prone to intermittent explosive episodes of aggression during which he or she causes bodily harm or destroys property.

Interpersonal therapy A form of psychotherapy that focuses on a patient's interpersonal relationships; it may be used to treat depression.

Interpretation A verbal comment made by the analyst in response to the patient's free association. It is intended to help the patient gain new insights.

Kleptomania An impulse control disorder in which one steals objects that are of little or no value.

Learning disorder When a child's academic ability is below what is expected for the child's age, schooling and level of intelligence. A learning difficulty is usually identified in reading, arithmetic or writing.

Major depressive disorder (also known as clinical depression) A major mood disorder characterised by one or more (recurrent) episodes of major depression, with or without full recovery between episodes.

Maladaptive Unsuitable or counterproductive; for example, maladaptive behaviour is behaviour that is inappropriate to a given situation.

Malingering Pretending to be ill in order to be relieved of an unwanted duty or obtain some other obvious benefit.

Mania An episode usually seen in the course of bipolar disorder characterised by a marked increase in energy, extreme elation, impulsivity, irritability, rapid speech, nervousness, distractibility and/or poor judgment. During manic episodes, some patients also experience hallucinations or delusions.

Manic depression (also known as bipolar disorder) Classified as a type of affective disorder (or mood disorder) that goes beyond the mundane or ordinary ups and downs. Manic depression is characterised by periodic episodes of extreme elation, elevated mood, or irritability (also called mania) and is contrasted with periodic, classic depressive symptoms.

Mood disorder (also known as affective disorder) A category of mental health problems including a disturbance in mood, usually profound sadness or apathy, euphoria or irritability, such as the disorder major depression.

Munchausen by proxy A factitious disorder in children produced by a parent or other caregiver.

Munchausen syndrome A factitious disorder in which the patient's symptoms are manufactured, dramatised and exaggerated.

Narcissistic personality disorder People with this personality disorder have severely overly inflated feelings of self-worth, grandiosity and superiority over others.

Negative symptoms Symptoms of schizophrenia characterised by the absence or elimination of certain behaviours. DSM-IV specifies three negative symptoms, namely, affective flattening, poverty of speech, and loss of will or initiative.

Neurosis A mental and emotional disorder that affects only part of the personality and is accompanied by a significantly less distorted perception of reality than in psychosis.

Neurotransmitters In the brain these chemicals transfer messages from one nerve cell to another and affect mental states.

Obsessive-compulsive disorder (OCD) An anxiety disorder in which a person has an unreasonable thought, fear or worries that he/she tries to manage through ritualised activity. Frequently occurring disturbing thoughts or images are called obsessions, and the rituals performed to try to prevent or dispel them are called compulsions. Individuals with OCD often become uncomfortable in situations that are beyond their control and have difficulty maintaining positive, healthy interpersonal relationships as a result.

Panic disorder (also called panic attacks) An anxiety disorder characterised by chronic, repeated and unexpectedly intense periods of fear when there is no specific cause for the fear. In between panic attacks, patients with panic disorder worry excessively about when and where the next attack may occur. Panic disorder may be accompanied by agoraphobia.

Paranoia An unfounded or exaggerated distrust of others, sometimes reaching delusional proportions.

Paranoid personality disorder Individuals with this disorder are often cold, distant and unable to form close, interpersonal relationships. Often overly suspicious of their surroundings, individuals with paranoid personality disorder generally cannot see their role in conflict situations and often project their feelings of paranoia as anger onto others.

Phobia An uncontrollable, irrational and persistent fear of a specific object, situation or activity.

Positive symptoms Symptoms of schizophrenia that are characterised by the production or presence of behaviours that are grossly abnormal or excessive, including hallucinations and thought disorder. DSM-IV subdivides positive symptoms into psychotic and disorganised.

Post-traumatic stress disorder (PTSD) A specific form of anxiety that begins after a life-threatening event, such as rape, a natural disaster, or combat-related trauma. A debilitating condition that is related to a past terrifying physical or emotional experience causing the person who survived the event to have persistent, frightening thoughts and memories or flashbacks of the ordeal. Patients with PTSD often feel chronically emotionally numb.

Poverty of speech A negative symptom of schizophrenia, characterised by brief and empty replies to questions. It should not be confused with shyness or reluctance to talk.

Psychotic disorder A mental disorder characterised by delusions, hallucinations, or other symptoms of lack of contact with reality. The schizophrenias are psychotic disorders.

Prognosis The patient's chances for recovery; a medical assessment of the probable course and outcome of a disease, based on the recorded history of the disease, the physician's own experience of treating the disease, and the patient's general condition and age.

Projection The attribution of one's undesired impulses onto another. This is considered a defence mechanism.

Psychiatrist A medical doctor who specialises in the treatment of mental, emotional or behavioural problems.

Psychodynamic An approach to psychotherapy based on the interplay of conscious and unconscious factors in the patient's mind. Psychoanalysis is one type of psychodynamic therapy.

Psychodynamic therapy A branch of psychotherapy that deals with the psychology of mental or emotional forces or processes developed in early childhood and their effects on behaviour and mental states. A therapeutic approach that assumes dysfunctional or unwanted behaviour is caused by unconscious, internal conflicts and focuses on gaining insight into these motivations.

Psychologist A specialist in the diagnosis and treatment of mental and emotional problems. Their role with patients usually involves testing, counselling and psychotherapy.

Psychomotor agitation Disturbed physical and mental processes (eg fidgeting, wringing of hands, racing thoughts); a symptom of major depressive disorder.

Psychomotor retardation Slowed physical and mental processes (eg, slowed thinking, walking, and talking); a symptom of major depressive disorder.

Psychosocial Involving both psychological and social aspects, or relating social conditions to mental health.

Psychotherapy The treatment of mental and emotional disorders using psychological methods, such as talk therapy.

Pyromania An impulse control disorder in which one is impelled to set fires.

Rage A state of intense emotional experience associated with uncontrolled destructive behaviour.

Reaction formation The converting of wishes or impulses that are perceived to be dangerous into opposite thoughts. This is considered a defence mechanism.

Regression The process in which the patient reverts to earlier or less mature feelings and behaviours. The reversion to an earlier stage of development in the face of unacceptable impulses. This is considered a defence mechanism.

Relapse The recurrence of a disease after apparent recovery, or the return of symptoms after remission.

Relaxation technique A technique used to relieve stress. Exercise, biofeedback, hypnosis, and meditation are all effective relaxation tools. Relaxation techniques are used in cognitive behavioural therapy to teach patients new ways of coping with stressful situations.

Repression The blocking of unacceptable impulses from consciousness. This is considered a defence mechanism.

Schizoaffective disorder Schizophrenic symptoms occurring concurrently with a major depressive and/or manic episode.

Schizophrenia A complex mental health disorder involving a severe, chronic and disabling disturbance of the brain. The symptoms may include hallucinations, delusions, disorganised thinking, disorganised speech and behaviour and inappropriate or flattened affect (a lack of emotions) that seriously hampers the afflicted individual's social and occupational functioning.

Schizophreniform disorder A short-term variation of schizophrenia that has a total duration of 1 to 6 months.

Schizoid personality disorder People with this disorder are often cold, distant, introverted and have an intense fear of intimacy and closeness. They are often so absorbed in their own thinking and daydreaming that they stay detached from others and reality.

Seasonal affective disorder (SAD) A mood disorder characterised by depression related to a certain season of the year, especially winter.

Sedatives A group of drugs used to produce sedation (calmness). Sedatives include sleeping pills and anti-anxiety drugs.

Serotonin A chemical messenger in the brain believed to play a role in mood regulation. A chemical that transmits nerve impulses in the brain (neurotransmitter), causes blood vessels to narrow at sites of bleeding and stimulates smooth muscle movement in the intestines. It is believed to be involved in controlling states of consciousness and mood.

Self-esteem Feelings about one's self.

Shared psychotic disorder Also known as *folie a deux* (when two individuals are involved); a shared psychotic disorder which is an uncommon disorder in which the same delusion is shared by two (or more) individuals.

Social phobia An anxiety disorder in which a person has significant anxiety and discomfort related to a fear of being embarrassed, humiliated, or scorned by others in social or performance situations.

Somatisation disorder A chronic disorder characterised by multiple, often long-standing physical complaints such as aches and pains.

Specific phobia A type of phobia characterised by extreme fear of an object or situation that is not harmful under normal conditions.

Street drug A substance purchased from a drug dealer; may be a legal substance sold illicitly (without a prescription, and not for medical use), or may be a substance that it is illegal to possess.

Stress management A category of popularised programmes and techniques intended to help people deal more effectively with stress.

Stressor A stimulus, or event, that provokes a stress response in an organism. Stressors can be categorised as acute or chronic, and as external or internal to the organism.

Suicidal behaviour Actions taken by one who is considering or preparing to cause his own death.

Suicidal ideation Having thoughts of suicide or wanting to take one's life.

Suicide The intentional taking of one's life.

Suicide attempt An intentional act aimed at taking one's life that is unsuccessful in causing death.

Supportive therapy Psychotherapy that focuses on the management and resolution of current difficulties and life decisions using the individual's strengths and available resources.

Symptom breakthrough The return of symptoms in the course of either the continuation or maintenance phase of treatment.

Tolerance A phenomenon whereby a drug user becomes physically accustomed to a particular dose of a substance, and requires increasing dosages in order to obtain the same effects.

Tourette's syndrome A tic disorder characterised by repeated involuntary movements and uncontrollable vocal sounds. This disorder usually begins during childhood or early adolescence.

Transference The process that develops during psychoanalytic work during which the patient redirects feelings about early life figures towards the analyst.

Trauma In the context of severe stress disorders a disastrous or life-threatening event.

Trichotillomania An impulse or compulsion to pull out one's own hair.

Tricyclic antidepressants Drugs used in the treatment of clinical depression. Tricyclic refers to the presence of three rings in the chemical structure of these drugs. Have now given way to a new generation of antidepressant drugs.

Vegetative symptoms A group of symptoms that refers to sleep, appetite and/or weight regulation.

Withdrawal Those side effects experienced by a person who has become physically dependent on a substance, upon decreasing the substance's dosage or discontinuing its use.

Word salad Speech that is so disorganised that it makes no linguistic or grammatical sense. Seen in some severe psychotic states.

Working through The repeated testing of insights, which takes up most of the work in psychoanalysis after the therapeutic alliance has been formed.

PART 1

GENERAL

CHAPTER 1

THE PSYCHOLOGIST IN FAMILY AND CHILD LAW

1.1 INTRODUCTION

Psychologists study behaviour. Where human behaviour is concerned psychologists may be found working in academic, educational, industrial, occupational and clinical settings among others. It is the clinical psychologists among these who are increasingly called upon to undertake assessments of children and families for the purposes of legal proceedings. Psychological assessments, when undertaken in the context of family and child law, aim to provide an understanding of mental, emotional and behavioural aspects of human functioning, which includes normal behaviour and psychopathology. The psychologist who is thus involved not only makes an important contribution to these proceedings in his own right but his findings and conclusions may also complement psychiatric assessments and other expert evaluations where these have also been commissioned.

In order to understand the role of the clinical psychologist it is worthwhile to look further at his work and the field of clinical psychology in general. Clinical psychology is a branch of psychology which is an applied science in which principles of psychology are utilised to understand and alleviate human problems; thus it comes to have a strong clinical basis. The clinical psychologist is focused on the understanding of psychopathology and psychological distress as well as in engaging in treatment methods and programmes. Additionally they undertake psychotherapy and psychological assessments which range from assisting patients who may suffer from a range of disorders from learning disabilities to the problems associated with severe psychotic illness. A clinical psychologist would typically undertake four or more years of graded university training beyond a bachelor's degree (which would include a full-time, one year internship to refine their clinical skills) and also be trained in research and in the conduct of psychological assessments. To clarify the distinction between psychiatrists and clinical psychologists: psychiatrists are physicians who specialise in psychiatry. They receive a medical degree after attending medical school to receive a general medical education. They then undertake specialised training to learn skills in the field of psychiatry. Since they are physicians, psychiatrists are legally permitted to prescribe medication; they are also especially skilled in diagnosing medically related psychiatric difficulties and in treating psychopathology. Some psychiatrists may train in the psychotherapies and some are trained to conduct research, but remain uniquely qualified to use biological treatments.

By the time a psychologist is instructed significant developments would normally have occurred within the family, with the involvement of the local authority, preliminary parenting assessments having been undertaken and possibly a range of services provided to the family to assist the parents in their role of parenting. Similarly, where private law proceedings involving contact and residence disputes arise, by the time a psychologist is instructed there could have already been a significant breakdown of trust between the parents and the children involved could possibly have been exposed to conflict and the battle between the parents. The instruction to a clinical psychologist in both private and public law proceedings would range from assessment of the emotional and psychological functioning of the child, the personality structure of the parents and their ability to parent their children. The psychologist is also required to assess the emotional well-being of the child and determine any emotional harm associated with neglect, physical abuse, non-accidental injuries, sexual abuse and fabricated or induced illnesses that may be present in the child.

Emotional abuse and neglect is intrinsically linked to the abuser-child relationship, and thus skills in undertaking assessment of the family system and relationships would be essential. This would involve the assessment of the parents' emotional and psychological functioning to highlight factors which are contributing to the harm and the neglect the affected children may be experiencing. An aspect of psychological assessments which is unique to the psychologist is the carrying out of psychological tests. This requires the psychologist to be in a position to use quantitative and qualitative psychometric testing. The psychologist would need to have knowledge of the reliability, validation and statistical underpinning of these tests in order to interpret the results. In broad terms, the psychologist's skills and expertise are based on scientific foundations and supported by empirical studies.

It is central to the assessment of children to determine whether they have suffered or are likely to suffer significant harm. The Children Act 1989 uses the term *significant harm* which is directly related to child abuse and neglect and the impact that this has on the child. Significant harm is the harm to and/or impairment of the child's physical or mental health as well as impairment of physical, intellectual, behavioural, emotional and social development which is attributed to the lack of adequate parental care. In proceedings relating to children, the paramount consideration of the law is the welfare of the child and the clinical psychologist who is engaged as an expert witness must also adopt this priority. To assess *significant harm*, comprehensive evaluation of the family would need to take place including the assessment of the child, the attachments and relationships it has, and of the parents individually in order to determine their psychological and personality functioning. Thus, the input of the psychologist is holistic and includes assessment of current and future risk, potential for change, likely timescales for any treatment to be successful and whether or not treatment in any given instance is indicated and, if so, of what kind.

1.2 FAMILY ASSESSMENTS FOR THE COURT

When undertaking family assessment, a sound and extensive knowledge of adult mental health and child psychology, personality and psychopathology are essential requirements for the clinical psychologist involved. An understanding of the psychological consequences and impact of abuse in all its forms would be necessary in determining how this may make an impact on interpersonal, social and emotional functioning as well as the cognitive functioning of the child. Interpersonal difficulties could relate to attachment disorders, while social and emotional impairment may be associated with anxiety states, depressive disorders, conduct disorders and possible substance misuse. Cognitive impairment could be related to developmental difficulties and under-achievement. Abuse and traumatic experiences could lead to psychiatric disorders, suicidal behaviour and aggression. The long term effects of childhood sexual abuse could have significant implications for interpersonal relationships in the future and the development of psychopathology and psychological disorders associated with depressive illness, eating disorders, self-harm, suicide, anxiety states and substance misuse.

When assessing the emotional and psychological well-being of children, the psychologist would be required to make recommendations with regard to treatment and management of the situation in order to reduce the emotional harm which had been experienced previously, and to prevent further harm from occurring. A range of therapeutic interventions, including family therapy, unstructured and structured play therapy, cognitive behavioural therapy and family therapy are widely used in these situations.

The psychological assessment would involve an extensive study of the child and family, with information derived from a broad base of data relating to the background history and derived also from clinical observation. This would include reviewing and gaining a thorough understanding of the background history from the documentation provided as well as from carrying out interviews with the persons involved such as the parents, foster carers, grandparents, siblings and the child or children involved. Clinical interviews would also be carried out on the persons identified in the letter of instructions as needing to be psychologically assessed. Subject to the nature of the instruction, and the needs of the case, observation of contact and interaction between parents and children would be a valuable way of noting prominent family dynamics and gaining insight into attachment styles. Psychometric assessment with the purpose of exploring cognitive function, behaviour, personality and emotional functioning could also be undertaken. When applying psychological tests, the psychologist would be able to provide a more extensive interpretive function to the assessment. The application and use of psychological tests should always be used in conjunction with other sources of data obtained, such as from clinical interview and the observation of contact.

1.3   THE SCOPE OF THE WORK BY PSYCHOLOGISTS IN CARE PROCEEDINGS

From a research review on Child Care Proceedings under the Children Act l989 carried out by Brophy (2006), the author highlighted key features in the profiles of children when the parents are subject to the proceedings are as follows:

(1)   Most cases contain multiple categories of child ill-treatment and multiple allegations of failure of parenting.

(2)   All applications which were subject to proceedings contain serious allegations of maltreatment.

(3)   Most children of parents in care proceedings were well known to local authorities.

(4)   The economic circumstances of parents are linked to difficulties in parenting and failure of parenting.

(5)   The concerns and allegations were related to parents who were highly vulnerable and had mental health problems, families who lived chaotic lifestyles, mothers injured in domestic violence and where parents were unable to control their children.

(6)   Half of all parents were likely to experience housing problems and over 70% of applicants failed to co-operate with welfare and childcare professionals.

From the research review it was established that clinical skills would be needed in order to identify the causes of child's problems, its difficulties and injuries, determine the prognosis in relation to future harm and the parental capacity for change. The research review found that experts have increasingly been required to assess psychological, developmental and emotional profiles of children together with providing skills in diagnosis and in seeking prognostic indicators. Brophy (2006) points out that the work of the psychologist:

> 'is not generally limited to the assessment of current harm. Rather the approach is holistic and contributes to 'form a package', this includes current and future risk but also the potential for change and likely timescales and whether the parents might benefit from parenting skills work. Clinicians also address the children's placement, contact and treatment needs.' (Brophy, J. 2006. Research Review, Child Care Proceedings under Children Act 1989.)

1.4   THE CLINICAL PSYCHOLOGIST AS AN EXPERT WITNESS

The subject of expert evidence in family and child proceedings has been discussed in detail in Chapter 1 of the companion to this volume, *Adult Psychiatry in Family and Child Law* (2006), and in relation to the *Code of Guidance for Expert Witnesses in Family Proceedings* which itself forms part of the *Protocol for Judicial Case Management in Public Law Children Act Cases*. Only an outline of the principles arising is therefore given here.

(1)   Expert evidence is required when the court would otherwise find it difficult, if not impossible, to resolve issues for want of the relevant technical knowledge.

(2)   An expert witness therefore gives evidence on the areas of technical knowledge he possesses. He must not go beyond this area of competence, for the court may thereby be misled and injustice may ensue. It is plain now that that most of the problems arising out of expert evidence are not due to lack of competence on the part of experts but are a result of an expert exceeding the boundaries of his skill, knowledge and experience.

(3)   An expert must be one recognised as such, for it is the evidence of such a person that a court desires to have. A chartered clinical psychologist would be normally deemed to possess the requisite expertise in the field of clinical psychology. He must, however, be able to show that he has the particular and relevant expertise in areas of family and child law where the issues concern this branch of the law.

(4)   An expert witness gives a specialised form of opinion evidence. He is not expected to, and should not; give his views on the facts which, if disputed, remain in the province of the court to decide. Thus, the business of the psychological expert is to demonstrate that, say, a child might have come to psychological harm, not whether harm, in fact, befell the child.

(5) An expert is an independent professional whose highest duty is to
the court. He remains independent of the parties including those
who might have given him instructions. He must therefore be able to
act and speak without fear or favour. There is no scope for
displaying any bias or exploiting the proceedings for the advocacy of
some personal belief.

1.5 SUMMARY

Clinical psychologists play an important role in assisting the court in
family and child care matters. The focus of psychological assessments is
on establishing the extent of any emotional harm suffered by the child,
exploring and assessing family functioning, and considering issues
involving attachment as well as making recommendations for treatment
and giving a prognosis for change. The purpose of the psychological
assessment in family and child care litigation is to evaluate the family or
individual's strengths and weaknesses in order to assist the judge in his
determination. Thus, in order to provide meaningful assistance to the
court a psychologist needs to take a holistic approach that takes account
of the family as a dynamic whole. Additionally, it is important for the
clinical psychologist to understand the legal as well as the clinical issues
pertaining to the case and the family being assessed.

CHAPTER 2

METHODOLOGY

2.1 INTRODUCTION

Methodology, to put it at its simplest, refers to the means by which a professional (for present purposes, a clinical psychologist involved in family and child care proceedings) goes about his business so as to arrive at his findings and draw his conclusions. Sufficient detail must be given by the clinical psychologist of the methodology employed so that, if need arises, these findings and conclusions could be challenged by another professional who is an expert in the same field. Methodology in psychological assessment involves studying and reviewing all the papers and documentation in order to gain an overview of the case and to be able to devise a strategy for the assessments to be undertaken. The psychologist would need to formulate a model for the understanding of the psychological issues involved in the subjects he has been instructed to assess and put forward various hypotheses, which would then need to be tested. Reading the documentation is essential to the differentiation of the fundamental aspects of the case from the peripheral issues which may also be involved. The methods and psychological techniques decided upon should be based on the psychologist's understanding of the case and involve those instruments which are appropriate for use with the family and the individuals within it who are being assessed.

2.2 THE CLINICAL INTERVIEW

The clinical interview is important for two reasons. First, the kind of information clients report to the clinical interviewer is not always shared by them with other persons, including those with whom the subjects could be in an intimate relationship. This information may concern their self-doubts, anxiety, sexual difficulties and the like, which are rarely spoken about to others. Thus, the interview could be a painful experience for the client. Secondly, for the same reasons, the initial interview may often also be paradoxically therapeutic for the subject as it affords him the opportunity to ventilate often painful feelings which he has previously kept concealed. When undertaking a clinical interview, the clinical psychologist is required to possess clinical skills to draw out information from a possibly highly distressed individual whilst at the same time attempting to reduce that distress and leaving the subject with some hope as to a positive outcome. This skill comes from having a sound knowledge about human behaviour as well as being able to carefully observe the client's behaviour. In addition to acquiring basic demographic data such as age, background and factual details of the family, recording observational data is an important part of the clinical interview. Through communication, paralinguistic aspects of speech could also be observed which include non-verbal behaviour such as changes of posture and eye contact, which may in turn reflect the underlying emotions. For example, the paralinguistic signs of anxiety include increased speech rate and speech dysfunctions, while at a non-verbal level; anxiety is often demonstrated by a rigid posture, foot movements and similar phenomena. Depression is often associated with decreased speech and increased muscular tension and anger or assertion are often indicated by reddening of the face, a rigid posture, tension and increased eye contact. Some aspects of the subject's behaviour during interview would indicate how he or she acts in other settings and his interpersonal and communication styles may reflect the presence or absence of social skills. Appraisal of body cleanliness and manner of dress would reflect knowledge of social nuance and the ability of an individual to maintain pride in his personal appearance. Gaining such a picture of the subject's skills would assist in clarifying and amplifying the self-reported data as presented by him.

It is the role of the clinical psychologist to integrate all the data that has been accumulated during the clinical interview and thus be in a position to be able to undertake a clinical analysis. This data cannot be interpreted without reference to normative data such as how much eye contact is within normal limits, how long a depressed mood lasts after the death of a parent and so on. Consequently, the interviewer must be familiar with the scientific literature about normal behaviour as well as that relating to psychopathology. It is only by comparing the various types of data provided by the client with those of other subjects as well as with the literature that the interviewer is able to reach a comprehensive and accurate conclusion.

2.3 PARENTAL INTERVIEWS

An interview with a child's parent is an essential part of the assessment in child care proceedings and provides a meaningful contribution to the information about the child's current functioning, the developmental history, its relationships, its involvement with its peers and its schooling. The aim of the parental interview would be to gather information concerning the onset of the child's specific difficulties and behaviour, the duration of those and any triggers or precipitating events which might have resulted in abnormal or disturbed behaviour. Furthermore, child rearing practices, attitudes to the management of behaviour, parental attitudes towards structure and discipline, punitive measures used by the parents and the effectiveness of the parenting are also to be taken into consideration. An assessment would need to determine if the children are within parental control, the nature of parental roles within the family and the degree of involvement of each of the parents. Reporting by parents is not always to be deemed to be totally accurate and is obviously subject to bias; but the parents' perspective and their perception of the situation are valuable pieces of information.

2.4   STRUCTURED PSYCHOLOGICAL INTERVIEW WITH PARENTS

A structured interview with the parents is always helpful to uncover the extensive background information needed to carry out a proper family assessment. Areas to be included in the interview would be related to general identifying data and presenting problems. It is useful to ascertain each family member's perception of the problem, the progression of the difficulties and precipitating factors, as well as how the parents have dealt with the difficulties. Enquiry into the child's personal and developmental history would include a detailed history from birth and through each developmental stage, the milestones achieved and difficulties experienced in each phase. Emotional, social and educational development, any separations during that time and the general health of the child may also be noted. Interpersonal relationships with parents and other adults in the child's life, siblings and peer group, school and extra-curricular activities and psycho-sexual development are important areas to explore. The family history to be taken includes general information about the father and mother with regard to age, secondary and tertiary education, career, religious affiliations, health, any use of alcohol or drugs, and illnesses suffered. Clinical exploration of the parent's personality, psychiatric history, drug and alcohol misuse and any problems with aggression is important. Social activities, social circumstances, financial standing, work, housing and recreation are also enquired into.

2.5   INTERVIEW WITH THE CHILD

Child interviews would need to be carried out in an environment which is appropriate to the child. The child's age and cognitive ability need to be taken into account, and when engaging with the child it is necessary to note not only what the child is saying, but how the child is saying it. The congruency between the expressed view and emotions displayed would be taken into account. How children talk about certain areas requires attention to be paid to varied responses, increased anxiety, and whether they are presenting as being emotionally blocked or unduly defensive.

The understanding a child has of why it needs to attend at the interview may indicate the level of communication a parent has with the child and also whether the child has in any way been prompted or coached to provide information to repeat during the assessment. Additionally, the child's ability to relate in a one-to-one situation with the interviewer, how it deals with separation from its parents, and its coping ability in new situations are all taken into account during the clinical interview. The child is asked how it experiences relationships, school, friends, what are its anxieties and fears and how it experiences or feels about the issues which are relevant to the proceedings.

2.6   OBSERVATION OF CONTACT

Assessment of the interaction between parents and children would be by means of observation of the interaction either in the home environment or in a more structured setting in an appropriate play room or other child-centred environment. Areas to be looked at would include the parent's ability to respond to the health and safety of the children, their attentiveness to issues concerning safety, the level of supervision they offer and the degree of attentiveness they pay to hygiene and nutrition, also noting if there is an over involvement with food or whether the children are being provided with 'junk' food with high colours and additives, etc, which have been reported to result in hyperactive behaviour and other difficulties.

Assessment of the degree to which the parents are actively involved with the children, whether they make use of physical, verbal and emotional contact, and whether they are attentive to their needs and their ability to address these are noted. Attachment and bonding responses such as eye contact, facial expressions including smiling and affectionate reassurance would all be assessed. The parent's ability to understand the children's needs and whether they are 'in tune' with their child would also be recorded.

The children's responses are assessed, noting whether the child or children are able to participate and to become actively involved in a way that shows they are able to reach out for their needs to be met. Does the child demonstrate an expectation that its needs would be met by the parent? An assessment of the child's response to controls and guidance given by the parents and whether the child attempts to manipulate and control the situation is also made.

The parent's ability to focus on educational stimulation and training, to provide positive feedback, show patience, tolerance and encouragement, would also be looked at. The parent's ability to play at the child's level, to offer help appropriately and whether the parent relates to the children by engaging in age appropriate play and interaction would be considered. Their demands for good manners, degree of indulgence of negative behaviour, and degree of modelling would also be considered, as will be the issue of whether the parents are able to deal with positive and negative behaviour appropriately and deal with sibling conflict within families.

2.7   PSYCHOLOGICAL TESTING

Psychological testing provides an opportunity to study a sample of behaviour under controlled conditions and in standardised situations. These tests do not reveal anything that could not be discovered through clinical interview and observation of the child over a period of time. Rather, psychological tests provide short, quick and effective ways of creating conditions under which particular behaviours will occur, rather than waiting for them to occur spontaneously in the course of time. They serve as an effective tool to obtain whole and systematic samples of certain behaviours in standardised situations.

In order to carry out assessment on children or adults it is important to make use of a battery of tests involving a series of psychological tests, psychological questionnaires and techniques. The advantage of using a battery of tests is to provide the opportunity for the different levels of functioning of the subject to be given the chance to manifest themselves in the tests. No single test can hope to reveal the diagnosis or the difficulties faced in these cases.

When clinical psychologists make use of a psychological test, basic familiarity with administration, scoring and interpretation of psychological tests is assumed in the presentation. The aim of using psychological tests when undertaking psychological assessments is to be able to make inferences from raw data and to draw conclusions about the presence or absence of various psychological states. The psychological testing, when used as part of the methodology, should go beyond the level of description; it should attempt also to understand individuals in a more holistic or global manner. A more detailed look at specific psychological tests and techniques will be taken in the next chapter and short descriptions of a variety of techniques and questionnaires are provided in Appendix II.

2.8   INTERPRETATION AND CLINICAL ANALYSIS

When all the information has been gathered, this needs to be analysed so that the variables which affect particular behaviours could be determined. Clinical interviews, psychological testing, observation of contact and background information, are all taken into account in formulating an understanding of the psychological issues and problems. The clinical psychologist must employ all his training, knowledge and experience to make interpretations and an analysis of the problems faced by individuals or within the system of their families.

2.9 PARENTING ASSESSMENT

In undertaking a parenting assessment, variables such as parental stress, mental health, psychiatric factors and psychological elements influencing the functioning of the parent need to be taken into account. Central to evaluating parents is the assessment of their motivation to bring about change to improve parenting behaviour or styles of parenting if these have been deemed deficient. Additionally, past parenting experience, levels of social support available and expressions of anger would highlight specific parenting problems such as child abuse or behaviour which may elevate the risk of child abuse. With the benefit of background information as well as clinical assessment, the clinical psychologist should be in a position to assess whether the parents have the basic ability to accept that emotional harm has occurred and to establish the role the parent had played in any harm and neglect that has occurred. Assessment would be made as to whether the parents are able to accept help from the local authority and/or the child care services. The extent to which parents are able to acknowledge the concerns that have been expressed by the authorities, and perhaps even a court, would indicate their motivation to bring about change.

The assessment of parenting capacity is a dynamic process. In order for parenting to be effective there needs to be a fundamental match between the needs of the child and the parenting resources available to the parent or carer. In this regard it is important to assess whether the parents have a capacity to provide competent parenting through childhood and adolescence so that they are able to meet the developmental and emotional needs of their child or children. Exploration would be made in the following areas:

- The parents' ability to provide basic care including medical and health needs, safety, protection from harm (which includes protection from domestic violence) and practical needs.

- The parenting capacity to provide emotional warmth, the attachment the parents have with the children, whether they have appropriate sensitivity to empathise with their children and their responsiveness to the needs of their children.

- The parent's ability and motivation to stimulate their children in order to promote learning, intellectual development and cognitive growth. This would include facilitating the child's cognitive development by ensuring school attendance.

- The parents' ability to provide appropriate and consistent guidance and boundaries which would enable the child to regulate its own emotional state; the ability to demonstrate and to model appropriate social behaviour and pro-social behaviours.

- The parent's ability to provide a problem solving strategy which is effective, rather than by means which are abusive or negative.

2.10 PARENTAL CAPACITY

Parenting competence in the face of a child with complex needs or a difficult temperament may remain intact if the parents' own needs for support are met and also if the parents' own capacities are relatively high. When making an assessment of parenting capacity, a consideration of the relationship between the partners within the course of the parenting assessment would be essential, as this is an important factor which influences overall parental responses as well as indicating the protective mechanisms in play in the parenting situation.

2.11 PARENTING STYLES

Assessments of parenting styles are concerned with the approaches parents adopt in their management of and control of their children. In particular, the extent to which the parents show control, emotional warmth, acceptance and involvement in regard to the children are studied. It is essential for a parent to strike a balance between being demanding and demonstrating responsiveness; when this is achieved, it reflects a child centred approach being taken by the parent. Where there is non-demanding parenting behaviour in addition to lack of parental control, this could reflect inconsistent parenting strategies, resulting in the child's ability for self-regulation possibly being under-developed; it may also lead to high levels of impulsivity being suffered by the child. Neglectful parenting occurs when the parent takes on an undemanding and unresponsive approach to the problems that may arise. In such a case the parents would not be equipping the child with the capacity to develop the ability for self-regulation. This feature is characteristic of homes where there is lack of monitoring or supervision and where emotionally deficient parenting exists. Problematic outcomes include children with impulsivity, low levels of academic achievement and poor self-esteem.

2.12 DOMESTIC VIOLENCE

Any parenting assessment would require an exploration of the level of domestic violence, if such is suspected. Whilst abused parents are usually regarded as the victims of domestic violence, it is in fact the children, when present, who are the true, albeit apparently secondary, victims. They may come to experience significant emotional harm and may also be subject to levels of conflict while living with parents who are not able to anticipate or give priority to their needs. This could be due to the parents' own extreme emotional chaos and distress. In homes where there is domestic violence, the parental figures could be experiencing emotional and psychological disturbances as a result of the impact of domestic violence, among the effects of which are sleep deprivation, social isolation, depression, loss of confidence, self-harm and increased tendency to commit suicide and, of course, having consequent difficulties in providing care for the children. Domestic violence undermines the general functioning and parenting ability which impacts directly on the capacity to parent. Women who are exposed to domestic violence are left with fundamental inabilities to mother and care for their children effectively. The physical, emotional and mental states of the abused mother would at times make mothering or parenting almost impossible. This could further increase the woman's feelings of failure and cause the mother to enter a vicious circle of ineffective parenting and increased emotional and psychological difficulties, which then in turn reduce her parenting capacity. The child's emotional needs are neglected owing to inconsistent emotional availability on the part of the mother in these cases.

2.13   PROGNOSIS FOR POSITIVE CHANGE

As part of the parenting assessment it is important to determine the prognosis for positive change and to ascertain whether the parents are able to make use of any treatment offered in order to improve their situation in respect of parenting. First, the parents' acceptance that the child has been abused or neglected has to be evaluated and then it is necessary to further assess whether the parents are able to accept responsibility for any abuse and neglect that has resulted. Exploration of the level of denial that abuse has occurred and the degree to which the parents apportion blame, whether attempting to cast it on each other and the child, must also be attempted. Secondly, it is necessary to assess whether the parents can show a commitment to meeting the children's needs by accepting that they need to change their parenting behaviour and to undertake parenting training. The parent's willingness to seek assistance and to utilise local resources in order to improve parenting and to gain support would reflect an ability to put the needs of their children first.

The parent's commitment to improving his own emotional and psychological functioning would also reflect a good prognosis for change. Positive prognostic indicators would include the degree of their engagement in services to address their psychological problems, be it of substance abuse, depression, anger management or marital discord. It is important that the parents do accept (where relevant) that they do have psychological problems which have had an adverse impact on their parenting. The parents' capacity to change would take into account their capacity and ability to learn new skills and whether they have the emotional strength and flexibility of personality required to benefit from the therapeutic process. The parents' capacity to maintain a co-operative relationship with teams from the local authority and independent professionals involved with child protection and rehabilitation approaches would also reflect a positive prognosis.

2.14 SUMMARY

The methods employed by a clinical psychologist are employed with the intention of formulating a model for the understanding of the psychological issues involved in the family and concerning the individuals he has been instructed to assess. Thereafter, he puts forward various hypotheses, which would then need to be tested. Clinical psychologists derive their evidence from a combination of material from the interview of the family or individuals, psychometric testing, studying documents and previous reports and from interviewing informants. It should be noted that when the clinical psychologists make use of psychometric tests and measures these may serve as effective tools in an attempt to obtain whole and systematic samples of certain behaviours in standardised situations, but only as an adjunct to the assessment undertaken as a whole. When all the information has been gathered, this needs to be analysed so that a formulation and an understanding of the psychological issues and problems could be achieved. The clinical psychologist needs to draw from all his training, knowledge and experience when making interpretations and an analysis of the problems faced by individuals or within the system of their families. This broad based approach is essential in order to provide the court with a comprehensive assessment and report of the family or individuals therein.

The court usually requires and is assisted by parenting capacity assessments. These involve exploring and investigating the parenting styles of the parents, studying conflicts and difficulties within the family dynamics, such as domestic violence and emotional abuse, as well as the emotional state of the abused parent. A program or therapeutic package would be influenced by the risk factors assessed to have been present as well as the positive and negative prognostic indicators that have been determined to exist.

CHAPTER 3

PSYCHOLOGICAL TESTING

3.1   INTRODUCTION

Psychological tests are carried out by a psychologist or a trained psychometrist for the purpose of systematically (and sometimes quantitatively) assessing psychological functions associated with behaviours involving the neurological, cognitive, and emotional and personality dimensions. The word 'test' could be misleading as some of the psychological tools used could be questionnaires or projective techniques.

The British Psychological Society (BPS), in its 'Users Guide on Psychological Testing' published by the Psychological Test Centre (PTC), defines testing as:

> 'including a wide range of procedures for use in psychological, occupational and educational or clinical assessments. Testing may include procedures for the measurement of both normal and abnormal or dysfunctional behaviours. Furthermore testing procedures are normally designed to be administered under carefully controlled or standardised conditions and embody systematic scoring profiles. These procedures provide measures of performance and involve the drawing of inferences from samples of behaviour; they also include procedures that may result in qualitative classifications or ordering of people.'

In evaluating the results of psychological tests perhaps the most important point to be made, especially in family and child care proceedings, is that no test result is to be taken and acted on in isolation. Not only should the results of a battery of tests be considered but the test results themselves should also be studied in relation to the known history of the subject and his recorded behaviour in various aspects of his life. The analogous situation in medical practice involves the doctor considering laboratory test results only in relation to the clinical findings on the patient and not placing reliance on test results alone.

3.2   RELIABILITY

The reliability of a psychological test refers to the consideration as to whether the test score actually reflects the characteristics being measured or is simply an indication of some random chance element. It is concerned with how accurate or precise the test score is. If a test is described as reliable, the psychological examiner should be able to accept a given score as being a true indicator of the characteristic being assessed. The test reliability is expressed as a correlation co-efficient (R=0.00 to 1.00). The closer it is to 1.00, the greater the reliability of the test. Measures of test reliability allow us to estimate the accuracy which is an important consideration when carrying out an in-depth individual assessment on which a psychologist may well be basing important decisions. An essential characteristic of reliability when the term is used in this context is that test results should be capable of replication on repeat testing within an acceptable range of scores.

3.3 VALIDITY

Validity is concerned with what the test score is actually measuring. Understanding the concept of validities is critical to competent test use. Face validity is the global impression that the test appears to be reasonable and that it seems to be measuring what it says it is measuring. Content validity reflects whether the behaviour demonstrates a representative sample of behaviours to be exhibited in a desired performance domain. Concurrent validity is where test scores correlate with an external criterion that is currently available, that is, at the time of testing, while predict validity is where the test score is correlated with an external criterion that may become available in the future. A simple example of the concept of reliability and validity may be given in the form of a thermometer. It is a valid instrument for the measurement of temperature but its reliability depends on whether or not it is in working order.

3.4 NORMS

Scores obtained in tests are typically converted into 'standard' form to facilitate interpretation. This may be carried out by using tables of norms or by references to criteria and scores. Norms refer to the range of scores obtained on a given test by the standardisation sample. The purpose of norms is to allow the test to compare an individual score with a score obtained by comparable individuals.

3.5 ETHICAL STANDARDS AND INTERPRETATION

The most important area concerning ethical standards is that involving test selection. The selection of tests with adequate norms, reliability and validity for diagnostic purposes is the clinician's ethical responsibility. The examiner must thoroughly understand the research literature for the tests used. A second ethical consideration relates to test security. This means that an examiner must safeguard the questions and the answers for many tests and inventories. Only those who administer, score and interpret the test should have access to such material. Without test scrutiny the validity of test scores would obviously be reduced.

3.6   COMPETENCY TO USE PSYCHOLOGICAL TESTS

In order to carry out psychometric assessments the PTC have set standards that an individual must be able to:

> 'demonstrate knowledge and understanding of psychometric principles underlying test construction, knowledge of the type of tests that are available, when it is appropriate to use them, and to be able to administer, score and interpret tests in order to provide accurate and meaningful feedback to others.' (PTC, *Psychological Testing; Users Guide*).

The International Test Commission (ITC) 2000, has stated that:

> 'the competent test user will use the test appropriately, professionally and in an ethical manner, paying due regard to the needs and rights of those involved in the testing process, the reasons for testing, and the broad context in which the testing takes place.'

3.7   EVIDENCE TO COURT AND LAWYERS

In 2004, the BPS issued a 'Statement on the Conduct of Psychologists providing expert psychometric evidence to the courts and lawyers' in association with the PTC. It is strongly advocated that whilst psychologists have a duty to the court, they also need to consider their obligation to the profession and the ethical standards required of those employing psychometric instruments. Obligations include ensuring that experts' opinions provided do not exaggerate the attributes of the tests, and that psychologists do not go beyond their competency in making comment. However, psychologists should at all times uphold the confidential nature of test material. Many tests are invalidated by prior knowledge on the part of the subject of the specific content of tests and their objectives. Thus, psychologists who use tests are required to respect the confidentiality of test materials and to avoid release of the test materials into the public domain (*Conduct of Psychologists*, BPS, 2004).

The Psychological Association in its *Statement of the Disclosure of Test Data 1996* makes the following points:

> 'Availability of test material to an unqualified person cannot only render the test invalid for any future use with that individual, but also jeopardise the security and integrity of the test for other persons who may be exposed to test items and responses. Because there are a limited number of standardised psychological tests considered appropriate for a given purpose they cannot

easily be replaced or substituted if an individual obtains prior knowledge of item, content or the security of the test is otherwise compromised.' (APA, *Disclosure of Test Data 1996*).

When a psychologist is required by law to release test data to persons whom he or she believes to be unqualified to interpret such material, or that such requirement would result in the release of test items into the public domain, thus invalidating the test, the BPS advises that the psychologist should inform those making such demands of the consequences of such compliance. The psychologist should make solicitors, barristers, and the court aware of BPS policy concerning the security of test materials and the psychologists' obligation under this and other ethical and professional codes, including the BPS *Code of Practice for Psychometric Testing*.

3.8   THE USE OF PSYCHOLOGICAL TESTS IN ASSESSMENTS

Clinical psychologists are usually instructed in the course of legal proceedings to assess the behaviour of individuals who have some forms of maladaptive experiences or disturbances which could prevent such a person from meeting his or her full potential. The causes of these deficiencies can vary from the consequences of disturbed interpersonal relationships to the effects of serious brain damage. The psychological term for potential is ego-strength; there are six broad areas and functions of ego-strength. The first of these is thought processes which consist of the cognitive ability to evaluate information selectively, the possession of reasoning skills, the ability to draw logical conclusions about relationships and events, and having the ability for concept formation which is the ability to interpret experiences at an appropriate level of abstraction. The second ego-strength is the relationship to reality, focusing on reality testing which is the accurate perception of one's environment and reality sense, which involve the experiences of one's body. The third ego-strength is defensive operations, which imply that there is the presence of healthy controls, adjustment and defences against anxiety. This is of great importance in maintaining psychological balance. In situations of acute distress, maladaptive defence mechanisms may also be established. The fourth ego-strength is object relations which are related to the ability to attach and to establish and maintain meaningful interpersonal relationships. Autonomic function is the fifth ego-strength, which develops independently from internal conflicts and includes such features as intelligence, language, memory, motor development and learning processes. Synthetic functions are the ability to organise all ego strengths and functions in a balanced way to lead a healthy psychological life.

Psychometric tests and techniques are used to assist the clinical psychologist in assessing a person's ego strength and ego functions as well as to determine the presence of any maladaptive processes contributing to mental illness or psychological dysfunction. Thus, psychological tests are used to assess the person's basic potential, to assess to what degree it may be impaired and how, where possible, these impaired potentialities can be renewed or repaired. The evaluation of the individual is done by means of reviewing and exploring the clinical history, undertaking clinical interviews, engaging in observation and administering psychological testing. The clinical psychologist remains among professionals the person in the best position to decide which of these tests to use. The psychologist would need to determine what psychodynamic factors are influencing the clinical picture and to establish if the presenting problems are psychological.

The tests in the psychological test battery used in most psychological assessment settings are usually chosen in terms of how well they serve the purpose of a psychodynamic formulation of personality functioning. The need of a battery of tests arises not only because of the possible invalidity of any single test, but because different tests detect different levels of functioning, as well as the fact that relationships between tests reflect the subject's multi-level system of functioning. Psychological tests tend to be divided into broad categories. The first category is Ability or Performance tests, which is designed to assess intelligence, aptitude and memory with tests such as the Wechsler Adult Intelligence Scales (WAIS), Wechsler Pre-Primary Scales of Intelligence (WPPSI), Wechsler Memory Scales (WMS) and the Wechsler Intelligence Scales for Children (WISC). Personality tests take the form of questionnaires or projective techniques. Examples of projective techniques include the Draw Person (DAP), Thematic Apperception Test (TAT), Child Apperception Test (CAT), Sexual Adaptation and Functioning Test (SAFT), and the Roberts Apperception Test for Children (RATC). Examples of questionnaires or inventories would include Minnesota Multiphasic Personality Inventory (MMPI), Edwards Personal Preference Schedule (EPPS), and the Trauma Symptom Inventory (TSI).

3.9   ABILITY TESTS AND TECHNIQUES

Ability or performance tests such as the range Wechsler Scales provide valid measures of global intellectual capacity in adults. With increased research and standardisation, new editions of the test materials are continually produced. The Wechsler scales measure the function of inherent potential which unfolds in the course of the process of the individual's maturation.

Psychological testing, be it the undertaking an intelligence test or personality test, occurs as *part* of the process of psychological assessment. This process includes the clinical interview, taking account of the demographic information, medical information, and personal history as well as making observations. Thus, the results of the psychological test are not used on their own. Undertaking cognitive assessments would involve this process and helps the examiner to come to an understanding of the person's intellectual functioning ability as well as an IQ score. The IQ scores reflect general capacity for performing intellectual tasks, such as solving verbal and mathematical problems.

The average IQ score is 100 where the standard deviation of IQ scores is 15, which means that 50% of people have IQ scores between 90 and 110, 2.5% of people are very superior in intelligence (over 130), 2.5% of people are mentally deficient/impaired/retarded (under 70) and 0.5% of people are near genius or genius (over 140).

Standard Score System

		Centile
Exceptionally high	*more than* 130	*more than* 97.5
High	120–130	90–97.5
High Average	110–120	75–90
Average	90–110	25–75
Low Average	80–90	10–25
Low	70–80	2.5–10
Exceptionally Low	*less than* 70	*less than* 2.5

Cognitive tests are carried out to obtain overall IQ, to examine interrelationship between the chronological age of the person with the functional intellectual level and potential intellectual level. The cognitive tests help to formulate a cognitive profile in order to identify areas of weakness and strength for possible remedial work, to assess at what level guidance and help needs to be given for the person to be able to make use of the information given. Not all people function at their potential intellectual capacity. Various reasons could account for this, including the mental state at the time of testing or general features such as lack of motivation, lack of impulse control, lack of perseverance, fear of failure, procrastination, inability to delay gratification and too little/too much self-confidence. Additionally, emotional and psychological factors such as anxiety, depression, emotional deprivation or disturbed behaviour as a result of mental disorder could interfere with performance. Neurological damage or difficulties could also impair an individual's performance on the cognitive test and general functioning on a day-to-day level.

3.10   THE WECHSLER INTELLIGENCE SCALES

David Wechsler designed intelligence tests made up of items that are appropriate for a wide range of ages. There are three main types of Wechsler intelligence tests:

(1) Wechsler Pre-school and Primary Scale of Intelligence (WPPSI): 3–7 years.

(2) Wechsler Intelligence scale for Children (WISC): 7–16 years.

(3) Wechsler Adult Intelligence Scale (WAIS): 16 years and over.

The first of these tests was the Wechsler-Bellevue Intelligence Scale published in 1939. There have been many revisions to this original scale and currently there are different adaptations of the scale, country by country. The scales are made up of 11 separate subtests, which are broken down into the Verbal scale (6 subtests) and the Performance scale (5 subtests). An individual taking the test receives a full-scale IQ score, a verbal IQ score, a performance IQ score, as well as scaled scores on each of the subtests.

The cognitive report would contain information and assessment of the intellectual functioning based on the scoring. The interpretation of the Wechsler scales would provide the following information.

Three IQ scores are obtained from the WAIS(R):

(1) Verbal IQ.

(2) Performance IQ.

(3) Full scale IQ.

Interpretation is fairly systematic and can be broken down into a number of areas. Firstly, the three IQ scores are given with an indication as to which standardised categories they fall into. Where there is any Verbal-Performance discrepancy, this should be discussed and the significance of this reported upon. The discrepancies could be due to a mental disorder, neurological factors, educational deprivation or emotional and psychological interference with intellectual function. Thereafter, the scores are broken down into the factorial sub-structures or index scores and a discussion follows if these are significantly high or low and on the degree of inter-subtest scatter (variations between the subtests) or intra-subtest scatter (variations of scores within the subtest). The **sub-structures or index Scores** are as follows:

(1) The **Verbal Comprehension Index** (VCI) involves verbal comprehension skills, as the name suggests, and is typically what we think of as intelligence at school or work involving vocabulary, verbal reasoning and general knowledge. VCI is made up of Vocabulary, Similarities and Information.

(2)   The **Perceptual Organisation Index** (POI) is made up of non-verbal skills. These are typically associated with abilities in the practical, 'doing' arena rather than with words. It involves non-verbal reasoning, three-dimensional problem solving and visual perception. POI is made up of Picture Completion, Block Design and Matrix Reasoning.

(3)   The **Working Memory Index** (WMI) relates to short-term memory such as remembering telephone numbers, sequences, or items to manipulate 'in the head' for immediate use. The Arithmetic, Digit Span and Letter-Number Sequencing subtests make up this Index.

(4)   The **Processing Speeding Index** (PSI) involves speed of information processing, in this case visual scanning and motor (written) response to symbols. It is not about thinking or reasoning speed, but dealing with information at a lower level. The subtests Digit-Symbol Coding and Symbol Search make up this Index.

The **Verbal** subtest comprises the following:

(1)	*Vocabulary*	A test of understanding and defining the meaning of words.
(2)	*Similarities*	A measure of abstract verbal reasoning involving verbal concept development. Single concepts between two words need to be identified.
(3)	*Arithmetic*	Measures mental arithmetic, involving a range of cognitive functions including short-term auditory working memory, tables and some mathematical skills.
(4)	*Digit Span*	A test of short-term auditory working memory, also involving sequencing of sounds. Digits have to be remembered in forward and reverse order.
(5)	*Information*	Measures general knowledge and ability to recall information from long-term memory.
(6)	*Letter-Number Sequencing*	A test of working memory involving remembering numbers and letters, but also re-ordering them. Attention, focus as well as auditory memory are required for this subtest.

The **Performance (non-verbal)** subtest comprises the following:

(1)	*Picture Completion*	A visual perception task involving attention to visual detail and completion of the pattern where a missing part in a picture is found.

(2)	*Digit-Symbol Coding*	A measure of short-term visual memory, speed and Visuo-motor co-ordination. Numbers are given a written code under timed conditions.
(3)	*Block Design*	A test of spatial imagery, three-dimensional problem solving ability and Visuo-motor co-ordination. Visually presented patterns are copied using blocks.
(4)	*Matrix Reasoning*	Tests non-verbal reasoning, pattern perception and the mental manipulation of shapes. Visually presented patterns have to be completed.
(5)	*Symbol Search*	A speed of visual processing test involving rapid scanning and detail perception. Sequences of symbols have to be scanned under timed conditions.

The WAIS has a good standardisation sample and it is also considered to be reliable and valid. The **reliability** coefficients (internal consistency) are 0.93 (high level of reliability) for the Performance IQ averaged across all age groups and 0.97 for the Verbal IQ, with an r of 0.97 for the full scale. Split half reliability of the WAIS is 0.95+ (very strong). Evidence supports the **validity** of the test as a measure of global intelligence. It appears to measure what it intends to measure. It is correlated highly with other IQ tests (eg The Stanford-Binet), it correlates highly with empirical judgments of intelligence; it is significantly correlated with a number of criteria of academic and life success, including college grades, measures of work performance and occupational level. There are also significant correlations with measures of institutional progress made among the mentally retarded.

3.11 PROJECTIVE TECHNIQUES

The term projection, on which the projective techniques are based, is not the same concept as is found in psychoanalysis (a defence mechanism by which certain feelings and actions which are characteristic and unacceptable to the individual are attributed to other objects). Rather, it refers to the spontaneous restructuring of material by the person using his own internalised frame of reference and structuring principles.

The projective technique reveals more than conscious attitudes and thought processes owing to the fact that an individual cannot try to create an impression that he believes is desired because he is not aware of the value of his responses. The person is presented with stimulus cards and asked to respond to these. By structuring an incomplete or unstructured situation, individuals are believed to reveal strivings, dispositions and conflicts. It is believed these spontaneous reactions are the best way of understanding an individual's motives as the person is free to do what he wishes with the material. What the individual seeks out of the unlimited variety of possible responses is believed to reflect his fears, anxieties, goals, desires, conflicts, fantasies, feelings of aggression and so on. It is generally considered to tap into underlying needs and feelings, conflicts, dynamics, motivations and defence mechanisms.

Projective tests and techniques are presented as stimuli whose meaning is not immediately obvious, which means that there is some degree of ambiguity facing the subject causing him to project his own needs onto or into amorphous, somewhat unstructured situations. Interpretation of the elicited free association data requires experienced knowledge and in-depth understanding of personality theory, developmental theory and psychodynamic understanding.

The most well known projective techniques are the Rorschach Ink-blot tests, the Thematic Apperception test (TAT), Draw Person test (DAP) and Family Relations test (FRT).

3.12   THE RORSCHACH INK-BLOT TEST

The Rorschach Ink-blot test is one of the most widely used techniques and best researched of tests. The Rorschach test was developed by Hermann Rorschach, a Swiss psychiatrist who began work on this technique in 1910, experimenting with ambiguous ink-blots to assess an individual's personality. The main focus of this technique is on the understanding of the unconscious factors affecting an individual's personality.

The Rorschach ink-blot is a standard set of ten ink-blots that serve as a stimulus for associations. The blots are essentially symmetrical, five with various shades of grey, two with grey and red and three with combination pastel colours. Instructions given to the subject are purposefully vague, in order not to create a set of instructions that might unduly influence the subject. The subjects are told they will be shown some ink-blots one at a time and that they are required to tell the examiner what each one looks like or might be. A verbatim record is kept of the subject's responses along with initial reaction times and total time spent on each card. After completion of what is called the free association, an enquiry is then conducted by the examiner to determine important aspects of each response crucial to the scoring. Occasionally a third phase, testing the limits, is included in the testing.

In scoring the responses quantitatively the important aspect of each response is converted into a symbol system related to the location areas, the determinants used and the content area. Location is scored in terms of what portion of the blot was used for the basis of the response, the whole blot, large unusual details of blots, small details or the white spaces. The determinacy of each response reflects what it was about the blot that made it look the way the patient thought it looked, making use of the form or shading or colour, movement, inanimate and various combinations of these determinants with varying emphasis. The content areas reflect the breadth and range of interests which include human and animal anatomy, sex, food, nature, etc.

In undertaking qualitative interpretation of the cards, the qualitative content reflects how the client handles new situations, his or her functional self-image and how the person experiences his environment. Handling of emotional stimuli from the environment, interpersonal relationships with father and authority figures as well as maternal or nurturing figures would be assessed. Idealised self-image versus functional self-image is assessed, handling of sexuality and affection needs and the impact of these is also considered from the responses. Finally, dealing with the full impact of emotional stimuli from the environment on the subject, those particularly relating to creativity, vitality and organisational ability are assessed.

3.13   THEMATIC APPERCEPTION TEST

The TAT was created by Henry Murray and C Morgan in 1943. This technique consists of a series of 30 pictures and one blank card. The choice of pictures used depends upon the subject's age and sex and the selection would also depend on the examiner's card preference and which area of conflict he wishes to clarify with a particular subject. The stimuli of the pictures are more structured than the Rorschach ink blots, but there is still ambiguity in all of the pictures. The TAT requires a person to construct or create a story, the instruction given to the client being:

> 'I'm going to show you some pictures one by one, you must tell me a story about each picture, tell me what is happening at the moment, what has given rise to the present circumstance, how the person feels and thinks and how the story is going to end.'

The subject is told that everything he says will be written down.

The selection of cards most commonly used relates to the hypotheses formulated and tests the individual's perception of and his reaction to demands made of him by the external world, and how he copes with demands and responsibilities set for him in his environment. Furthermore interpersonal and family relationships are assessed where the subject's attitude towards his parents, his environment and his aspirations could be assessed. Reaction to frustration, handling of aggression and coping with conflicts is also assessed. Mother/son relationships, mother/daughter as well as father/son and father/daughter relationships are assessed and explored. Handling of aggression, affectional and psycho-sexual development as well as the attitude present towards heterosexual relationships could also be assessed by various cards.

The TAT cards have different stimulus value and can be assumed to elicit data pertaining to different areas of functioning. The TAT is most useful as a technique for making inferences about motivational aspects of behaviour.

3.14   DRAW PERSON TEST (DAP)

Machovers in 1949 developed the Draw Person Test, which is an extremely popular technique both with children and adults. The subject is given a blank piece of paper and is told to draw a person. After the first drawings are complete the subject is told to draw another person of the opposite sex to the first figure drawn. After both figures are drawn, the subject can be asked to tell something about the personal characteristics of each figure including name and age.

Interpretation of the DAP is entirely intuitive and based on Machovers' hypothesis concerning the relationship between the structural (size, placement on the page and so on) and content (eg body detail or clothing) aspects of personality. The DAP is used in this way to assess personality characteristics. They are easy to administer and this technique is believed to have considerable face validity. A general assumption is that the drawing of a person by the subject presents the expression of the self or of the body and environment. Interpretive principles rest largely on the assumed factual significance of each body part. Modifications include asking for a drawing of a house and a tree (house, tree-person test), one's family and other animals.

3.15   ROBERTS APPERCEPTION TEST FOR CHILDREN (RATC)

RATC is also a technique similar to the Thematic Apperception Test, created for the evaluation of children's psychological development by Roberts in 1958. The RATC is intended for children and adolescents aged from 6–15 years. Its primary purpose is to assess the person's perception of common interaction situations as an aid to general personality description and clinical decision making undertaken by the assessor. More specifically, it can be used as an effective technique for initial clinical assessment and treatment planning, as an outcome measure to assess change over the course of treatment or over time, as well as an assessment tool in clinical research. The interpretation of the RATC is based on the assumption that children, when presented with ambiguous drawings of other children and adults in everyday interaction, will project their characteristic thoughts, concerns, conflicts, and coping styles into the story they create.

The test applies two additional assumptions. First, because children are generally unfamiliar with the test rationale they will respond with a minimum of distortion due to the interaction or undue defensive elaboration. In general their responses would reflect how they would feel or act in interpersonal situations similar to those portrayed in the picture. Secondly, even if the manifest content of the story does not directly affect their feelings or actions in real situations, it provides important clues about obvious psychodynamic issues which may be clinically useful. Both these assumptions require empirical validation.

General themes of the cards involve family confrontation, maternal support, school attitudes, a child's support, aggression, parental affection, peer and racial interaction, dependency and anxiety, physical aggression towards peers, fears, parental conflict and depression, aggression release, maternal limit setting, nudity and sexuality, and paternal support.

3. 16   CRITICISMS OF PROJECTIVE TECHNIQUES

There is a debate in the literature and in professional fields in relation to projective techniques and testing. The main criticism is that projective techniques are not scientific or subjective. It is accepted that there is subjectivity in the interpretation of results obtained through projective techniques. However, psychodynamic formulations are used which rely on an understanding of emotional and psychological functioning. Owing to the subjectivity that attends the projective techniques, there are basic guidelines and principles to be observed when undertaking these assessments. First, the projective techniques primarily serve to supplement qualitative interviewing aids in the hands of a skilled clinician and they are used to acquire a range of information to use in conjunction with clinical interviews and observations. Tests should never stand alone or be accepted as final. They must be constantly tested against information elicited through enquiry, test responses and the results of interviewing. Thus the special value that projective techniques has will emerge when they are interpreted along with qualitative clinical procedures, rather than when they are scored and interpreted as if they were stand-alone objective psychometric instruments.

3.17   SUMMARY

Psychological testing is generally used as a study of samples of behaviour under controlled conditions and, thus, psychological tests do not reveal anything that could not be revealed in the clinical interview and/or through observation of the patient over a period of time. Therefore psychological testing can be regarded as a short, quick and effective way of creating conditions under which a particular behaviour will occur rather than waiting for these to occur spontaneously in time. Projective testing can tap personality dynamics which reveal any changes that the individual subject experiences and, thus, within a brief period of time, can uncover hidden personality dynamics that might otherwise take a busy clinician months to spot.

Psychological testing forms an important component of the tools used by clinical psychologists in litigation. Psychologists are of particular assistance to the court as they are in the unique position to apply reliable and valid psychometric tests and measures which are relevant to the legal issues before the court. Areas that can be addressed to assist the court include cognitive functioning, neurological status, personality, areas of clinical concern, anger, sexual problems, emotional impairment and various legal competencies.

In childcare cases the psychometric assessments and evaluations look at the capabilities of the parents and the needs of the children, and an arrangement may then be recommended which, ideally, would make the best use of each parent's strengths. Psychological testing improves the objectivity of these evaluations, helps to look beyond the deception which may be practised by individuals in cases involving an adversarial aspect and may help to elicit information about which parent of a child can best serve its needs without directly asking it to choose between parents.

CHAPTER 4

CHILDHOOD ABUSE AND EMOTIONAL HARM

4.1 INTRODUCTION

In order to assess risk to a child from a psychological point of view, an understanding of child development and child psychopathology is essential. Psychopathology is a term used for emotional, psychological and psychiatric disturbances and disorders including personality disorders.

When one examines factors which are causative of neuroses and allied disturbances, they appear invariably to centre on the concept of trauma. There are two elements involved in the concept of trauma. Firstly, there is the event itself, of course, but an equally relevant consideration is the predisposition of the individual who is experiencing the effects of the traumatic event. That is, the trauma is a function of the interaction in which an experience is observed to evoke an unusual pathological reaction and acute stress as it comes to make excessive demands on the personality of the individual.

4.2 DEVELOPMENT OF PSYCHOPATHOLOGY

It is generally held in developmental psychology that there is a particular phase of life, the first 5 or 6 years, during which every human being tends to be more vulnerable to stress. From a Freudian perspective the reason for this is that the ego or developing self is immature and incapable of resistance. As a result the ego fails to deal with psychological tasks or stress at this early stage, which it could have coped with if faced later on in life with the utmost ease. Instead, the imperfect ego resorts to defences such as splitting or repression.

When considering life experiences within this frame of reference, separation from the mother, for example, can be seen to be a traumatic experience. The prolonged distress of separation could bring about psychological changes due to the child having had to make use of repression, splitting and denial in order to cope with the loss and in an attempt at the prevention of the loss. In the same way, being exposed to stressors in the form of abuse would lead to the child making use of maladaptive coping mechanisms which serve to reduce endured anxiety and/or protect the individual from emotional pain.

The effect on a child of separation from its parent has proved to be one of the key issues in child psychiatry and developmental psychology. Extensive research has shown that early separations could cause a variety of psychiatric disorders that could persist into, or appear for the first time in, adult life. These range from anxiety and depression to the development of a maladaptive personality. It is, however, important to consider the context and circumstances of the separation. The quality of the relationship from which the child is removed and to which it may be returned as well as the quality of the care received during the time of the separation need to be taken into account. It has also been found that children may be damaged by seriously disturbed patterns of parent-child interaction even in the absence of any separation.

The mother, as the centre of the infant's earliest environment, plays a crucial role in the successful development of the child and specifically in the development of its ego. Thus, any disturbance of the mother-child relationship may be associated with trauma and some level of developmental arrest. Inconsistent emotional availability of the parent, unreliable parenting and/or absent parenting have been proved to have detrimental effects on the child. Patients who have been diagnosed to be suffering from personality disorders have been shown to have experienced early maternal deprivation and/or difficulties in the resolution of the separation-individuation phase, and these conditions may also be related to actual loss. Thus, the pathology appears to be a consequence of a developmental failure in one or other phase of the early development of the child.

The family dynamic approach views the childhood of individuals diagnosed to be suffering from personality disorders as being characterised by neglect and deprivation, resulting in object hunger and affective instability which represents the child's searching for the parenting they never had. Furthermore, repetitive and continuous stress and distress arising from chronic disturbances in family structure and relationships are also viewed as being capable of causing pathology.

It should also be noted that both parents may play a contributory role in the development of psychopathology, which points towards bi-parental failure in some cases. In cases where a troubled relationship with one parent is offset sufficiently by a more positive relationship with the second parent, this could serve as a buffer or protection against the development of psychopathology. Thus bi-parental failure occurs where both mothers and fathers show significant impairment and a failure to properly carry out their parental functions. The absence of parental protection contributes significantly to the development of disturbance, whereas a parent who intervenes and protects the child may offset the influence of the more disturbed parent and possibly protect against the developing psychopathology in these children.

When assessing risk and exploring contributory past experience, help may be derived from research studies that support an association between psychopathology and personality disorder with bi-parental failure, parental over-involvement, separation, loss, neglect as well as physical and a sexual abuse.

Characteristics of families associated with psychopathology would include:

(1) Frequent separations and disruptions.

(2) Violent arguments witnessed by the children and serious marital discord.

(3) Atmosphere in the home of turmoil and impending violence.

(4) Lack of adequate role models with which to identify.

(5) The degree of neglect and parental rejection accounting for a degree of pathology.

(6) Unstable and inconsistent mothering.

(7) The continued abuse of children makes the child feel helpless and results in it experiencing a significant angry affect.

(8) Psychiatric disorders present in family members.

Growing up in such a disruptive environment could impair the child's development of a secure sense of self which would have served to contain anxieties. The disruption can also impede the social development required for satisfactory peer relationships that are necessary for adequate latency-age (ie teenage years) functioning. These extreme stresses may give rise to difficulties in reality testing and to preoccupation with self annihilation and destruction, which may involve deliberate self-harm including the misuse of substances.

Children from families in which both parents have psychiatric illness may be at a double disadvantage. They could inherit the illness of one or both of the parents, and they may also develop an intense vulnerability to adult object loss as a result of the tempestuous early home environment. Childhood experiences of children from grossly disturbed family settings reveal a typical childhood pattern which characterises psychopathology. There are two basic hypotheses within the psychodynamic framework which attempt to explain personality disorders and psychopathology. The first hypothesis is that the development of psychopathology is strongly associated with day-to-day contact with chronically disturbed parental figures or caregivers, in other words being exposed to chronic stress. The second hypothesis suggests that the trauma of abuse or separation from such caregivers is of primary aetiological significance, in other words being exposed to isolated trauma. Thus a combination of these two leads to a developmental arrest as a result of a loss of bad object, which is the loss of a parenting figure that was experienced as causing conflict. Research into the relevant literature reveals that personality disordered patients predominantly recall their family experiences as having been a combination of traumatic early events, emotionally or psychologically unavailable parents and family conflict.

Exposure to chronic stress as well as to isolated trauma reflects a non-nurturing and unstable environment, where a pattern of emotional neglect is characteristic. Often superimposed on this unstable environment are traumatic experiences of sexual and physical abuse. These life experiences would directly impact upon difficulties in establishing age-appropriate relationships in school and a failure in the development of ego identity. Ultimately, the person views himself or herself as a loner, isolated and separate from others, and may then turn to drugs, alcohol, and promiscuity as avenues in the search for satisfying interpersonal contact.

4.3   RISK ASSESSMENT AND RISK MANAGEMENT

A significant part of clinical assessments undertaken in care proceedings by psychologists is related to the assessment and management of risk or violence or abuse of others. When assessing risk, the historical characteristics such as frequency and type of previous offending behaviour on the part of the parent or other carer, the age of onset of offending behaviour, drug and alcohol misuse, and aggressive or violent behaviours would need to be explored and determined. While psychometric instruments can be used to guide clinicians through comprehensive assessments, experience is required to make clinical judgements, the collection of the relevant information and the interpretation of structured risk assessment findings. Undertaking a risk assessment is essential to the development of an appropriate and effective risk management plan.

4.4   RISK TO CHILDREN OF PARENTS' SUBSTANCE MISUSE

While it is the case that not all alcohol and drug addicted parents physically abuse or seriously neglect their children, there are many components to the lifestyle within drug taking families that may predispose a child to abuse as well as protecting a child from abuse within such families. There are various factors which relate to higher risk or lower risk to children. Characteristics and features of the parents which are associated with high risk to children were surveyed by L Alison (in Harbin et al, 2000) and identified as follows:

(1)   Addictive parent being the mother.

(2)   Long period of drug use by parents.

(3)   Continuing substance misuse.

(4)   Continuing substance misuse in pregnancy.

(5)   Use of other drugs in addition to methadone.

(6)   Drug taking affecting lifestyle.

(7)   Greater degree of poverty.

(8)   Presence of domestic violence.

(9)   Lack of social support.

(10) Low parental education.

(11) Young mothers.

(12) Infant withdrawal syndrome.

(13) Previous child abuse.

(14) Previous child in care.

(15) Poor parenting skills, for example in disciplining of children and a lack of knowledge of child development.

Factors associated with improved outcome:

(1)   Voluntary participation in drug treatment programmes.

(2)   Living with older family members not using drugs.

(3)   Previous demonstrated ability to raise other children satisfactorily (Harbin et al, 2000).

4.5 SEXUAL OFFENDING AND ASSESSMENT OF RISK

Assessment of risk in sexual offending tends to focus on the evaluation of risk and whether any risk identified could be sensibly managed. Assessment of risk requires an understanding of the psychological, interpersonal and practical features which contribute to an offender's risk of offending or re-offending. Central to such an assessment is the identification of what features need to change in the individual if the risk is to be reduced. Assessment of treatment needs is part of the risk assessment and would be considered among the factors involved in attempting to manage risk.

4.6 LEVELS OF RISK

The basic level of assessment of risk involves gathering historical and factual information which would include the person's age, past convictions for sexual or violent offences and the characteristics of past victims. Having this information may help to identify long-term risk, as this information is objective in nature and predictive in character and could be subject to empirical verification. Risk Matrix 2000 is an assessment also used by probation officers to identify historical information to estimate risk levels in individuals which then helps to classify offenders as posing low, medium, high or very high risk.

The second level of risk assessment involves the intrinsic features of individual persons which are relatively stable over time such as psychological characteristics, personality, cognitive processes and behaviour patterns. Although these factors are stable, they do have the potential to change if therapeutic intervention is provided as it may be possible to modify these features with treatment. These features consist of areas of behaviour requiring change for risk to be reduced, for example cognitive distortions. Characteristics of these second level risk factors include features such as sexual interest and sexual drive, thinking processes, cognitive patterns, emotional management, ability to self-regulate, impulse control, and lifestyle management. An important area to assess is victim empathy. Where this is lacking, it may suggest that there is a lack of emotional intimacy, lack of emotional congruence with children (that is, identifying emotionally with them and feeling more comfortable in their presence), and thereby could be an indicator of a high risk of re-offending. Cognitive distortions, which are thought patterns, processes and beliefs associated with offending such as, for example, believing that a young child has enticed an adult into a sexual relationship would need to be assessed alongside levels of victim empathy.

A third level of risk assessment involves acute features, that is, those behaviours and circumstances that are current and ongoing. These are liable to change over short periods of time and could be associated with short-term high risk. It would be considered a high risk situation if the offender's behaviours and interests were bringing him into contact with potential victims, or if they were engaging in hobbies, interests and employment which placed them in contact with potential victims and where they could engage in the grooming of potential victims. High risk could be considered where there has been deterioration in lifestyle such as the breakdown of relationships, loss of accommodation, loss of job, change in mood states and the perception that the individual is suffering from stress. Where supervision and treatment of the offender are involved, missed appointments, lying to the provider of the treatment, being otherwise deceitful and the breaking of the rules generally would be indications of acute risk.

4.7   PROGNOSTIC INDICATORS

According to M Calder et al (2000), positive or good prognostic indicators for sexual abuse assessments would be identified as:

(1)   Perpetrator attends treatment sessions.

(2)   Perpetrator does not prefer children as sexual partners.

(3)   Abuse was situational (eg when the usual partner was away).

(4)   Abuse was limited to touching.

(5)   Perpetrator referred himself for treatment and was not ordered to attend treatment.

(6)   Abuse was minimal and/or only began recently.

(7)   Perpetrator displays many areas of appropriate parental functioning.

(8)   Abuser experiences guilt regarding the abuse and displays a genuine empathy with the child.

(9)   Perpetrator accepts full responsibility for the abusive behaviours.

(10) Abuse involved the use of verbal persuasion only.

(11) There is no history of abuse in the perpetrator's family.

Poor prognostic indicators were identified as:

(1)   Perpetrator wishes to leave treatment.

(2)   Perpetrator prefers children as sexual partners and/or same-sex victims.

(3)   Abuse was not limited to specific situations.

(4)   Severe forms of abuse were inflicted.

(5)   Perpetrator was compulsorily ordered to attend treatment, or he persistently denies the abuse and refuses help.

(6)   Abuse was over a long period and with frequent encounters, or involved children outside the family as well.

(7)   Perpetrator has a long history of extensive antisocial behaviour, alcohol or drug addiction, or many areas of problem behaviours.

(8)   Perpetrator's guilt relates to their apprehension in regard to the consequences rather than concern for the damage caused.

(9)   Blame for the abuse is directed at the non-abusing family members or external stressors.

(10) Abuse involves physical force.

(11) Perpetrator was himself sexually abused as a child (M Calder, 2000).

Thus, in sum, when undertaking a risk assessment of offenders, an in depth assessment of the individual's past and current functioning, assessment of his thought processes, personality functioning and sexual development are all important to consider. All information would need to be clinically analysed taking into account the risk factors as well as prognostic indications. Most importantly, the offender's ability to accept that abuse had occurred, accepting full responsibility for it, recognising his need to make fundamental change within himself and the motivation to undertake all appropriate treatment, and commitment to long term treatment will need to be evaluated. The offender's ability to make use of the therapeutic offers and his psychological ability to translate what he has gained into demonstrating an ability to make the necessary emotional psychological and behavioural changes and growth will also need to be assessed. This risk assessment of offenders is an ongoing process undertaken over a long period of time.

4.8   PHYSICAL ABUSE

Physical abuse is described as being a deliberate act to inflict physical harm or injury to a child. There are obvious physical injuries as well as psychological harm capable of accruing as a result of physical abuse. Emotional effects in the child include affect deregulation, loss of self worth, poor self image and emotional symptoms of depression and anxiety. Additionally, cognitive, social, educational and interpersonal disturbances resulting in developmental delay may be caused. Physical abuse is usually triggered by behaviours of a child which the parent perceives as being aversive or undertaken in opposition to the parent. These include crying, wetting itself, refusing to eat, and stealing, lying and aggressive conduct. The parent is then provoked into using physical punishment as a response to the child's trigger behaviour.

Where the punishment is severe, and the parents lack sufficient inhibition, this may become abusive behaviour. The high level of anger which fuels the parent's abusive act is determined by the parent's arousal level and also the parent's appraisal of the child's trigger behaviour. The parent's level of anger is clearly displaced onto the child and other factors such as marital conflict or a stressful conflict with someone in his work situation may also help displace their arousal and anger onto the punishment he metes out to the child. Parents who abuse their children have difficulty empathising with children and may use self-justification to increase their negative appraisal of the child and therefore their own levels of anger.

Risk factors of physical abuse relating to the child are higher with younger children, where there is developmental delay, frequent illnesses, and a difficult temperament and where the child itself is aggressive. Parental risk factors need to be explored and in this process assessment of the presence of psychological problems, alcohol and substance abuse, history of being abused or whether the parents themselves come from aggressive families would need to be undertaken. The parents who pose a high risk usually have unrealistic and fanciful expectations of the child, little knowledge of child development and poor mood and anger regulation skills along with deficient skills in showing empathy with a child. An additional area which raises risk involves attachment problems involving the child, marital discord and poor social networks available to the parent.

Parents who have low self-esteem, low self-efficacy, immature defences and poor coping strategies would be more likely to pose some level of risk. Poor emotional regulation and poor empathy skills are two of the most important components of these broader psychological disorders from the point of view of increasing risk. Without adequate empathy it would be impossible to engage in sensitive parenting where it is necessary to be able to tune appropriately into a child's emotional state. Additionally, without adequate emotional regulation, parents would have difficulty giving priority to the needs of or to respond to the child in a way that regulates the child's own emotional state. Good parental adjustment is seen as a protective factor. Where parents have internal loci of control, high self-efficacy, high self-esteem, secure attachments, mature defences, and capacity to empathise, this would be reflected in a low risk of physical abuse.

4.9   SUMMARY

Where children have been exposed to neglect, physical abuse, sexual abuse and inadequate or inconsistent parenting, it is highly likely that the courts will become involved. The psychological assessment of the family and the individuals therein are central to assisting the court in making difficult decisions which could have far reaching implications for the children and the family as a whole. When undertaking psychological assessment in cases where there is childhood abuse, neglect and emotional harm, it is vital to have an understanding of the underlying emotional experiences, developmental processes and the consequence of these experiences. The parenting a child receives and the personality and behaviour of the parents could either enhance or undermine the attachment processes. Thus, when assessing risk, in-depth assessments would need to include parenting experiences, personality and psychological functioning of the parents as well as the emotional experiences of the child.

CHAPTER 5

UNDERSTANDING EMOTIONAL HARM

5.1 INTRODUCTION

In attempting to understand the effects of child abuse and neglect, it is important to recognise that there is no specific post-maltreatment syndrome that follows the abuse of a child. The nature of experiences would be so different that no one syndrome would become evident in children and therefore no one specific mode of treatment would be indicated. A child having been exposed to abuse and neglect would have undergone a psychological assault and suffered traumatic experiences. There are, however, broad common experiences of children found in those who have suffered abuse and/or neglect, in particular those which affect the child's ability to empathise with others. These children usually also have difficulty in self-regulating their emotions as a result of a lack of impulse control and have difficulty also in modulating their emotional responses. This could be seen in the form of mood swings and intense shifts of emotional responses displayed by the child. Furthermore, children who are maltreated come to learn about models of aggression, with a lack of impulse control affecting them leading possibly to disruptive and destructive behaviour on their part. Abused and neglected children invariably experience deprivation of life experiences and developmental experiences, resulting in developmental delay which is caused by emotional and social deprivation. This could be associated with mood swings and intense shifts of emotional responses. Trauma and fear could be associated with child abuse and neglect, and, thus, it is not unusual for these children to present with post trauma symptoms. Associated use of defence mechanisms and strategies in the form of avoidance, hyper-arousal and the re-experiencing of the symptoms could be expected. Arousal symptoms, including being easily startled, irritability, anger and sleep disturbance may all be found. Re-experiencing symptoms take the form of nightmares, flashbacks and experiencing acute emotional reactions when faced with or reminded of their traumatic experiences. These could undermine the emotional and psychological well-being of the child.

Glaser (2000) highlighted that brain and neurological changes accompany the psychological manifestations following abuse and neglect. The first 2 years are crucial to the emotional development in the child as it is during this period that emotional foundations are established through changes in the brain. Emotional experiences of a child activate the brain to stimulate synapses which in turn trigger and stimulate other neurological connections. Some of these synapses could only be activated with certain emotional experiences, for example when the primary caregiver to the child consistently responds to the infant. This is believed to stimulate synapses in the infant's brain responsible for recognition of that caregiver. The attachment process would then begin to develop. Synapses may be thought of as connections waiting to be wired and, if this does not occur, no growth of that part of the brain would take place. The development of stranger wariness is one such emotional development which is dependent on early experiences to develop. If the neurological synapses are not stimulated during the sensitive period for this development, it could be missed and remain underdeveloped. With consistent care giving and appropriate responses to the infant's needs, at the age of 6 months the child usually begins to distinguish between different people, familiar as against unfamiliar, and by the age of 9 months stranger wariness would normally have been formed. Thus, if the child does not have a primary caregiver or is reared by a mother who is emotionally unavailable, the child will not develop the stranger wariness as the sensitive period for this development in the brain has been missed. This would be evident in children who keep looking for a primary attachment, displaying emotional neediness, attention-seeking responses and indiscriminately looking for their unmet needs to be met.

Affect regulation is another neurological development reliant on the stimulation of synapses and neurological connections. There is also a sensitive period for development of affect regulation, and, if the centres responsible are left unstimulated, this could result in an impaired capacity for affect or mood to be regulated. Where a child experiences extreme deprivation, lack of emotional consistency and lack of stimulation there could be irreversible damage and the child may continue to have impaired affect regulation.

Additionally, the basic ability to control aggressive responses is also dependent on life experiences. If a child is brought up in a context of negative affect, anger and aggression, the particular synapses relating to responding to aggression will develop and even overdevelop. The child would then develop an adaptive process and become acutely sensitive to aggressive responses and aggressive nuances. They are likely to become unduly responsive to aggressive stimuli and the child would then respond inappropriately to cues and stimuli which need not necessarily be aggression-inducing stimuli. However, owing to being hyper-alert and over sensitive to these stimuli, the child would constantly react as if it were faced with aggressive responses. A critical factor is that stress-invoking responses result in a release of cortisol, which is one of the hormones affecting the brain, released when a child experiences undue stress. Cortisol in this situation, along with other neurochemicals, could cause damage to the brain and brain development. Thus, in a child facing excessive stress or repeatedly facing such stress, the damage caused may be associated with potential for emotional deregulation.

5.2   SIGNIFICANT EMOTIONAL HARM

Significant emotional harm could occur as a result of emotional abuse, neglect, sexual abuse and exposure to domestic violence. Situations experienced which directly relate to and bring about emotional harm include road traffic accidents, witnessing domestic violence, witnessing rape, receiving inconsistent emotional care, suffering experience of rejection, insecure attachments, neglect of educational, health and social needs, sexual abuse and emotional inconsistencies, emotional unreliability or emotional absence on the part of significant caregivers.

Emotional abuse is thus a pattern of behaviours that attacks a child's emotional development and sense of self-worth. It includes unreasonable demands being placed on the child, and the failure of a parent or caregiver to provide the child with love, emotional support and guidance. All the while the parent is unable to provide emotional support as a result of his own trauma, psychological problems or with the preoccupation with the struggle to cope with his own survival. A clear failure to provide care is evident in these cases. The child depends on adults for physical survival, emotional warmth and protection from external and internal threats. Thus, abuse and neglect in the home creates an atmosphere of fear and pain and puts a child's growth and emotional well-being at risk. When a child observes the mother, say, being abused by a partner, the child may learn to equate love with pain, force with problem solving and submission with keeping of the peace in the home. Children who experience emotional difficulties associated with abuse often present with particular symptoms or a constellation of symptoms which include anxiety-related symptoms such as fearfulness, apprehension, and anxiety about loss and separation. Post trauma symptoms could also be experienced in such forms as nightmares, high levels of stress, bedwetting, sleep disturbances and psychological inhibition and not being responsive to their own needs and feelings. In addition, they could present with difficulties dealing with emotional responses relating to anger, sadness, fear, guilt and helplessness as well as an inability to act for themselves. Emotionally abused children may present as indiscriminately seeking affection with unfamiliar adults, lacking empathy and presenting with psychological symptoms associated with diarrhoea, abdominal pain and skin rashes.

Neglect is defined as the failure of a parent or caregiver to provide a child with the necessary care, protection and supervision. Educational neglect affects a child and the impact of neglect can be devastating, particularly since it affects disproportionately infants and pre-school children who are in their most vulnerable developmental phases. Long-term effects of neglect can result in serious and lasting cognitive and emotional harm to children of a young age and increased rates later of delinquency, drug and alcohol abuse, sexual promiscuity and teenage pregnancies.

Sexual abuse can take the form of either sexual exploitation of children, non-touching sexual offences or touching offences. Sexual exploitation of children can include engaging a child for the purpose of prostitution or using a child to film or to model pornography. Touching offences include sexual fondling, making a child touch an adult's sexual organs, or forcing a child to engage in sexual intercourse or activity. Non-touching sexual offences include indecent exposure or exhibitionism, exposing children to pornographic material and deliberately exposing a child to acts of sexual intercourse and/or masturbation in front of a child. Covert sexual abuse in the form of verbal abuse involves inappropriate sexual talk, the father figure for example, being derogatory in a sexual manner of the mother and the mother depreciating men in sexual terms. Boundary violation is a form of covert sexual abuse which involves children witnessing their parents' sexual behaviour; this could involve the children walking in on sexual behaviour frequently because parents have not provided closed or locked doors to their bedrooms. It also involves the children not being allowed sufficient privacy in their own right.

5.3   CONSEQUENCES OF CHILDHOOD ABUSE

Children exposed to any form of childhood abuse, be it sexual or physical abuse or emotional disturbance, typically come from a disrupted home and a grossly disturbed family setting. Such family settings are associated with conflict, neglect, abuse, loss and a highly punitive environment which lead to subjective distress experienced by a child, with insecure attachments and other trauma accompanying. Trauma, in turn, evokes unusual pathological responses in the child as it attempts to cope with the traumatic events, and excessive demands are thereby made on the personality of a child. In the process the child would begin to make use of defence mechanisms in order to cope with the high levels of subjective distress that have been aroused. This could involve internalised anger and anxiety which leads to hostility towards parents in the adolescent years, for example through antisocial behaviour, disruptive behaviour, disciplinary difficulties, truancy and fighting and alcohol and drug use. As a result the child then repeatedly fails to meet society's expectations and the internalised conflicts continually interfere with the parent-child relationship. Should the child prematurely leave the family home, it could find that the inconsistencies and intolerance of authority associated with the parents are replaced by even more intolerant authorities in the workplace, and with relationships with which the child is ill-equipped to deal. As a consequence, ongoing maladaptive coping mechanisms, psychological disorder and personality disturbances may feature in the outcomes for these children.

It has been found that personality disorders are associated with childhood experiences of neglect, deprivation and continuous trauma arising from chronic disturbance in family structures in the course of early relationships. The child is left with unmet needs and affective instability which results in the child searching for parenting, stability and security that it has never experienced. The non-nurturing and unstable environment during the formative years of such a child underlies such patterns of behaviours which are the end products of emotional neglect.

5.4 SUMMARY

All forms of neglect, abuse, trauma and inadequate parenting could have a negative effect on a child's development, both at psychological and neurological levels. Protecting the child from harm or risk of harm may involve litigation. In order to assist the court and maintain the focus upon the child, whose needs are paramount, the clinical psychologist needs to have a sound understanding of emotional harm, what constitutes emotional harm and how to assess the nature and extent of the harm.

CHAPTER 6

CHILDHOOD SEXUAL ABUSE

6.1   WHAT IS SEXUAL ABUSE?

Any sexual activity between an adult and a child where the child is used by the adult as an instrument of sexual gratification constitutes child sexual abuse. Sexual abuse may also occur between children. The kind of sexual activity involving one or more adults and a child is a fundamental abuse of trust and the activities could include interfamilial sexual abuse, the most common form of which is father-daughter incest, and extra familial sexual abuse, where the abuser resides outside the family home and the activity may involve friends and family members. Sexual abuse includes acts and behaviours associated with obscene phone calls, fondling, exposure, penetrative sex, pornography, prostitution or rape.

Estimates based on research in the UK reflect the fact that 20.83% (just under one in four) of the population has been exposed to some form of sexual abuse. Thus, in excess of 10,400,000 individuals could be survivors of sexual abuse in the UK. The concern is that even more cases are unreported. An estimated 50% of cases get reported and, of those reported, only in 35% is there a likelihood of criminal charges being brought. The threat that disclosure is deemed to pose to the integrity of the family structure has been found to be the main factor preventing disclosure in victims abused by parental figures. Furthermore, fear of harmful consequences at the hands of the abuser due to threats made at the time of abuse also hinders disclosure. It was found that among men convicted of a sexual offence against a child, five or more undetected sexual assaults were also admitted to.

Sexual abuse occurs with both boys and girls of all ages. The group where the highest incidence of sexual abuse has been seen to occur is amongst girls at the age of 6–7 years and also at the onset of adolescence. In approximately 67% of cases the abuse appears to have started before the age of 11 years. It has been evident that vaginal intercourse was most common in victims aged between 6 and 11 years of age and in victims who were abused on a daily basis.

Girls are more commonly abused within families and boys are more commonly abused outside of families. In the UK 16% of boys are sexually abused before the age of 18 and those men who were sexually abused as boys or as adults often experience serious psychological consequences in later life, including an increased likelihood of trying to kill or harm themselves.

In 2000, there were 5,190 sex offenders in custody in England and Wales and in September 2003 it was determined that 21,000 individuals, mostly men, were registered as sex offenders. The cost of dealing with child abuse to the statutory and voluntary agencies is in excess of £1 billion a year, almost all this money being spent on dealing with the aftermath of abuse rather than in its prevention.

6.2   UNDERTAKING CLINICAL ASSESSMENT OF THE CHILD

When assessing the emotional and psychological functioning of children who have been sexually abused, or where sexual abuse has been alleged, the child's account of the sexual abuse needs to be clinically assessed. In this process the child's ability to differentiate fact from fantasy, whether its disclosure and description contain appropriate contextual details, any idiosyncratic detail present in its account and whether the child is using its own language without adult phrases or sentences being present are matters to be evaluated. It would also be important to consider the child's emotional and behavioural presentation, such as whether its mood is labile, the level of depression that is present, the presence of nightmares, and the nature of the child's play and its sense of security. Research has shown that adolescents showed deterioration in their school work after disclosure of sexual abuse while pre-school children displayed a greater degree of clinging behaviour following disclosure.

The child's medical condition and its social background need to be considered, taken into account and clinically analysed. It needs to be remembered that there are empirical findings that indicate that fewer than 10% of allegations are fictitious, and in most of those cases the fictitious allegations arose as a consequence of conflict in relationships during acrimonious divorce proceedings. In other cases there is also the presence of parental alienation (see below).

When undertaking an assessment and interview of the child, in evaluating how and what the child says, the most prominent indicators which give credence to the child's disclosures and allegations appear to be as follows:

(1)   Sexualised behaviour.

(2)   Sexual knowledge that is not age-appropriate.

(3)   The use of age-inappropriate language.

(4) Where the disclosure is contextually detailed and consistent with each re-telling of the events.

(5) An account given in an emotional way which describes attempts by the abuser to silence the child through the use of coercion or bribery.

(6) The responses of the child are spontaneous to non-leading questions and there is no evidence of a rehearsed account.

(7) Where anatomically correct dolls or drawings were used in the assessment, the account given by the child was consistent with the formal assessment undertaken.

(8) Medical evidence was seen to be consistent with the child's disclosure.

(9) The account given by the child correlates with the history of allegations and events corroborated by witnesses.

Following initial disclosure and assessment, if it had been considered that the child's account has credibility, action needs to be taken in order to protect the child. Where the alleged abuser lives outside of the child's home, or in the case of sibling abuse, the parents need to be able to put protective measures in place. Where the parents do not accept the disclosure, some level of family intervention would need to be carried out to determine whether the parents would be able to protect the child against further harm taking place. If the child had made a disclosure concerning a parental figure living within the home, the child returning to the situation may find it intimidating and in all likelihood this may result in the child retracting its statement. The abuse could continue and the child may well be unlikely to make further allegations owing to the threat of violence and the child will also continue to feel unsafe because of the apparent ineffectiveness of the professionals to protect it after the disclosures and statements it had made. It would, however, be acceptable for the child to return to the home environment if the non-abusing parent believes the child and agrees to protect it and the abuser leaves the home.

Assessment and clinical interviewing of children as part of a medico-legal or clinical assessment should be focused upon the following:

(1) To assess the impact of the abuse on the child.

(2) To assess any abnormal behavioural patterns and the trauma-related dynamics of sexual traumatisation, stigmatisation, betrayal and powerlessness.

(3) To assess the child's perception of risk and the protective factors within its family.

(4)   An account to be obtained of the child's perception of the non-abusing parent's capacity to be protective.

(5)   To establish the ways in which the child has coped with the abuse and its personal strengths and resources, particularly its capacity for assertiveness and the possession of self-protective skills (A Carr, 1999).

6.3   ASSESSMENT CHILD INTERVIEWS

In addition to talking in a one-to-one situation with the child, the making use of play, sand play, drawing and using anatomically correct dolls are useful aids to interviewing. It is recommended that the child be interviewed alone as the presence of a parent could inhibit the child and there could also be an element of fear of repercussions present from what the child could come to say. The pace of the interview should always be in line with the child's pace, its abilities in coping with the interview and the level of anxiety that is aroused in the child. There has been much research on the use of anatomically correct dolls in this situation. The most significant feature that has been discovered is that children who have not been sexually abused inspect and touch sexual body parts but do not enact sexual activities such as oral, anal or genital intercourse with the dolls. Anatomically correct dolls do not lead, when used, to undue distress or traumatisation suffered by the child and this approach provides a useful way into communication with the child and also allows the child to talk about difficult experiences. This serves as a medium through which to communicate about sexually abusive acts committed on the child.

It is only after the child has given a spontaneous general account of the abuse that information about specific details should be obtained. Specific areas to be covered would include:

(1)   The location of the abuse.

(2)   The frequency and duration of the abuse.

(3)   The use of violence or threats.

(4)   The presence of other people during the abuse.

(5)   The use of drugs or alcohol by the perpetrator or the child.

(6)   Whether photographs or recordings of the abuse were made.

(7)   The child's psychological reactions to the abuse.

In addition to the psychological assessment of the child a full physical and medical forensic examination of the child should be conducted as part of a comprehensive assessment following guidelines for good practice. Individual interviews with non-abusing parents should be conducted to assess their capacity to protect the child in the future.

6.4 THE RISK OF REPEATED ABUSE

The risks of abuse and/or repeated abuse are related to factors in a child that prevent children resisting the abuser. Children who are targeted for sexual abuse could often be likened to a 'broken-winged bird', the child who tends to be more vulnerable by the nature of a poor relationship with the non-abusing parent, where there is poor communication and insecure attachment between that child and the non abusing parent. Children who lack assertiveness, lack physical strength, have physical disabilities or hold the belief that they should always obey adults, could be considered susceptible owing to the nature of the vulnerability which is being targeted by the abuser. It needs to be recognised that sexual abuse is a process of the abuser gaining the child's trust and targeting it by 'grooming' or preparing it for the abuse. Once a pattern of abuse becomes entrenched, the use of threats inhibits disclosure by children due to fears that their own safety could be undermined or out of fears for the breakdown of their family. These children could also be locked into the abuse by having been given bribes or rewards they receive from the abuser and low self-esteem or low self-efficacy further renders these children vulnerable to repeated abuse. Once absorbed into the process, children make use of coping strategies and defence mechanisms in order to cope with the abuse. These include accommodation of the abuser's wishes, denial of the abuse, self-blame, recanting, and attempts to avoid disclosure and its consequences.

Where a child has positive personal characteristics such as assertiveness, intelligence, high self esteem and open communication with others, repeated abuse would be less likely. Successfully functioning coping strategies may be viewed as protective factors.

As indicated, sexual abuse of a child is a process, a course of events which is usually planned by the abuser who needs to manipulate the situation, then manipulates the child and finally overcomes its inhibitions. Reducing inhibitions involves a process of cognitive change on the part of the abuser, in particular reframing his thinking to neutralise the belief that sexually abusing the child is wrong and illegal and may lead to negative consequences for the abuser and the child. Alcohol or drugs may be used to overcome inhibitions. It is also the case that aspects of the abuser's personality, difficulties in controlling impulses associated with personality disorder and intellectual disability could predispose a person to overcome such internal inhibitions. When manipulating the environment, the abuser could take advantage of factors such as lack of parental supervision, social isolation, and crowded living conditions to create opportunities to abuse the child he has targeted. The abuser takes on the position of control or power over the child.

Some families are more vulnerable and thereby are prone to be at high risk for abuse to take place. Where family functioning is chaotic and disorganised there would, for example, be fewer external inhibitors preventing family members from abusing children present in the family. The father, say, could dominate the family and assert his control and power and the abuse could be seen to serve to regulate the conflict within the family. Where a family is over-organised or rigid it is more likely that the father will come to abuse a single child and a greater degree of secrecy is also evident in these families. Sexual dissatisfaction within the marital relationship and a non-supportive relationship between the abused child and the mother also tend to characterise these families. In both these dysfunctional family systems the absence of a supportive and protective relationship between the non-abusing parent and the child is evident (A Carr, 1999).

6.5 THE EFFECTS OF CHILD SEXUAL ABUSE (CSA) ON THE CHILD'S PSYCHOLOGICAL FUNCTIONING

Children who have been sexually abused suffer from significant short and long-term effects on their psychological functioning and could go on to develop psychological symptoms and disorders. A third of persons abused are left with psychological disorders, the figure being higher in the case of men who were abused as children. A study by Mullen et al (1988) reported that 20% of the women who had been exposed to sexual abuse in childhood had a history of a psychiatric disorder in later life, mostly of a depressive nature, compared with only 6.3% of the non-abused population. There is no specific post sexual abuse syndrome or disorder. However, many victims do present with some degree of post trauma reaction, with associated behavioural and emotional features. Sexualised behaviour is common, although not always evident, and social, interpersonal and educational functioning was usually adversely affected to some degree. In an attempt to categorise symptoms experienced, Browne and Finklehor (1986) proposed that there are 'traumagenic dynamics' which include traumatic sexualisation, stigmatisation, betrayal and powerlessness that account for the wide variety of symptoms shown by children who have been sexually abused.

With traumatic sexualisation, the child's concept of normal sexual behaviour and morality is distorted by the abuser, by the child being rewarded for sexual behaviour inappropriate to its developmental level. Consequently, sexual arousal becomes associated with rewards, receiving care, love and attention. Furthermore, sexual activity becomes associated with negative emotions and memories.

The child may also experience stigmatisation by way of the abuser blaming and denigrating the child and threatening the child into maintaining secrecy. Additionally, after disclosure, where the family network blames the child for participating in the abuse, the child may go onto develop negative beliefs about the self, which may result in such behaviours as self-blame and self-denigration. These beliefs lead to self-destructive behaviours such as avoidance of relationships, drug abuse, self-harm and suicide.

Abuse is an extreme violation of trust which results in the child experiencing overwhelming betrayal, with the generalised expectation developing that other adults will also betray their trust and fail to be protective. This fundamental loss of basic trust forms the basis of relationship problems, delinquency and the experiencing of intense feelings of sadness and anger. Where a child is unable to prevent the abuse because the abuser has used power and control, it is left with an overwhelming sense of powerlessness. The child is left with a sense of ineffectiveness, inadequacy and being a victim, and may experience associated features of depression, anxiety and somatic symptoms.

Sexually abused children may develop or present with a variety of behaviours which tend to be short term symptoms. These could, however, have long term implications for social and emotional development and functioning and include:

(1) unusual interest in or avoidance of all things of a sexual nature;

(2) sexualised behaviours;

(3) statements that their bodies are dirty or damaged, or fear that there is something wrong with them in the genital area;

(4) refusal to go to school, social withdrawal and isolation;

(5) delinquency/conduct problems, unusual aggressiveness, fighting;

(6) secretiveness;

(7) aspects of sexual molestation in drawings, games or fantasy play;

(8) suicidal behaviour or self harm;

(9) clinging behaviour and moodiness;

(10) sleep problems or nightmares;

(11) depression or withdrawal from family and peers.

Long term psychological effects would depend upon a variety of factors which could be assessed as being either risk or protective factors. Risk factors are associated with the degree of stress associated with the abuse which would include the frequency of the abuse, the degree of trauma and aggression involved and the relationship that existed between the child and the abuser. Additionally, the feature of the abuse, the child's personal attributes and the social context within which the sexual abuse occurs may also affect the level of stress experienced by the child and influences also the risk of further abuse.

6.6   SEXUALLY REACTIVE CHILDREN

When a child is reported to have engaged in sexual behaviour, it needs to be assessed whether the child has been exposed to any form of sexual abuse. An assessment needs to be made as to whether these behaviours are due to natural or normal experiences, or are a reflection of disturbance or concern.

Children of a pre-pubescent age who have had contact with inappropriate sexual activity or have been exposed to sexual abuse tend to present as sexualised or sexually reactive. A sexualised child may engage in a variety of inappropriate sexual behaviours as a result of the exposure to sexual experience, may act out or engage in sexual behaviours or relationships that include obsessive sexual play, inappropriate sexual comments or gestures, mutual sexual activity with other children or sexual molestation or abuse of other children. When undertaking assessment to determine sexual abuse, there are various signs and behaviours which alert one to the possibility of the child having been exposed to inappropriate sexual exposure or sexual abuse. The following behaviours would be of concern and require further assessment.

(1)   Excessive masturbation or demonstrating a preoccupation with sexual activities.

(2)   Mutual sexual play with same age or younger children.

(3)   Demonstrating precocious sexual activities, gestures, language and knowledge.

(4)   Interest in or attempting sexual contact with older children, adolescents.

(5)   Engaging in sexual behaviour in public such as rubbing, masturbation or sexual exposure.

(6)   Engaging in or attempting sexual encounters and intercourse with same aged or younger children, including masturbation, physical penetration and intercourse.

(7)   Sexual play when a child is preoccupied with sexual play.

(8)   Directing sexual behaviours towards adults or adolescents.

Although sexual play of young children does not necessarily indicate abuse or exposure to sexual abuse, where these behaviours lead to complaints from or have negative effect on other children they should be further investigated. Sexual play between very young children should not have features of sexualised or sexual reactive indicators.

6.7   PSYCHOLOGICAL TREATMENT OF CHILDREN WHO HAVE BEEN SEXUALLY ABUSED

Sexual abuse is a psychological assault on the child's psyche and may have an overwhelming and pervasive impact upon the psychological development of the child. Whether or not the child responds with behavioural and/or emotional problems, the abuse is fundamentally damaging to the psychological state of the child and there could be long term consequences with behavioural and emotional problems persisting into adult life. Identifiable reactions and responses to sexual abuse would vary depending on the age and developmental stage of the affected child. Owing to the debilitating impact of sexual abuse, from a very early age and stage the child would begin to develop strategies and defensive responses to cope with the acute distress. Consequent maladaptive responses and symptoms may become evident such as anxiety, fears, depression, academic difficulties, disturbed peer and family relationships, sexualised behaviour, sexual dysfunctions, post-traumatic stress disorder (PTSD) and poor self-esteem. Additionally, suicidal or self-injurious behaviour, substance abuse, dissociative disorders, sexual dysfunction and anorexia nervosa are effective, albeit maladaptive, ways of blocking or avoiding the traumatic experience. Childhood abuse often disrupts children's development by stimulating primitive coping strategies and by creating cognitive distortions of self, others and the future.

As there is no specific post-sexual abuse syndrome, and there are different forms of abuse-related distress or dysfunction that may appear in these individuals, treatment interventions would need to be tailored to address the specific aspects of the abused child or adult survivor of child sexual abuse. However, in establishing a therapeutic relationship, the therapist would need to be well versed with the psychodynamics of the psychological impact of sexual abuse. Owing to the often traumatic nature of the experiences and any difficulties present involving disclosure, it is essential that the therapist does not react with embarrassment, anger or shock to what he hears but responds, instead, with tact and empathic understanding. The specific interventions should be based upon the issues raised, the nature of the experience and on the survivor's unique response

ectic therapeutic approach taking into account cognitive,
ical and social aspects should be considered.

schools of thought which suggest that recalling the
could be more harmful than letting things be, since
.... the trauma could induce an increase of such symptoms. It is held that if the person does not present with acute symptoms, treatment is not indicated. Research has however shown that recalling the details of the abuse experience is a necessary therapeutic intervention, as this would enable the client to experience a cathartic release. The precaution to be taken would be to ensure that a positive rapport has been established with the client and that the therapist has established the capacity of the client's coping mechanisms which are aimed at reducing anxiety, stress, anger and fear. The therapist assisting to develop these inner resources would enable the client to experience this release without further emotional decomposition. Therapeutic interventions would be aimed at alleviating guilt and shame, attributing responsibility for the abuse to the abuser and the ventilation of anger. Therapeutic intervention would also need to focus on the development of a positive self-image, reinforcing the survival skills and personal strengths as well as re-establishing a sense of self acceptance.

The level of distress and the speed of a victim's recovery would be dependent on the parental support available, in particular maternal acceptance of the disclosure. Research has revealed that the lack of maternal acceptance of the disclosure creates significant harm to the child and inhibits the potential for recovery and also increases distress and the conflict experienced. Similarly, maternal upset assists the child by reducing feelings of guilt, sparing it from having to take all responsibility itself and also leads to it feeling accepted by the mother. The non-abusive parent's active seeking of help and thereby protecting the child from further abuse assists the recovery of the child and engenders closeness and healthy conflict management. The more the family are involved in the treatment plan and package, the more effective is likely to be the treatment.

Cognitive behavioural interventions should focus on reframing the negative, erroneous and distorted beliefs which the child has been exposed to, such as self denigration. The child should also be encouraged to express abuse-related feelings such as anger, ambivalence and fear. The therapeutic interventions should assist to empower the child by teaching abuse prevention skills and self assertion techniques. Additionally, the cognitive behavioural approach could assist in diminishing the sense of stigma and isolation experienced by the child through reassurance and/or exposure to other victims. Psychodynamic psychotherapy and other eclectic approaches may all be effective in addressing the psychological consequences of sexual abuse. All the approaches should incorporate general support and psychological education. As the child's psychological needs change during the various stages of its development, therapeutic interventions of varying kinds would be needed to address different issues which may become relevant at different developmental stages, and thus therapy could turn out to be an ongoing and intermittent process well into the adult life of the child.

6.8 SUMMARY

The first step in assessing sexually abused children is learning to recognise the signs of child sexual abuse and understanding the psychodynamics involved in children who have been abused. The presence of a single sign does not indicate that sexual abuse has taken place. However, when these signs appear repeatedly or in combination the clinical psychologist should take a closer look at the situation and consider the possibility of abuse having occurred. In order to arrive at a conclusion about the likelihood of sexual abuse, the clinical psychologist needs to weigh the clinical findings from the child's interview with any corroboratory evidence from other sources. Additionally, the clinical psychologist undertaking an assessment for the purposes of litigation needs to identify and make recommendations upon the levels of risk faced and the treatment needed for the child and the family as a whole.

CHAPTER 7

PARENTAL ALIENATION

7.1 INTRODUCTION

Parental alienation is the creation of a singular relationship between a child and one parent, to the exclusion of the other parent. It is where the one parent turns the child against the other parent, with, characteristically, accusations and counter accusations made by the parties. The fully alienated child is a child who does not wish to have any contact whatsoever with one parent and who expresses only negative feelings for that parent and only positive feelings for the other parent. This child has lost the range of feelings for both parents that is normal for a child (Ward & Harvey, 1993).

Perpetuating conflict, blocking contact and vilifying the non resident parent, when undertaken by the resident parent, are likely to endanger the child's mental health and seriously compromise its emotional and psychological well-being. Preventing contact, giving the message that the child is unsettled by the contact and the non-resident parent being treated rather as an unimportant acquaintance, all in the name of 'protecting' the child could, in fact, be instruments inflicting severe emotional suffering on the very person whose protection and well-being is being sought.

When viewing the interests of the child as being paramount, it is essential to understand that it is psychologically harmful to children to be deprived of a healthy relationship with any parent. There is substantial research which supports the view that children need contact with both parents for a balanced development and that this should be maintained. Where parents separate or divorce, it is the visiting and contact agreements which should ensure that the emotional bond of the child with both parents is being protected. It is the case that with the exception of situations of proven abuse there is no reason why a child should not want to spend some time with each of its parents, and it is found that, even with abuse, most children still want to maintain some relationship with the abusive parent. Should it be the case that a child insists that it does not want contact without good reason, it needs to be determined and assessed whether the residential parent is acting as a kind of gate keeper, putting himself forward as the parent who is superior and in charge, whilst creating the impression that the non residential parent is on the periphery and not important to the child. This would have an erosive effect on the relationship and the child is placed in a severe loyalty or double bind conflict, a position wherein the child believes it must choose which of its two parents it will 'love' more. To have to choose between parents is itself damaging and could cause significant emotional harm to the child. Furthermore, if the end result is the exclusion of a parent from the child's life, the injury may well be irreparable.

In an attempt to understand the psychodynamics of a parent who engages in an alienation process, one needs to look at the previous relationship between the parents and whether there remain unresolved issues with associated intense anger and resentment as the result. The alienation process involves the resident parent attempting to ward off these powerfully hostile and intensely uncomfortable feelings, and thereby coming to develop behavioural strategies that involve the children. The child or children are used as a way to punish the other parent by seeking his or her exclusion. The motives could be conscious or subconscious, and in the latter case the parent involved would be unaware of his alienating behaviour. Where the motivations are conscious the parent may be consciously attempting to protect the child. Additionally, not all bitterly contested divorces are alienating; this would only be a feature when the children are willingly used as weapons and vehicles to express the parties' intense emotions. In these cases the child is used to inflict retribution on the non residential parent.

Ward & Harvey (1993) take the view that there are degrees of alienation. Mild alienating behaviour is subtle, involving subliminal and subtle messages being given directly to the child. Features of mild alienation would include:

(1) Little regard for the importance of visiting/contact with the other parent.

(2) Lack of value regarding communication between visits.

(3) Inability to tolerate the presence of the other parent even at events important to the child.

(4) Disregard for the importance of the relationship to the child.

Moderate alienation is where there is an awareness of the alienating parent's emotional motivations (fear of loss, rage) and little sense of the value of the non-residential parent. The features of moderate alienating parents are:

(5) Their statements and behaviours are subtle but damaging to the child.

(6) Communications of dislike of visits.

(7) Refusal to hear anything about the other parent.

(8) Delight in hearing negative news about the other parent.

(9) Refusal to speak directly with the other parent.

(10) Refusal to allow the target parent physically near.

(11) Not allowing the other parent out of his car or even on the property, being kept in the driveway.

(12) Doing and undoing statements.

(13) Subtle accusations.

(14) Destruction of memorabilia of the target person.

(15) Parent is interacting with the spouse or former spouse or partner in a manner designed to produce conflict.

When the alienation is overt, the motivation to alienate is blatant. The alienating parent holds the view that the other parent is destructive and presents a danger to the child. The past history with the non resident parent would be considered as all bad. Features of severe and overt alienation would be as follows:

(1) Statements about the non resident parent are delusional or false.

(2) Inclusion of the children as victims of the parent's bad behaviour.

(3) Overt criticism of the parent.

(4) The children are required to keep secrets from the target parent.

(5) Threats of withdrawal of love.

(6) Extreme lack of courtesy to the other parent.

In these extreme cases the alienating parent holds no value at all for the other parent and the hatred is completely overt. At this stage the child is so enmeshed with the alienating parent that it may agree totally that the target parent is a villain. The child itself may come to take on the alienating parent's desires, emotions and hatreds and verbalises them all as if it were its own (Ward & Harvey, 1993).

7.2 ASSESSMENTS

When undertaking a family assessment, in-depth clinical interviews would need to be carried out with the children as well as with both parents. Observation of contact between the child and both parents separately would be beneficial to assess intentional patterns, levels of enmeshment and attachment. The assessment should focus on the needs and feelings of the child, the reasons the child has given for not wanting to see the non residential parent and attachment it has with both parents. The assessment would also look at the emotional and psychological functioning of both parents. The clinical assessment would aim to identify the specific motivations and behaviours and to assess whether or not individual therapy could be beneficial. Should there be indications of an alienation process; the development of a behavioural plan to intervene in the alienation process would be indicated. Recommendations would need to focus on re-establishing contact, initially indirect with a gradual progression towards direct face-to-face contact. Clear direction as to the nature of the indirect contact needs to be given, for example how often letters or cards are to be sent, the residential parent to encourage the child to send a picture or painting in the post, say, once per week. Clear guidelines should be given as to contact arrangements once direct contact commences. A suggestion would be for the non-residential parent to provide a photograph of himself to his child, and the resident parent to encourage the child to display it.

This contact program would need to be monitored and the children's guardian could be the person best placed to support the family and monitor the progress. Furthermore, individual therapy to address the impasse and unresolved issues experienced by the alienating parent would need to take place. It is, however, essential in these circumstances that the guardian has the support of the court behind such a program. Owing to the level of resistance for contact by the alienating parent, clear and unambiguous sanctions must stand behind any court orders and directions made, as compliance at this stage would in all likelihood be motivated only by fear. The ultimate sanction is a change of residence. However, other sanctions such as fines and loss of liberty could be used to motivate the parent to co-operate for contact to be reinstated. If the alienating behaviour continues despite the education, post divorce counselling and impasse resolution therapy, it could only be concluded that this parent does not have the capacity to foster a relationship with the other parent. At that stage the issue for the court is the determination of whether the residential parent has sufficient parenting capacity to outweigh the very serious harm it could be inflicting on the child by the behaviour shown to the other parent.

7.3 PSYCHOLOGICAL IMPACT OF PARENTAL ALIENATION

Children who experience high degrees of conflict as between their parents during divorce show more emotional difficulty than those whose parents are better able to resolve their difficulties. Children whose parents are in conflict are more likely to feel trapped, and children who feel caught are more likely to experience depression, anxiety, and, to a lesser degree, participate also in deviant behaviour. A parent who attempts to alienate the child from the other parent is considered to be perpetrating a form of emotional abuse in that such alienation could not only produce lifelong alienation from a loving parent, but lifelong psychiatric disturbance in the child. The ultimate emotional state of an alienated child is that its behaviour could become fully enmeshed with the alienating parent's behaviour and incorporates the alienating parent's hatreds, emotions and desires with regard to the non resident parent. In some of these cases, the enmeshment is so complete that it would cause the child to suffer an emotional breakdown of devastating proportions if residence were to be awarded to the, in its eyes, hated target parent. According to Ward & Harvey (2003) in these cases the child's sense of self is totally dependent on the relationship it has with the alienating parent, and a loss of that relationship would mean destruction of the self. Certainly, attempts to switch residence would be fought against and undermined by the child, using tactics including attempts to run away.

In the process of parental alienation it is not uncommon for the alienating parent to make false allegations and accusations of abuse. The empirical literature has referred to this as 'Sexual Allegations in Divorce Syndrome' (SAIDS), highlighting the use of sexual abuse allegations as a weapon to prevent contact from taking place. Other weapons could include accusations of threats of or actual domestic violence, physical abuse of the child, emotional abuse of the child, mental illness on the part of the non-resident parent, alcoholism/drug abuse and homosexuality. Caution should however always be expressed that even when such allegations are made in the context of high conflict litigation that these accusations should be taken very seriously and fully investigated to determine their truth. The clinical literature suggests that the emotional harm to a child who is induced into making false allegations of sexual abuse is of a similar degree to the emotional harm that is experienced from actual sexual abuse.

A significant indicator of parental alienation is where the child has had a positive relationship with the now non-residential parent, and the deterioration in the child's behaviour had occurred following his departure from the family home. It has been seen that children do not naturally lose interest in or become distant from their non-residential parent simply by virtue of the fact of absence of that parent. By the nature of the alienation processes the child is placed in a situation involving divided loyalty and conflict, believing it needs to choose which parent to be loyal to. Furthermore, due to the level of conflict and hostility between the parents, alienated children become overly alert to the nuances of emotion and tend to keep the peace by joining the alienating parent in the negative emotions shown towards the alienated parent.

7.4 SUMMARY

Parental alienation is an extremely complex issue in psychological assessments in cases of residence and contact disputes. Clinical interviews with all parenting figures, psychological tests, and observation of contact of child with both parents, where appropriate, are the basic approach when undertaking assessments. However, due to the complexity of the dynamics involved with parental alienation, the clinical psychologist should go well beyond the confines of the individual clinical assessment model and utilise more comprehensive assessment and investigation techniques such as critically analysing case material from a longitudinal perspective and comparing information provided by the parties during interviews with data from other sources.

Adding to the complexity is the fact that, in the context of divorce proceedings, parental alienation is one of several possible explanations for allegations of abuse. Thus, any clinical psychologist conducting assessments of alleged sex abuse, not just in family law proceedings, should be knowledgeable about parental alienation as a possible motivating factor for false allegations. Parental Alienation Syndrome is a pervasive social problem with far reaching and potentially permanent repercussions for the child. When alienation becomes complete, it can amount to a complete termination of parental rights, the alienated child having experienced the loss of nuclear and extended family, in addition to other long-term, detrimental effects. The judgments that courts and professionals make are difficult, complex and have far reaching consequences. Therefore, achieving a sound understanding of the issues by a clinical psychologist and the undertaking of a broad based assessment by him is of considerable importance in advising and assisting the court.

CHAPTER 8

UNDERSTANDING ATTACHMENT

8.1   INTRODUCTION

Attachment is a biological instinct, not learned behaviour. The fundamental universal need and instinct of an infant is to get nearer to the person offering attachment in the belief that it will be protected and its needs will be met. All behavioural and affectional systems of an infant/child strive for proximity to an attachment figure. This attachment response in seeking an attachment figure is activated by both internal and external stressors. When a child receives sensitive care giving and has its needs anticipated and appropriately met, a state of emotional contentment is achieved allowing appropriate development of affect regulation. Thus, having these needs met by a caregiver who is able to anticipate needs is crucial for attachment and for a child learning to regulate its needs. It needs to be understood that basic physical care is not part of the attachment paradigm, neither is stimulation, affection, and play or positive feedback. These have nothing to do with attachment, which is a biological instinct, but they may be part of the interactions that take place when a parent provides sensitive caregiving. The function of the primary caregiver is to be a secure base from which the child is able to explore its world, but at the same time the secure base is also a safe haven to which the child returns or reaches out towards when needed.

8.2   SECURE ATTACHMENTS

When experiencing secure attachment, the child will be confident that its parents or parent figures are responsive, emotionally available and will anticipate its needs should it encounter any threatening, insecure or difficult situations. Consequently, a child who receives significant reassurance and has the confidence within itself and security in its environment in order for it to explore its world may begin to individuate or separate appropriately from the parent figure to become an autonomous individual in its own right. A secure attachment within a child is reflective of the relationship between a child and a parent whose parenting is sensitive and in tune with the child's signals, anticipating and responding appropriately to the needs of a child. The parent who is emotionally available to a child would be in a position to provide protection, comfort and a secure attachment.

Positive attachment behaviour on the part of the parent is being in harmony with the child's physical, emotional and mental needs and responding to its needs in such a way as to regulate arousal, to create a sense of security and to promote growth. Attachment behaviour on the part of the child is the behaviour that evokes this response in a parent so that he comes to attend to its needs. This relationship creates thereby a strong bond between the two. A child would thereafter begin to experience appropriate anxiety from a perceived loss of a person on whom it has come to depend for a sense of security.

8.3   INSECURE ATTACHMENTS

If there is no sensitive care giving, the attachment process could be disturbed, particularly during the first 18 months to 2 years of the child's life. The failure to attune or respond to the children's basic needs could result in the child developing a pattern of interaction where it does not hold the parent in its mind as a person upon whom it can depend and turn to when in need. It is when the parents are unable to engage in sensitive parenting that insecure attachments could develop. This is usually the case where parents have poor emotional regulation, or the parents have difficulty giving priority to the needs of the child, or they fail to respond to a child in a way that regulates the child's emotional state. With consistent sensitive parenting, the child is left feeling secure and would generally have lower cortisol levels influencing the brain, owing to being less afflicted by stress because its needs are being appropriately met. However, with inconsistent emotional availability on the part of a parent, a child could not depend on the caregiver and will experience increasing levels of stress. Where the parenting is inconsistent, involves rejection or is unavailable, the child adapts to and learns to suppress its distress and may react in a defensive way through avoidance or withdrawal. Avoidance is where a child suppresses its responses and tends to withdraw. However, when it has an overriding need, it would still know where to look for the primary caregiver. In situations of inconsistent parenting, where the primary caregiver is sometimes available, sometimes not, the child then desperately holds on to the hope and expectation of its attachment needs being met. Owing to this uncertainty these children experience increased levels of anxiety and this may lead to resistant or ambivalent attachment styles.

Anxious resistant attachment is when the child is uncertain whether the parent would be available when the child exhibits or presents a need. Because of this uncertainty there is always a tendency towards separation anxiety and thus a child could come to cling unduly and may be anxious about exploring its world. The child could be thrown into conflict by the inconsistent availability of the parent and may become anxious on separation owing to fears of abandonment by the parent when it begins to individuate from the parental figure.

Anxious avoidant attachment is found when a child has little or no confidence that, when it seeks care, its needs will be responded to and, in fact, may begin to expect that its needs will not be met and anticipates a degree of rejection or negative emotion. It could result in a child attempting to live a life without the support of others, trying to become emotionally self sufficient and presenting with varying degrees of psychological inhibition. These children may have great difficulty relating to and responding within interpersonal relationships.

While avoidant, resistant or ambivalent attachment styles may cause concern, these defensive styles could be corrected with positive and adaptive parenting. The attachment process which is significantly more serious and gives a lower chance of the child making some form of recovery with reparative parenting could arise when it has developed disorganised attachment styles. In situations where the behaviour of parents or caregivers is confusing, violent and/or unpredictable, it would leave the child either to be afraid of or afraid for the parent and thus the child is faced with a frightening parent upon whom it is reliant for the purposes of meeting its needs. This process suggests that the parent frightens the child; the fear raises distress and anxiety which activate attachment behaviour whose purpose is to get that child into the safe and close proximity of the carer. This occurs when children have no strategies to deal with their distress and/or to deal with the type of parenting that they receive. They become aggressive and in this way tend to take charge and attempt to be in control of their situation. These children may develop into compulsively controlling individuals. Research has indicated that 55 to 80% of maltreated children have disorganised attachment. These children may be deeply troubled and may have considerable difficulty in forming attachments to others. The child is left with anxiety and in a state of conflict in that if it approaches the parent it feels anxious and, yet, if it separates from the parent it continues also to feel anxious. The main conflict in the child will be whether or not it should approach the carer.

Disturbed developmental pathways developing as a result of such disorganised and confused attachment may lead to reactive attachment disorders. The children remain in a continual high state of arousal, fear and distress and may have experiences that are frightening and disturbing to the child. The child could also present with aggressive behaviours that can be exacerbated by frequent changes of carers or intense violence and aggression being present in the home. The essential features of reactive attachment disorder are a markedly disturbed and developmentally inappropriate capacity for engaging in social relationships. In most cases this difficulty begins before the age of 5 years. The child persistently fails to initiate and to respond to most social interactions in a developmentally appropriate way. This condition is associated with grossly pathological parental care that may take the form of persistent disregard of the child's basic emotional needs for comfort, stimulation, affection, and persistent disregard of the child's basic physical needs or where there have been repeated changes of primary caregivers so that stable attachments have been prevented from forming. The pathological care given to the child is presumed to be responsible for the disturbed capacity rising in the child for forming appropriate social relationships later in life.

8.4   SUMMARY

Establishing and maintaining secure attachments with the primary caregiver is crucial for healthy emotional and psychological development. Where there are difficulties with parenting, losses, separations and any form of abuse and/or neglect, the primary relationship with the child could come under threat. The clinical psychologist undertaking an assessment for the court would need to understand the development of attachment, the presentation of any disturbed or insecure attachment styles and the nuances of interpersonal dynamics. Attachment disorders in childhood refer to a persistent disturbance in a child's ability to interact and relate to others across social situations. It needs to be understood that an attachment disorder usually begins before the age of 5 years, and has its roots in a child's earliest relationships with caregivers. Attachment disorders are associated with 'grossly pathological care' which could include disregard for the child's basic social needs for affection, comfort and stimulation as well as basic physical needs, and the need for the presence of a stable primary caregiver leading to a consistent child-caregiver attachment. Attachment disorders, which overlap with the developmental concept of disorganised attachments, are commonly linked to unresolved loss and/or traumatic experiences in the caregiver, capable of being identified with some reliability by the Adult Attachment Interview.

Thus, a sound knowledge of attachment theory and the evidence base for explaining the development of a child's capacity to establish meaningful relationships with primary others is essential. The clinical psychologist when assessing the attachment of a child and parent would need to take account of the child's history, social circumstances, relationships and life experiences. When making recommendation to the court, the psychologist should also indicate the treatment available to address the attachment difficulties and the support required for the parents and the child.

CHAPTER 9

UNDERSTANDING DEFENCE MECHANISMS

9.1 INTRODUCTION

The experience of stress and distress by its very nature makes an impact on our day-to-day functioning. The impact stress makes depends not only on the nature and severity of the stressor but also on the individual's pre-existing vulnerabilities and psychological make up. In the case of an individual who is quite vulnerable to begin with, stressful situations may precipitate more serious psychopathology. Furthermore, severity of the stress is measured by the degree of disruption it causes in the individual experiencing it. People's responses when faced with stress or distress could be seen as a way of repairing or addressing the impact of psychological damage it has caused. Thus, crying, repeatedly talking about the event or mourning at the outcome of the situation are in effect psychological damage repair mechanisms. It is when a person is vulnerable that there is a greater tendency to use more maladaptive coping mechanisms such as denial and repression. These are ways of protecting the self from hurt or emotional pain. The use of defence mechanisms are in effect ways to protect the self and this could be done either by denying or distorting the experience, countering the threat or reducing emotional or self-involvement.

The human mind has the capacity to invent mechanisms that shield a person from becoming aware of unpleasant emotions and acute distress. These mechanisms are not always conscious and could be present in disguised form. It is important to uncover and understand these mechanisms as most emotional difficulties result from a combination of problematic defence mechanisms and affects. However, understanding feelings is not enough to help people overcome their problems. It is also necessary to explain why unconscious defences are keeping a person from knowing about those unpleasant feelings. In order to understand the meanings and origins of the irrational behaviour, symptoms and attitudes, individuals need to be assisted to gain insight into their pathological defence mechanisms and feelings.

9.2   THE PSYCHODYNAMICS OF DEFENCE MECHANISMS

According to Blackman (2004), any behaviour or action could be a defence, and actions or responses such as looking away, preferring to watch the television rather than engage in conversation with another who is present, going to sleep or screaming at someone could all be defence mechanisms. Whatever the mental activity or behaviour, if it shields a person from experiencing unpleasant emotions, it is defensive. Defences could be conscious or unconscious, as individuals may consciously and deliberately take control of emotions. For example, suppression indicates purposeful forgetting. In contrast, repression is unconscious forgetting. It is a subconscious way of regulating defences. Defences could be used adaptively or be maladaptive. As maladaptive defence mechanisms interfere with interpersonal relationships or prevent meaningful interaction in social, emotional or interpersonal settings, it is believed they could contribute to psychopathology. Defences are developed or triggered when a person is faced with abuse or trauma, and has limited coping capacity, limited internal resources or psychological potential.

Defence mechanisms are thus learned reactions which become automatic and habitual when the individual attempts to deal with inner hurt, anxiety, emotional pain, and self-devaluation in the absence of coping capacity and emotional strength. Defence mechanisms are maladaptive in the sense that they interfere with effective resolution of actual problems and, if they become the predominant means of coping with stressors, these then become dysfunctional ways of coping. When assessing a person's defensive behaviour, their cognitive styles and their means of dealing with emotions and ways of solving problems could all be explored. The individual's flexibility in adapting to changing situations, his coping styles in the face of conflicts and frustrations and the coping strategies he deploys in the face of demands and responsibilities imposed on him are all to be assessed (Blackman, 2004).

9.3   TYPES OF DEFENCE MECHANISMS

There are unlimited ways in which individuals come to cope with stress and trauma, as any behaviour or action, as stated, could serve as a defensive mechanism. Defensive strategies commonly assessed when working with children and families would include the following.

Projection is a defence mechanism that involves taking our own unacceptable qualities or feelings and ascribing them to other people. For example, if you have a strong dislike for someone, you might instead believe that he or she does not like you. This may be seen when an angry spouse accuses his partner of hostility. Projection functions to allow the expression of the desire or impulse, but in a way that the individual does not recognise it, therefore reducing anxiety.

Denial is the refusal to accept reality and to act as if a painful event, thought or feeling did not exist. It is considered one of the most primitive of the defence mechanisms because it is characteristic of very early childhood development. Denial is probably one of the best known defence mechanisms, used often to describe those who seem unable to face reality or admit a truth. Denial is an outright refusal to admit or recognise that something has occurred or is currently occurring. Drug addicts, alcoholics and sex offenders often deny that they have a problem, while victims of traumatic events may deny that the event ever occurred. It is not unusual for victims of sexual abuse to deny that the abuse has occurred. Denial of reality is a defence mechanism which tends to screen out or block out painful realities by ignoring or refusing to acknowledge the situation. In other words, denial is a way the mind has of not paying attention to reality. There is an important diagnostic distinction to be made between individuals who have some defect in their ability to test reality and those who can see or understand reality but avoid doing so in order to resolve a conflict. Denial is a mechanism which protects the ego from things that the child or adult cannot cope with. While this may save the individual from the immediate experience of anxiety or pain, denial also requires a substantial investment of energy. As a result, other defences are also used to keep these unacceptable feelings from consciousness.

Reaction formation is a defence mechanism which attempts to reduce anxiety by taking up the opposite feeling, impulse, or behaviour. It aims to convert the person's underlying wishes or impulses that are perceived to be dangerous into their opposites, in other words to hide their true feelings by behaving in the exactly opposite manner. For example, a woman who is furious with her child and wishes her harm, might become overly concerned and protective of the child's health. Alternatively, it could be understood when one treats someone one strongly dislikes in an excessively friendly manner in order to hide one's true feelings.

Repression is a defence mechanism characterised by the blocking of unacceptable impulses from consciousness. It is a process whereby the threats of painful thoughts or desires are excluded or pushed away from the consciousness. This may take the form of forgetting, selective forgetting or selective recall. Repression is a means of protecting the self from sudden traumatic experiences until such time as the individual has increased his resources to cope with the situation or the individual has become desensitised to the shock. Repression acts to keep information out of conscious awareness. However, these memories do not simply disappear; they continue to influence one's behaviour. For example, a person who has repressed memories of abuse suffered as a child may later have difficulty forming relationships. Where unwanted information is consciously forced out of our awareness, the phenomenon is known as **suppression**.

Splitting is a defence mechanism used by individuals suffering from psychosis or borderline personality disorganisation. It involves the process of dividing people as purely hostile and others as purely loving. Splitting is a defence where the individual splits each incoming element into separate entities and is unable to consider the possibility that these elements are able to coexist. Therefore, the splitter usually attributes only love or hostility to a particular person, not seeing that most people potentially possess both loving and hostile qualities.

Rationalisation is a defence mechanism that involves explaining an unacceptable behaviour or feeling in a rational or logical manner, avoiding the true explanation for the behaviour. It is a process of cognitive reframing of one's perceptions to protect the ego in the face of changing realities. For example, a person who is turned down for a date might rationalise the situation by saying they were not attracted to the other person anyway, or a student who blames a poor examination result on his teacher rather than on his lack of preparation. Rationalisation not only prevents anxiety, it may also protect self-esteem and self-concept. When confronted by success or failure, people tend to attribute achievement to their own qualities and skills while failures are blamed on other people or outside forces.

Isolation is the removal of sensation or feeling from conscious awareness.

Fabulation is a defence that shows up in automatic lying, which is unconsciously motivated and is usually undertaken to relieve lower self-esteem associated with having forgotten the details of something.

Regression is a mechanism used when one returns to previous patterns of behaviour used earlier in development or could be explained as retreating from reality to a less demanding personal status. Regression is reverting to an earlier stage of development in the face of unacceptable impulses. An example is an adolescent who is overwhelmed with fear, anger and growing sexual impulses and could become clinging and begin thumb sucking or bed wetting. When confronted by stressful events, individuals sometimes abandon coping strategies and revert to presenting with behaviours such as sulking, crying, curling up into a ball or assuming the foetal position upon hearing unpleasant news.

Emotional insulation is a mechanism where the individual reduces emotional involvement in difficult, hurtful or conflict-inducing situations by a form of anaesthesia and is commonly seen in a grief reaction following a significant loss. It is a defence mechanism used in the face of increased stress and can be compared to a protective shell that prevents a repetition of pain previously experienced.

Intellectualisation works to reduce anxiety by thinking about events in a way which is devoid of emotion and which is cold and clinical. This defence mechanism allows us to avoid thinking about the stressful, emotional aspect of the situation and focus only on the intellectual component. For example, a parent who has seriously emotionally neglected a child who is presenting with disturbed behaviour, might focus on learning everything about autistic spectrum or ADHD disorders in order to avoid distress and remain distant from the reality of the situation. A further example could be that of an individual who when told he has a life-threatening disease focuses exclusively on the statistical chances of recovery to avoid coping with his fear and sadness.

Avoidance is a defensive mechanism used to stay away from situations because their symbolism generates feelings of conflict.

Fantasy, when used as a defence mechanism, is the channeling of unacceptable or unattainable desires into the imagination. This serves to protect the person's self esteem. For example, when educational or social expectations are not being met, one imagines success in these areas and attempts to ward off self condemnation. It is the re-creation of one's own reality to compensate for the experience of painful reality.

Passivity occurs where a person adopts a compliant or submissive attitude. As a defensive structure it occurs when a person is acquiescing in situations where activity is needed. The passivity thus becomes a maladaptive defence. Pathological defensive passivity usually involves unconscious guilt experienced over wishes to retaliate against harm or to kill another human. Where an apparently yielding attitude simultaneously expresses also resistance and anger, the term passive aggression is used.

Somatisation involves conscious symbolic fears about one's body and its functions despite the lack of obvious medical symptoms. The focus of this defence is to avoid depression, loneliness or being unfulfilled when the painful effects generate deprivation.

Dissociation as a defence mechanism occurs when a person not only forgets a thought (repression) but is unaware of the whole aspect of himself, such as elements of identity, drive, urges, guilt reactions, memories and defences.

Displacement is the redirecting of thoughts, feelings and impulses from an object that gives rise to anxiety to a safer, more acceptable one. Being angry at the social worker who removes a child who has been subjected to non accidental injuries is an example of displacement. It is generally observed when someone takes out his frustration, feelings, and impulses on people or objects that are less threatening. Displaced aggression is a common example of this defence mechanism. Rather than the single mother expressing anger and frustration in ways that could lead to negative consequences she may express her anger towards a person or object that poses no threat such as the children or domestic pets.

9.4 SUMMARY

When undertaking assessment of children and adults who have experienced some levels of trauma or psychological distress, it will not be unusual to encounter an individual who has developed and is utilising defence mechanisms. In fact, the presence of defensive strategies and defensive behaviour would suggest that the person is attempting to cope with internalised anxiety. In many cases these defences could be occurring unconsciously and working to distort reality. Not all defense mechanisms are unhealthy; in adult life some of these could be adaptive and allow the individual to function normally. As defense mechanisms are our way of distancing ourselves from a full awareness of unpleasant thoughts, feelings and desires, it is usually a matter of concern when a child is assessed to be using these strategies. This would suggest that the child has endured life experiences which are so disturbing and anxiety producing that it has needed to develop coping strategies which it is not normal for it to have created. By creating defensive strategies and mechanisms the child or adult would be altering and distorting their awareness of the original impulse in order to make it more tolerable and protect itself from unpleasant emotions. The greatest problems arise when defence mechanisms are overused in order to avoid dealing with problems.

CHAPTER 10

MALADAPTIVE PERSONALITY DEVELOPMENT

10.1   INTRODUCTION

Personality should be viewed in the context of the growth and the developmental history of a child. The child's personality develops over time when its initial range of behaviours becomes shaped and gradually narrowed, selected and crystallised by preferred ways of relating to others and coping with its world. A child acquires patterns or traits that become deeply etched, and also become entrenched and difficult to change. These constitute habitual ways of psychological functioning that make up a child's style and patterns of relating to others and the world. Ever since the ancient Greeks identified four temperaments, each associated with one of the four humours, psychiatry has taken an interest in the classification of personality disorders. There is consensus in the clinical literature that personality disorder has now come into its own as a diagnostic entity. With the advent of the Diagnostic and Statistical Manual of Mental Disorders (DSM III) devised by the American Psychiatric Association 1980, it became a generally held view, supported by research, that there were characteristics that all personality disorders share, the chief among these being an inflexible and maladaptive response to stress, a disability in working and with loving, characteristics generally more serious and always more pervasive than when found in neurosis. Personality disorders almost always occur in response to social and interpersonal situations. Additionally, people with personality disorders constantly fail to see themselves as others see them; they lack empathy with other people, may not get on with other people and may also annoy others with whom they attempt to relate. There exists a tendency to create a vicious cycle in which already precarious interpersonal relationships are made worse by the person's mode of adaptation and behaviour.

10.2   CHARACTERISTICS OF MALADAPTIVE PERSONALITY

Personality disorder is identified when behaviour traits, patterns or styles become inflexible and maladaptive which then leads to significant impairment in interpersonal, social or occupational efficiency as well as causing subjective distress such as anxiety and depression. When studying the psychodynamic aspect of personality disturbance (in contrast to a neurotic person whose symptoms result primarily from intra-psychic conflicts), the diagnostic psychopathology of a personality disorder is seen to result from rigid personality traits and patterns. A personality disorder would arise when some distortions of the personality develop early in life and persist as part of a person's style and characterise the way in which he copes with and in his environment, how he defends himself against real or imagined threats, and his personal competence or integrity. Persons with personality disorder may never consider or admit they may have something abnormal or intrusive and thus may never come to suffer feelings of anxiety once these traits become established. The change occurs in childhood resulting in a distortion of personality and the sufferers may come to see things with compensatory changes made by them to offset the distortion. Cameron and Rychlak (1985) note that:

> 'personality disorders suffer from more severe disturbances in that they are distorted strategies in living that enable the person to achieve a stable level of functioning with this distortion included. There is a distortion of personality style that more or less permanently alleviates anxiety.'

After extensive research and clinical experience, Kaplan & Sadock (1981) highlighted that the most outstanding characteristics of all personality disorders includes:

(1)   an inflexible and maladaptive response to stress;

(2)   a disability in occupation and relationships that is generally more serious and pervasive; and that

(3)   the personality disorder almost always occurred in response to a social context.

The literature highlights those with personality disorders as being individuals who constantly fail to see themselves as others do, and also lack meaningful empathy (Leaff, 1981). However, it is important to recognise that persons who have a personality disorder are not out of contact with reality. They do demonstrate non-specific manifestations of ego-weakness, namely lack of anxiety tolerance and lack of impulse control. Furthermore, they experience difficulties associated with shallowness of emotional reactions as well as significant difficulty in or capacity for forming deep and enduring interpersonal relationships (Leaff 1981).

It is widely documented that growing up in a disruptive environment may impair a child's development and his or her sense of self. The disruption can also impede the social development required for satisfactory peer relationships necessary for adequate latency-age (adolescence to adulthood) functioning. The primary difficulties are associated with role confusion, lack of identity and a lack of capacity for intimacy.

Difficulties encountered during the adolescent period of individuals diagnosed with personality disorders held similarities with features such as:

(1)   Hostility expressed in subtle ways towards the parent by the child.

(2)   Onset of antisocial and disruptive behaviour.

(3)   Repeated disciplinary problems, expulsions from school and truancy.

(4)   Poor motivation, failures and keeping late hours.

(5)   Frequent fights, alcohol and drug use, and recklessness in their behaviour.

10.3   PSYCHODYNAMICS OF MALADAPTIVE PERSONALITY

Looking at the development of personality maladaptive patterns and their dynamics, Ogata et al (1990) found in his studies and within the literature that these patients experience more conflict and less cohesion with their family during their adolescent years, and concluded that adolescent periods spawned problems for the family at a time when the identity and the individualities of an individual became salient features. Personality dysfunction, in particular borderline personalities, 'experience significant peer related problems in school especially during high school years, further underscoring possible difficulties with identity and affectional relationships' and reported feeling left out and isolated in their adolescent years (p 99).

From the research studies it appears that personality disordered patients recall family experiences as a combination of traumatic early years, emotionally or psychologically unavailable parents and family conflict. All of the above reflect a non-nurturing and unstable environment where the pattern of emotional neglect characterises personality-forming maladaptive experiences.

Persons who go on to develop personality disorders might have experienced trauma at an age when they would have been particularly vulnerable (between the ages of 5 and 10). Defence mechanisms employed by children at this age to deal with prolonged distress include denial, splitting and repression. Unmet needs during vulnerable developmental phases in early formative years have a direct impact on development of an immature ego which is incapable of resistance along with other vulnerabilities which lead to the development of these defences (Ogata et al, 1990; Stone, 1990; Leaff, 1980).

The developmental consideration of pathological personality development leads to the observation of developmental failure, particularly in disturbed family relationships, inadequate parenting received and dysfunctional mother/child relationships with repeated instances of children feeling rejected in their childhood. This developmental failure underscores the psychodynamics of personality disorders.

Past childhood experiences of personality disorders are also characterised by neglect and deprivation in childhood. This leads to repetitive and continual trauma arising from chronic disturbance in family structures and relationships. As a consequence, this results in object hunger (seeking for emotional needs to be met) and affective instability. This constant seeking of needs to be met and affective instability represents a child searching for the parenting it never had. This dynamic would be evident and replicated in future relationships and interactions and is reflective of personality dysfunction (van Rooyen, 1993).

10.4   PERSONALITY DISORDERS

Personality disorders do not stem from reactions to stress in the form of an adjustment disorder or post traumatic stress disorder, nor are they defences against anxiety such as neurotic disorders. These disorders stem from immature and distorted personality development resulting in individuals with persistent maladaptive ways of perceiving, thinking and relating to the world around them. These maladaptive approaches usually cause significant impairment in functioning. Individuals may behave in a way that is contrary to prevailing social attitudes or expectations of others. It is only when personality traits are inflexible and maladaptive that they cause significant impairment in social or emotional functioning or subjective distress that they constitute personality disorder.

Characteristics found in all personality disorders would include patterns of disruptive personal relationships; problems that would be long-standing and marked by behaviour that is consistently troublesome to others. Whatever the particular trait that the person develops, it would affect and influence new situations and would lead to repetitive or maladaptive behaviour patterns. A further characteristic feature of personality disorder is that the behaviour of individuals may be more marked by the impact their behaviour has on others rather than the pain felt by the individuals concerned themselves. Patterns of behaviour reflected in personality disorders are highly resistant to change.

Types of personality disorders are described in the DSM IV which characterise these personalities as being found in three clusters.

(1)   Cluster 1 includes paranoid, schizoid and schizo-typal personality disorders. Individuals with these disorders are often seen as odd or eccentric and their habitual behaviour may take different forms.

(2)   Cluster 2 includes histrionic, narcissistic, antisocial and borderline personality disorders. Individuals with these disorders have in common a tendency to be dramatic, emotional and erratic. The impulsive behaviour often involves antisocial activities, which are more colourful and more forceful and more likely to get them into contact with mental health or legal authorities than the other clusters.

(3)   Cluster 3 includes avoidant, dependent, compulsive and passive-aggressive personality disorders. In this cluster, the disorders, unlike others, often feature anxiety and fearfulness making it difficult in some cases to distinguish them from anxiety-based disorders and anxiety states.

These issues are further developed in Section III of this book.

10.5   SUMMARY

In order to carry out a family assessment it is important for the clinical psychologist to have a knowledge and understanding of how individuals behave and how their behaviour affects others. As part of this process it is also important to assess thought processes that may lie behind the behaviour. An understanding and knowledge of the features and characteristics of a normal and healthy personality as well as maladaptive personality functioning is important. Interview-based assessments are the preferred approach in assessing personality, making use of semi-structured and unstructured clinical interviews. Self report questionnaires do have validity in the broader assessment of personality traits, but are less useful in the diagnosis of personality disorders. When undertaking assessments for the court it is always advisable to have multiple sources of information and attempts should always be made to confirm or refute significant claims made by the patient.

CHAPTER 11

PSYCHOLOGICAL TREATMENT

11.1 INTRODUCTION

Clinical psychology, psychiatry and psychiatric social work and other disciplines make use of psychotherapy which is a widely practised procedure and treatment method. Psychotherapy involves two individuals engaging in private verbal interaction, usually face to face, and deals with highly personal material. The process of psychotherapy could be prolonged, as psychological and behavioural change is both difficult and painful to achieve. The therapist and client are required to invest in hard work to explore, evaluate and alter long-standing feelings, thoughts and behaviour patterns on the part of the client. Thus, psychotherapy is generally viewed as a special type of verbal interaction that is prolonged, highly personal and occurs for the benefit of the client.

Psychotherapy is psychological treatment to address significant life changes, decisions that an individual needs to make and difficulties he has at home or work. It is also used for assisting with serious problems that interfere with day-to-day life, such as physical or mental illness. It is also suitable for people when they feel an overwhelming and prolonged sense of sadness and helplessness, and they lack hope in their lives. It could be that their emotional difficulties make it hard for them to function from day to day. Psychological treatment may also be needed when a person's actions are harmful to himself or to others, for example, if he drinks too much alcohol and becomes overly aggressive or has suicidal ideations. Where people are troubled by emotional difficulties facing family members or close friends, or have problems with interpersonal relationships, psychological treatment could effectively bring concrete and positive results.

In **the process of psychotherapy**, psychological treatment initially involves the therapist getting to know the patient/client and building a rapport. Exploration of the person's life, getting to know him or her, asking about family and friends and trying to find out why the person is attending therapy is part of this process. This information helps the therapist to assess the situation and develop a plan for treatment. Psychotherapy involves an active collaborative effort between therapist and client.

It is not uncommon for patients to undergo psychotherapy while being assisted also with medication. For many individuals, this is the best approach to treatment; for example, patients with moderate-to-severe depression typically do best with a combination of antidepressant drugs and some form of psychotherapy.

11.2   LEVELS OF PSYCHOLOGICAL TREATMENTS

11.2.1   Supportive therapy

Supportive therapy involves formal counselling, which of all the psychotherapeutic approaches available has the most modest and conservative of goals. It is designed more to prevent the patient from getting worse rather than to produce improvements. This approach is usually provided on a short-term basis or to assist the patient through a crisis or period of great stress, or to help more chronically disturbed patients over the long-term. Supportive therapy does not attempt to produce any fundamental change in the patient's personality or manner of functioning. It is designed to strengthen existing defences, review and improve coping mechanisms in order to maintain control and restore levels of adaptation. General approaches of supportive therapy include guidance, counselling, and relaxation techniques. Supportive therapy is often offered at GP surgeries over six sessions.

11.2.2   Re-educative therapy

Re-educative therapy attempts to produce a substantial change with an approach which focuses on overt behaviour and conscious processes. It proposes that meaningful change can be achieved by focussing on current issues in the patient's life, for example ongoing relationships, current attitudes and behaviours and by dealing directly with sources of conflict and distress. Interventions could include readjustments, goal modification and gaining insight into conscious conflicts. Cognitive behavioural therapy, psychodynamic therapy, rational emotive therapy and psychodrama are some examples of re-educative approaches.

11.2.3   Re-constructive therapy

Re-constructive therapy aims to address extensive personality re-organisation. Psychotherapy attempts to reduce irrational impulses, to increase the individual's repertoire of adaptive defences and to make him more flexible and to gain insight into his inner needs so that the individual can adapt to social and interpersonal functioning. The approach is based on the notion that psychological difficulties are due to some unconscious drives, and psychological issues or inner turmoil. Thus the treatment focuses on making the client aware of inner conflicts and drives and the development of insight. The main objective would be to gain insight into unconscious conflicts with an aim of achieving change of personality and character structure. It is hoped to achieve some level of personality growth as well as development of new adaptive potentialities. The approaches would include analysis, psychoanalytic psychotherapy and analytic group therapy.

11.3 TYPES OF THERAPIES

11.3.1 Group therapy

In group therapy, a small group of people meets regularly to discuss individual issues and help each other with problems with the guidance of a trained therapist. Group methods are also commonly used to treat individuals with similar specialised problems, such as parents of children undergoing treatment, patients with alcohol and drug addiction problems and those with chronic psychiatric conditions, as these individuals share common problems and experiences. Groups are especially useful for providing support and understanding, communicating information and teaching members how to solve common problems. Psychodynamic approaches to group therapy usually fall into different categories depending on the emphasis of the individual therapist and the group. The approach could either involve treating of the individual patient in the group or treating of individuals by or through the group. There are economic advantages as large numbers can be treated at the same time, but a limitation could be that such group therapy could involve a less intense therapist/client relationship than individual therapy.

11.3.2 Family therapy

Family therapy typically focuses on the family unit, with varieties to include all family members living under one roof, the nuclear family, the parents alone, or even just one family member. Family or couple therapy is indicated when the physical or mental health of one of the family members is directly affecting family dynamics or the well-being of significant relationships. Family therapy can also consist of alternating sessions with different sub-sets of family members. Regardless of who is actually present at the sessions, the family would be the focus of treatment, with the goals established to strengthen the family system, increase separation-individuation and strengthen the marriage. Family systems are strengthened by improving communication between members and changing pathological interactional patterns. By focusing on increased separation-individuation and development of individual family members to achieve their individuality and independence one could hope to improve family functioning.

As a disturbed marital relationship is often the basis for broader family pathology, a focus on the marriage along with couple therapy is included in this approach. The actual process of family therapy includes various techniques, such as role play, taking the observations made to the family for comment and discussion and making the members undertake work assignments.

11.3.3   Individual psychotherapy

Individual psychotherapy is not limited to a particular type or technique. Generally speaking, most therapists are trained in several different approaches. They then combine techniques from these various approaches that fit their own style and personality and the needs of the patient.

11.3.4   Behaviour therapy

Behaviour therapy, also called behaviour modification or behaviourism, sets up rewards and punishments to change thinking patterns and shape behaviour. Behavioural therapy can involve relaxation training, stress management, biofeedback and desensitisation of phobias. Behavioural therapists help patients learn how to get more satisfaction and rewards through their own actions and how to unlearn the behavioural patterns that have contributed to, or have resulted from, their problems.

11.3.5   Cognitive therapy

Cognitive therapy seeks to identify and correct thinking patterns that can lead to problematical feelings and behaviours. Beliefs and expectations are explored to identify how they shape a person's experiences. If a thought or belief is too rigid and causes problems, the therapist helps the client to modify his or her belief so that it is less extreme.

11.3.6   Cognitive behavioural therapy

Cognitive-behavioural therapy (CBT) helps a person to recognise his or her own negative thought patterns and behaviours and to replace these with positive ones. Used both with and without medication, cognitive-behavioural therapy is the most popular and commonly used therapy for the treatment of depression. A major aim of CBT is to reduce anxiety and depression by eliminating beliefs or behaviours that help to maintain problematic emotions.

CBT generally lasts about 12 weeks and may be conducted individually or in a group. There is evidence that there are beneficial effects of CBT for patients with panic disorder, obsessive-compulsive disorder, post traumatic stress syndrome and social phobia.

11.3.7 Gestalt therapy

In contrast to the psychotherapy approaches which look at the unknown and subconscious processes, gestalt therapists look at the **here and now** of living. Gestalt therapy also focuses on the relationships people have with all things. With this approach focusing on the here and now, this enables the client or to understand himself more fully and to develop a greater self awareness.

11.3.8 Interpersonal therapy

Interpersonal therapy (IPT) is a short-term therapy often used to treat depression. This treatment approach focuses on an individual's social relationships and how to improve his social support. IPT therapy seeks to improve a person's relationship skills, working on how to communicate more effectively, expressing emotions appropriately and being properly assertive in social and work situations. In depression, IPT helps patients learn how to deal more effectively with others to reduce conflict and gain support from family and friends. It is usually conducted, like cognitive-behavioural therapy, on an individual basis but can also be used in a group therapy setting.

11.3.9 Movement/dance/art/music therapy

Movement/dance/art/music therapy methods include the use of movement, art or music to express emotions. This type of therapy is effective for those who have difficulty expressing their feelings.

11.3.10 Phototherapy

Phototherapy (light therapy) is used for people who suffer from seasonal affective disorder (SAD), a form of depression that is related to the change of the seasons within their geographic location. These may benefit from bright light phototherapy. Phototherapy uses special light bulbs which emit 'white light', which is much brighter than ordinary lights and is specially made for this purpose. The therapist would instruct the patient in how to use these high-intensity lights to improve symptoms of seasonal depression.

11.3.11 Psychodynamic psychotherapy

The psychodynamic psychotherapy approach helps a person look inside him or herself to discover and understand emotional conflicts that may be contributing to emotional problems. The therapist helps the client 'uncover' unconscious motivations, unresolved problems from childhood and early patterns of behaviour to resolve issues and to become aware of how those motivations could influence present actions and feelings. This is a lengthy process, typically taking several years.

11.4 AN IN-DEPTH LOOK AT SELECTED THERAPEUTIC APPROACHES

11.4.1 Cognitive behaviour therapy

Cognitive behaviour therapy (CBT) is an action-oriented form of psychosocial therapy that assumes that maladaptive, or faulty, thinking patterns cause maladaptive behaviour and 'negative' emotions. The treatment focuses on changing an individual's thoughts (cognitive patterns) in order to change his or her behaviour and emotional state.

CBT is indicated when a person has a pattern of unwanted behaviour accompanied by distress and impairment. It is a recommended treatment option for a mood disorders, personality disorders, social phobia, obsessive-compulsive disorder (OCD), eating disorders, substance abuse, anxiety or panic disorder, agoraphobia, post traumatic stress disorder (PTSD), and attention-deficit hyperactivity disorder (ADHD). It is also frequently used as a tool to deal with chronic pain for patients with illnesses such as rheumatoid arthritis, back problems, and cancer. Patients with sleep disorders may also find cognitive-behavioural therapy a useful treatment for insomnia.

CBT is a hybrid of cognitive therapy and behavioural therapy. Cognitive therapists attempt to make their patients aware of these distorted thinking patterns, or cognitive distortions, and change these (a process termed cognitive restructuring). Behavioural therapy, or behaviour modification, trains individuals to replace undesirable behaviours with healthier behavioural patterns. This approach does not focus on uncovering or understanding the unconscious motivations that may be behind the maladaptive behaviour. In other words, strictly behavioural therapists do not try to find out why their patients behave the way they do, they simply teach them to change the behaviour. With these approaches combined cognitive-behavioural therapy (CBT) integrates the cognitive restructuring approach of cognitive therapy with the behavioural modification techniques of behavioural therapy. The therapist works with the patient to identify both the thoughts and the behaviours that are causing distress, and to change those thoughts in order to readjust the behaviour.

Techniques used in cognitive-behavioural therapy to help patients uncover and examine their thoughts and change their behaviours would include:

(1) **Behavioural homework assignments**. Cognitive-behavioural therapists frequently request that their patients complete homework assignments between therapy sessions. Patients are encouraged to try out new responses to situations discussed in therapy sessions.

(2) **Cognitive rehearsal**. The patient imagines a difficult situation and the therapist guides him through the step-by-step process of facing and successfully dealing with it. The patient then works on practising, or rehearsing, these steps mentally. Ideally, when the situation arises in real life, the patient will draw on the rehearsed behaviour to address it.

(3) **Journal**. Patients are asked to keep a detailed diary recounting their thoughts, feelings, and actions when specific situations arise. The journal helps to make the patient aware of his or her maladaptive thoughts and to show their consequences on behaviour. In later stages of therapy, it may serve to demonstrate and reinforce positive behaviours.

(4) **Modelling**. The therapist and patient engage in role-playing exercises in which the therapist acts out appropriate behaviours or responses to situations.

(5) **Conditioning**. The therapist uses reinforcement to encourage a particular behaviour. For example, a child with ADHD gets a gold star every time he stays focused on tasks and accomplishes certain daily chores. The gold star reinforces and increases the desired behaviour by identifying it with something positive. Reinforcement can also be used to extinguish unwanted behaviours by imposing negative consequences.

(6) **Systematic desensitisation**. Patients imagine a situation they fear, while the therapist employs techniques to help the patient relax, helping the person to cope with their fear reaction and eventually eliminating the anxiety altogether. For example, a patient in treatment for agoraphobia, or fear of open or public places, will relax and then picture herself on the pavement outside her house. In her next session, she may relax herself and then imagine a visit to a crowded shopping centre. The imagery of the anxiety-producing situations gets progressively more intense until, eventually, the therapist and patient approach the anxiety-causing situation in real-life (a 'graded exposure'), perhaps by visiting a shopping centre. Exposure may be increased to the point of 'flooding', providing maximum exposure to the real situation. By repeatedly pairing a desired response (relaxation) with a fear-producing situation (open, public spaces), the patient gradually becomes desensitised to the old response of fear and learns to react with feelings of relaxation.

(7) **Validity testing**. Patients are asked to test the validity of the automatic thoughts and schemas they encounter. The therapist may ask the patient to defend or produce evidence that a schema is true. If the patient is unable to meet the challenge, the faulty nature of the schema is exposed.

11.4.2   Family therapy

Family therapy is a form of psychotherapy that involves all the members of a nuclear or extended family. It may be conducted by one therapist or a team of therapists. In many cases the team consists of a man and a woman in order to treat gender-related issues or serve as role models for family members. Although some forms of family therapy are based on behavioural or psychodynamic principles, the most widespread form is based on **family systems theory**. This approach regards the family, as a whole, as the unit of treatment, and emphasises such factors as relationships and communication patterns rather than traits or symptoms in individual members.

Family therapists may be either clinical psychologists or other professionals trained in marriage and family therapy. They will usually evaluate a family for treatment by scheduling a series of interviews with the members of the immediate family, including young children, and significant or symptomatic members of the extended family. This process allows the therapist(s) to find out how each member of the family sees the problem, as well as to form first impressions of the family's functioning. Family therapists typically look for the level and types of emotions expressed, patterns of dominance and submission, the roles played by family members, communication styles, and the locations of emotional triangles. They will also note whether these patterns are rigid or relatively flexible.

Family therapy is often recommended in treatment of a family member with serious mental health disorders. Family therapy helps other family members understand their relation's disorder and adjust to the psychological changes that may be occurring in the relation. It is also suitable in families who scapegoat a member or are undermining the treatment of a member in individual therapy. Additionally, family therapy is indicated where the identified patient's problems seem inextricably tied to problems with other family members or families with adjustment difficulties.

Some families are not considered suitable candidates for family therapy. They include:

(1)   families in which one, or both, of the parents is psychotically ill or has been diagnosed with antisocial or paranoid personality disorder;

(2) families with members who cannot participate in treatment sessions because of physical illness or similar limitations;

(3) families with members with very rigid personality structures;

(4) families whose members cannot, or will not, be able to meet regularly for treatment;

(5) families that are on the verge of breakup.

Family therapy tends to be short-term treatment, usually several months in length, with a focus on resolving specific problems such as eating disorders, difficulties with school, or adjustments to bereavement or geographical relocation. It is not normally used for long-term or intensive restructuring of severely dysfunctional families. The therapists seek to analyse the process of family interaction and communication as a whole. They do not take sides with specific members. They may make occasional comments or remarks intended to help family members become more conscious of patterns or structures that had previously been taken for granted. Family therapists, who work as a team, also model new behaviours for the family through their interactions with each other during sessions.

11.4.3 Psychodynamic psychotherapy

Psychodynamic psychotherapy is a form of psychotherapy used by qualified psychotherapists or clinical psychologists who are trained in this approach to treat patients who have a range of mild to moderate chronic life problems. It is related to a specific body of theories about the relationships between conscious and unconscious mental processes, and should not be used as a synonym for psychotherapy in general.

'Psychodynamic' refers to a view of human personality that results from interactions between conscious and unconscious factors. The purpose of all forms of psychodynamic treatment is to bring unconscious mental material and processes into full consciousness so that the patient can gain more control over his or her life.

Classical psychoanalysis is the least commonly practised form of psychodynamic therapy because of its demands on the patient's time, as well as on his or her emotional and financial resources. This treatment approach focuses on the formation of an intense relationship between the therapist and patient, which is analysed and discussed in order to deepen the patient's insight into his or her problems.

Psychodynamic psychotherapy is a modified form of psychoanalysis based on the same theoretical principles as psychoanalysis, but is less intense and less concerned with major changes in the patient's character structure. The focus in treatment is usually on the patient's current life situation and the way problems relate to early conflicts and feelings.

Not all patients benefit from psychodynamic treatment. Rather, it is indicated where the client has the capacity to relate well enough to form an effective working relationship with the therapist. The client would also need to have at least average intelligence and be psychologically minded. It is important for the person to have an ability to tolerate frustration, sadness, and other painful emotions as well as the capacity to distinguish between reality and fantasy. Problem areas and disorders best suited for psychodynamic psychotherapy would include depression, personality impairment, neurotic conflicts, and chronic relationship problems.

In psychodynamic psychotherapy, the therapist does not tell the patient how to solve problems; rather the focus of treatment is the exploration of the patient's mind and habitual thought patterns. Such therapy is non-directed and insight-oriented, thus the goal of treatment is to increase the understanding by the client of their inner conflicts and emotional problems.

Interpretations made during psychodynamic therapy may be either focused on present issues or to draw connections between the patient's past and the present. The patient is also often encouraged to describe dreams and fantasies as sources of material for interpretation. **Exploration and working through** is the primary work of the therapist. This allows the patient to understand the influence of the past on his or her present situation, to accept it emotionally as well as intellectually, and to use the new understanding to make changes in his present life. Working through helps the patient to gain some measure of control over inner conflicts and to resolve these or minimise their power.

The cost of psychodynamic psychotherapy is prohibitive for most patients without insurance coverage as a course of this treatment would involve at least weekly sessions for up to 2 years. The NHS does offer this treatment but resources are low and demand is high, consequently there are extremely long waiting lists. This limited and costly resource has led to the development of and preference for the use of short-term methods of treatment and the use of medications to control the patient's emotional symptoms.

11.5   CHILD PSYCHOTHERAPIES

11.5.1   Play therapy

Play therapy is a well established discipline based upon a number of psychological theories. Play therapy uses a variety of play and creative arts techniques to alleviate psychological and emotional conditions in children which cause behavioural problems and prevent children from realising their potential. Play therapy can be non-directive (where the child decides what to do in a session, within safe boundaries), directive (where the therapist leads the way) or a mixture of the two. Play therapy is particularly effective with children who cannot, or do not want to, talk about their problems.

The play therapy situation provides and creates a safe, confidential and caring environment which allows the child to play with as few limits as possible but as many as necessary (for safety). This allows emotional containment, a sense of security and unconditional acceptance. The child is given special time and assisted to apply strategies to cope with difficulties it faces in life and which it cannot change by itself. Sessions may last typically from 30 to 45 minutes. These sessions may be with individuals or groups of children. A variety of creative art methods are used according to the child's wishes which include storytelling, drama, puppets and masks, music and dance, sand play, painting and drawing, clay, and play dough as well as games.

The therapist must develop a warm and friendly relationship with the child. The child needs to be accepted as she or he is where there is a freedom of expression of feelings. The therapist needs to be alert to recognise the feelings the child is expressing and to reflect these feelings back in such a manner that the child gains insight into his/her behaviour. Through the medium of play children are able to express their feelings and play out their fears, anxieties and conflicts. The therapist should not attempt to direct the child's actions or conversations in any manner. The child leads the way, the therapist follows. Additionally, the child should not be hurried along. Clinical supervision is an essential part of working therapeutically with clients, be they adults or children. The purpose of clinical supervision is for the supervisor to help the supervised become more effective in helping the child.

Therapeutic play improves the emotional well-being of the child. It may be used to alleviate emotional, behavioural or psychological problems that are preventing the child from functioning normally. Therapeutic play is often used to prevent a minor problem becoming worse. The play therapist forms a short to medium term therapeutic relationship and often works with the child's peers, siblings, family and school as well.

11.5.2 Child psychotherapy, clinical psychology and psychiatry

Child psychotherapy, clinical psychology and psychiatry address more severe mental health and personality problems. Practitioners in these fields may use therapeutic play in addition to 'talking therapies' and possibly, in the case of psychiatry, medication. Support may be provided by a play therapist working in a multi-agency team.

11.5.3   Cognitive behavioural therapy with children

The use of CBT has been extended to children and adolescents with good results. It is often used to treat depression, anxiety disorders, and symptoms related to trauma and post traumatic stress disorder.

Features of cognitive behaviour therapy with depressed children and adolescents involve 8 to 12 weekly sessions. The therapist and child work together to solve problems and the emphasis would be on dealing with current difficulties the child is experiencing. CBT with children takes the form of a structured approach with intervention in accordance with the child's particular developmental stage. Treatment includes the cognitive elements such as challenging negative styles of thinking as well as the behavioural elements such as advice about poor sleep, social skills and change in behaviour.

Whilst principles of CBT are similar to those used with adults, particular adaptations are made when working with children with respect to the pace of work, the content of work and the speed of therapy at a level appropriate to the child. With younger children, the therapist is likely to be more active and will make use of a higher proportion of behavioural to cognitive techniques. While with adults much work in CBT is concerned with correcting maladaptive and dysfunctional distortions of thinking, the focus with children is with deficits in social skills or interpersonal problem-solving. Additionally, training in social skills and problem-solving are a part of interventions not only for children with conduct disorder, ADHD or empathy disorders, but also for children with depression or anxiety and those who experience impaired social relationships.

A typical treatment program would include gaining an awareness of the problem, guidance in developing strategies to cope, for example identifying maladaptive self-talk, then using positive self-talk as a strategy. The final stage would be the self evaluation with associated awards and reinforcements of positive outcomes.

11.5.4   Theraplay

Theraplay is a structured play therapy approach developed by Jernberg (1979) in working with children who had failed to make proper early attachment to their parents and where children were deprived of positive stimuli. It is primarily used for children who need a therapy that can bond poorly bonded parents and children at a nonverbal level; the therapy will, in effect, replicate parent-infant bonding.

A core to the Theraplay philosophy is the belief that parent-infant attachment is a developmental necessity and that the interactive play and engagement which is central to this approach facilitates growth and therefore health. The goal of Theraplay is to enhance the children's view of themselves and to increase their joy in the world. This cannot be made to happen quickly without an intensely personal and physical relationship between child and therapist with plenty of eye contact. The activities and interventions by the therapist are modelled on the healthy, attachment-enhancing behaviours between parent and infant. The child must 'come to see, reflected in the therapist's eyes, the image of himself as both lovable and fun to be with'.

The process of Theraplay is based on four core categories of the interaction that occurs between parent and child:

(1) **Structuring** behaviours occur when the primary carer engages in interactions that somehow create boundaries for the child. The effects of the structuring interactions are to teach the child how to regulate his or her own behaviour and to create an atmosphere of safety and security. Theraplay input and activities relating to structuring would be with equal turn-taking, the practical structuring of the session, not changing the plan of the session and the therapist always remaining in charge and not giving in to the child.

(2) **Challenging** behaviours of the primary carer are to encourage the child to perform at the upper end of their present abilities. Verbal mimicry, reflex grabbing, sports, teaching new skills are all examples of challenging interactions. Activities related to challenging would take the form of setting challenges for the child such as who could blow the biggest bubble, draw the straightest line and such like. Any fun competition type activity would challenge the child.

(3) **Intruding** primary carer behaviour has the effect of keeping the child's level of arousal at an optimal level. Any sort of intrusion into physical or psychological space exposes the child to new or surprising stimuli. In early childhood, a mother may engage in tickling games and tossing games which are healthy intrusions, particularly if they occur when the child needs them, not when the primary carer needs to dominate. Theraplay activity related to intrusion would include tickling games, keeping close physical proximity, counting freckles and such like.

(4) **Nurturing** activities provide for physical and emotional needs. Interactions between a mother and a very young infant are almost completely nurturing in nature and include feeding, changing, soothing, kissing, bathing and hugging. Nurturing related Theraplay activities would involving caring, soothing activities such as rubbing lotion on hands, feeding activities and such like.

Generally speaking, problems arise when a parent is unable to provide these four interactive experiences in the right mix, in the right amount and at the right time. A primary carer requires empathy and sensitivity to provide these interactions and there are many opportunities for the process to break down. Environmental factors such as intrusions, competing demands, external stress and lack of time may present barriers to a healthy mother-infant relationship.

Theraplay aims to increase self-esteem by engaging the child in activities which, regardless of age, duplicate the essential parent-child interaction which normally occurs with a 6-month-old infant. Thus, Theraplay initially requires an active role played by the therapist and then the transfer of this relationship to the parents. The child is helped to generalise these interactions in the world outside the playroom. Theraplay's bonding and attachment-enhancing properties are central to this treatment approach.

Theraplay is suitable for a wide range of children. However, it is contraindicated for children who are traumatised or abused owing to the intensity of the physical contact and the invasion of the child's personal and emotional space.

The therapist assumes the primary responsibility for the activities that are carried out in a session and these are not limited to what the child 'wants' so much as to what the child 'needs'. It is a play therapy approach that does not use traditional play therapy equipment. In fact, the therapist primarily uses him or herself in the activities. The child must feel the therapist's interest. The therapist is there to lead the child in constructive interactions and the following qualities of a Theraplay therapist are crucial:

(1) confident with leadership qualities;

(2) appealing and delightful;

(3) responsive and empathic;

(4) in charge;

(5) uses every opportunity for making physical contact;

(6) maintains eye contact;

(7) provides intensive and exclusive focus on child;

(8) initiates child's behaviours, anticipating the resistance;

(9) responsive to cues;

(10) ability to differentiate self from child;

(11) helps child see self as unique;

(12) able to describe and label affect;

(13) spontaneous, flexible;

(14) willing to use self as the primary object in therapy;

(15) can structure sessions clearly;

(16) cheerful, optimistic, positive;

(17) attentive to the present, past, future and here and now;

(18) unconditionally accepts child as he is;

(19) can provide sessions with beginnings, middles and ends.

A Theraplay therapist must accept the proposition that physical contact is not only appropriate but therapeutically mandated. Theraplay sessions are always characterised by a beginning, middle and end. Within this structure, there are always moments of spontaneity, but there is a need for time to be sequenced, planned and finite and for space to be ordered and safe.

Theraplay sessions are 30 minutes long. The first four sessions involve no expectations on the part of the parents, who from behind a mirror observe the interactions of the therapist and child. A second 'interpreting therapist' sits with the parents and talks them through what is occurring, keeping in mind the assumptions about the parent-child interaction style that is guiding the interventions. After these sessions, there is a general discussion/orientation about what went on with all four, therapists and parents. The final four sessions begin like the first, but during the last 15 minutes, the parents join the child and the participating therapist. It is the parents who ultimately become the full-time 'Theraplay therapists'.

Differences between Theraplay and other play therapy approaches are as follows:

(1) Does not focus on pathology.

(2) Uses direct, physical, personal active engagement.

(3) The therapist is in charge, not the child.

(4) Theraplay is playful and frivolous, not serious.

(5)   Does not use dolls, toys.

(6)   Does not ask questions.

(7)   Does not use verbalisations.

(8)   Does not let the child take the lead.

(9)   Has an outlined agenda.

(10) Does not discourage regressive behaviour.

11.6   SUMMARY

Psychotherapy is an interpersonal, relational intervention used by trained psychotherapists to aid clients in the problems of living. This usually includes increasing the individual sense of well-being and reducing subjective discomforting experience. Psychotherapists employ a range of techniques based on experiential relationship building, dialogue, communication and behaviour change that are designed to improve the mental health of a client or patient, or to improve group relationships (such as in a family). Most forms of psychotherapy use only spoken conversation, though some also use various other forms of communication such as the written word, artwork, drama, narrative story, or the therapeutic touch. Psychotherapy takes place within a structured encounter between a trained therapist and client(s). Therapy is generally used to respond to a variety or specific or non-specific manifestations of clinically diagnosable crises. Treatment of everyday problems is more often referred to as counselling but the term is sometimes used interchangeably with 'psychotherapy'.

When making assessment related to family and child care proceedings and for the purposes of assisting the court, treatment recommendations to address the areas highlighted in a report court could be complex. On the one hand, there are short term treatments which could be carried out which would assist the parties within the timescales of the proceedings. The difficulties often arise when the treatment recommended may require many months or years for a positive outcome to be seen. Despite these recommendations, this therapeutic work is rarely taken up for two reasons. In the first instance there would be little incentive for a parent, for example, to undertake long term reconstructive therapy if the child has been romoved from her care. From a practical perspective the psychological treament provided by the NHS is limited with long waiting lists and funding from the primary care trusts is notoriously difficult to secure. The parents, having undergone care proceedings, could also be disinclined to undertake the therapeutic work recommended owing to the distrust of and resistance towards professionals, particularly if the professionals had be instrumental in the recommendations that the child or children could not be returned to their care.

PART II

DISORDERS OF CHILDHOOD AND ADOLESCENCE

CHAPTER 12

COMMON CHILDHOOD DISTURBANCES

12.1 ENURESIS AND ENCOPRESIS

Children normally develop bladder and bowel control within an accepted age range. However, occasionally, delay can occur due to immaturity, delayed nervous system development, inadequate learning or emotional/stress related experiences.

With regard to enuresis, it is considered that children attain bladder control by the age of 5 and the diagnostic criteria for enuresis would only be satisfied when there is repeated involuntary voiding of urine by day and night, there being at least two such events a week for a child between the age of 5 and 6, and at least once a month for older children. Such a diagnosis is only made where there is found not to be a physical disorder responsible. Enuresis could be either primary or secondary. Primary enuresis occurs when a child never develops control over urination, whilst secondary enuresis is described when the problem has developed after the child had initially become continent for a period of time.

Encopresis refers to difficulty controlling defecation after the age of 3 or 4 years. By this age most normal children would have achieved bowel control and continual soiling after the age of 4 could suggest a deviation from normal development. The diagnostic criteria for encopresis would include repeated voluntary or involuntary passage of faeces of normal or near-normal consistency in a place not appropriate for the purpose. In an individual's own cultural setting, at least, one such event a week would occur after the age of 4, and the occurrence is not found to be due to any physical disorder.

Both enuresis and encopresis could have a negative impact on children's social, educational and personal development. These children often experience anxiety, low self-worth and lowered mood associated with the response of their peers, exclusion from school and generally from feeling different and ostracised. Children with encopresis often develop conflicting and clashing interactions with parental figures. Enuresis and encopresis are considered in some cases to involve hereditary factors. However, there are strong links between high levels of stress, which interferes with development and maintenance of bladder and bowel control, and these conditions, particularly with secondary enuresis and encopresis. When assessing and managing enuresis and encopresis evaluation is made also of the emotional functioning, family relations and levels of stress the child is experiencing. Before any conclusions are reached as to the possible emotional causes of these disorders, all physiological causes will need to be excluded. It is often the case that a combination of underlying causes is at play.

With enuresis, underlying emotional conflicts, small bladder capacity and failure to learn an adequate response to the sensation of a full bladder are cited as the most usual explanations for the condition. There are, however, no causes of these urinary problems which have been established conclusively. In child care proceedings, enuresis is a common feature and at times is observed to be an external indicator of emotional distress experienced by the child. In certain situations, such as when a child is exposed to conflict and violence in the home, or when having to make adjustments when placed in foster care or when placed in a situation of conflict, the child's behaviour may often be accompanied by periods of secondary enuresis.

Effective methods for bladder control and treatment programmes for encopresis would include behavioural procedures and behavioural modification programmes such as night-time awakening, practice of retention control and a reduced fluid intake. Medication has been found to be extremely useful and effective with enuresis, as has the alarm-based programmes such as the bell and pad. A vital element of treatment would include a psycho-educational component to assist parents and children to understand the physiological dynamics of these conditions. The parents' approach should be such that they are reassuring and assist to reduce the child's anxiety surrounding the wetting or soiling. Breaking the cycle of conflict with encopretic children is essential. Owing to the frustrating nature of these conditions, the parents would also require support and reassurance. For encopresis, family based approaches have been found more useful in conjunction with medical care involving laxatives and increased intake of dietary fibre. Behavioural therapy and techniques involving the maintenance of toilet routines, rewarding the child for engaging in such routines and the learning of sphincter control are included in the family work and psycho-education.

12.2 CHILDHOOD FEARS

General childhood fears are, of course, common and most normal children display specific age-related fears at one time or another. The fears could take the form of concrete stimuli such as fear of animals or strangers, to somewhat more abstract situations such as fear of getting lost, or being kidnapped and of death. Childhood fears are primarily learned experiences from past events, stimuli and experience of situations and events in the child's environment. The child's life experiences could at times have resulted in the association of a normal situation with a feared response. This could be developed through the means of classical conditioning, where fear responses in a young child are associated with a feared response within a neutral situation. Additionally, fear could also develop when a child observes other individuals who show evidence of fear; children generally pick up on the anxieties and fears of others in this way. Most childhood fears are transient in nature and spontaneously decline or resolve with increasing age, settling without any form of intervention. Mild fears are therefore viewed as being a normal part of childhood rather than as a pathological condition. Typical childhood fears in certain age groups could be, for example, of loud, sudden noises and loss of support could elicit fear in infants between 0–6 months of age. Between 6 and 9 months of age fear of strangers is fairly typical, and in the first year of life, separation, injury and the toilet could be the basis of common fears involving these situations. Children at the age of 2 typically fear imaginary creatures, death and robbers, while at the age of 3 the most common fears have been found to be the fear of dogs and of being alone. In the fourth year fear of the dark is typical. Then, between the ages of 6 and 12, school, injury, incidents or disasters involving a national dimension, death and social situations cause fear, whilst between the ages of 13 and 18, fear of social situations and of injury are common phenomena while natural disasters, sexual situations and injury are normal fears for adolescents of 19 years or older.

As mild childhood fears are common and disappear spontaneously with age, formal treatment would not be indicated, unless the fear is causing specific levels of distress to the child. Where therapeutic intervention is required procedures such as modelling are effective in dealing with normal fears as well as phobias. It is important to consider that there is a significant distinction to be made between fear and phobias, as phobic disorders would require therapeutic intervention. Fear is essentially a normal response to some object or source of danger, whereas phobias are excessive fears beyond voluntary control and are not age specific. Furthermore, phobias result in maladaptive avoidance behaviour, whereas fears do not necessarily bring this about.

At different points along their span of life, the social environment may present different challenges to individuals. This requires children to develop skills in managing and coping with fears and anxieties. It is only through learning to cope with these fearful situations in early childhood that the child becomes equipped for later management of and coping with any fearful and anxious situations that may arise.

12.3   TEMPER TANTRUMS AND AGGRESSIVE BEHAVIOUR

Temper tantrums could be viewed as a child's responses to frustrating situations. Children usually do not have the verbal capacity to express their frustration and anger and thus respond in a physically expressive way. Behaviour involving temper tantrums includes screaming, hitting, pounding the floor, and the general showing of displeasure through behaviour. While temper tantrums are common in normal children it is not, however, uncommon for parents to seek assistance to manage this normal behaviour. Temper-involved behaviour could be reinforced by parental response and any inconsistency in the parental response to the temper tantrum could increase the intensity and frequency of these behaviours. Whenever a parent gives in to the demands of the child, the parent is reinforcing the child's temper tantrum behaviour and increasing the probability of a child displaying such behaviour in similar situations in the future. Behaviour modification techniques, teaching parents to be consistent in setting boundaries, and psycho-education is indicated for parents to assist in reducing and/or eliminating certain behaviours rather than to reinforce them. Time-out procedures are extremely effective and are based on the principle that if a child is removed from a reinforcing situation as soon as that behaviour occurs, the probability of the recurrence of a temper tantrum will weaken and decrease. Temper tantrums never occur when a child is on his/her own, for a child displaying temper behaviour is seeking a response from his reaction. Thus, should the tantrum behaviour not be followed by attention, and instead results in a period of brief isolation, a decrease in such behaviours could be expected and, indeed, usually occurs. Temper tantrum behaviour requires a combination of positive reinforcement for positive behaviour; in effect, catching the child being good and then reinforcing that behaviour, rather than focusing on negative responses of the child.

Tantrum-related behaviour is seen as being different from *aggressive behaviour*, in that tantrum behaviour does not usually pose a threat to others, whereas aggressive behaviour involves a child hitting, shoving, biting, and scratching other children or adults. In some cases a child can direct the negative and aggressive behaviour towards himself. With aggressive children, learning how to handle and manage aggressive impulses and behaviour is an important aspect of child development and the socialisation of the child. It is the responsibility of the parent to assist the child in learning appropriate behaviour responses and learning how to deal with situations in non-aggressive or non-violent ways, in particular by channelling aggression through assertiveness, competitiveness and social learning. Learning to deal with aggression appropriately is an important task of early childhood. It is important that parental figures and role models to children should not display inappropriate aggressive behaviour, as the learning of aggressive models through observation of others being aggressive is very potent and results in increased aggressive behaviour. It is also essential that aggressive behaviour is never dealt with through aggressive means, as this would always reinforce, increase and entrench the child's aggressive behaviour. Where the parenting is inconsistent, ineffective and/or is showing a lack in some way, this learning process does not occur and, thus, as seen in childcare proceedings where parenting is an issue of concern, the ongoing aggressive, oppositional and antisocial behaviour of children can be observed to have its origins in impaired parenting.

12.4   SOCIAL WITHDRAWAL

Learning to relate to peers and to adults is another important task which continues throughout childhood. This aspect of socialisation is essential for future successful interpersonal and social interaction. It is however not uncommon for children to be hesitant to interact with others or to be socially shy, introverted or withdrawn. A failure of a child to interact on a consistent basis without any improvement does, however, raise concern for parents and does suggest that the child needs assistance to improve socialisation. A child with withdrawal or introverted behaviour could be showing behaviour which is part of his/her temperament or personality. However, it may be the case that the child has begun to associate anxiety with interaction from previous learned experiences. Where a child fails to acquire social skills necessary for interacting with others as a result of emotional and social deprivation, lack of parental involvement and insufficient exposure to other children during important developmental phases of growth, this would be a matter of considerable concern for future appropriate emotional and social functioning.

Children who remain socially withdrawn and extremely anxious on a social level, should be assisted to develop appropriate social skills and helped in reducing anxiety, particularly through behaviour modification, modelling experiences and anxiety reduction programmes. Parental and family involvement would be beneficial with psycho-education and support provided.

As can be seen, children experience common disturbances, difficulties and fears. These require adequate, appropriate and positively involved parenting experiences to successfully cope with these normal and common behavioural and emotional experiences. Should the parenting be inadequate, absent, uninvolved and generally not good enough, these common and normal experiences could and sometimes do evolve into more serious cases of emotional and social impairment. Positive and adequate parenting experiences are the key to normal adjustment.

CHAPTER 13

EMOTIONAL IMPAIRMENT AND DISORDERS

13.1   INTRODUCTION

Underlying emotional disorders and deficiencies may cause varying degrees of social and emotional impairment. Distress and anxiety erode emotional functioning and psychological well-being. Anxiety develops when a child experiences the results of an unrealistic or irrational appraisal of threat to his or her well-being. The coping strategies employed and reactions in the face of this anxiety would be determined by the extent and duration of anxiety symptoms experienced and how the child attempts to deal with this. This could present in the form of symptom constellations and emotional responses. Internalised anxiety, significant lowering of mood and experiences of anger could in turn fuel destructive and disturbed behaviour. These emotional experiences could also impact upon ideas of self-worth, levels of competency and sense of self, which in turn undermine emotional functioning. Childhood disorders could be viewed as attempts to cope with high levels of distress which has developed as a means of avoiding, blocking or defending against overwhelming emotional pain and anxiety.

13.2   SEPARATION ANXIETY

The essential feature of separation anxiety is excessive anxiety concerning separation from the child's primary attachment figure. For a diagnosis of separation anxiety to be made it is considered that the anxiety experienced by the child is beyond that expected for that individual child's developmental level. When separating from the attachment figure, the child becomes preoccupied with fears that the attachment figure will not return and this induces increased feelings of insecurity and distress in the child. Children with separation anxiety express fear of being lost, of never being reunited with their parents and thus tend to refuse to attend school or be in situations away from the primary carer. In early childhood, separation anxiety plays an important part in attachment. However, when separation anxiety occurs in a child much older, beyond the normal developmental timetable, the separation anxiety could lead to maladaptive adjustments, in particular related to school refusal, social anxiety and feelings of insecurity.

13.3   GENERALISED ANXIETY DISORDER

Generalised anxiety is defined as ongoing apprehension and anxiety without any particular focus or particular situation of concern. The anxiety experienced tends to be free floating and generally unrealistic. It is the excessive anxiety and worry arising from non-specific situations such as family events, social activities, health issues or any situation which is unknown to the child. Children presenting with generalised anxiety are usually over-anxious, and given to consistently worrying and fretting about new situations. They could experience difficulties with concentration and attention which may have implications for academic progress as well as for social development.

13.4   PANIC DISORDER

When a child is extremely anxious and experiences recurrent or unmanageable panic attacks of acute intensity, the diagnosis of panic disorder could be made. In childhood, panic disorders commonly result in some degree of agoraphobia, in particular where the child fears leaving the safety of home in case a panic attack occurs in a public setting. Consequently, a typical consequence could be the increased withdrawal and avoidance of going out, with implications with regard to the social, interpersonal, educational and emotional growth and development of the child.

13.5   OBSESSIVE COMPULSIVE DISORDER

This condition involves recurrent obsessional thoughts and compulsive acts that are extremely time consuming for the child to deal with and create great levels of distress. The child makes use of rituals or obsessive thoughts to reduce anxiety associated with the obsession. A vicious cycle of anxiety is experienced as the rituals and obsessions lead the child to maladaptive and dysfunctional behaviour and responses, which in itself increases internalised anxiety. The compulsions and obsessions are then increased with the primary purpose being to reduce the increase of anxiety and distress experienced. Typical obsessions and compulsions are related to compulsive hand washing due to obsessions with germs and cleanliness, or compulsions to order and count items, behaviour which is underlined by feelings being out of control.

13.6   SCHOOL PHOBIA

School phobia is seen in children with a fear and avoidance particularly relating to the school environment. It is often found that children who have this anxiety relating to school attendance do not have similar anxieties associated with interaction with their peers or going into situations away from school. Anxiety and phobia associated with school tends to lead to the avoidance of the school environment and the experience of fear in that setting. The irrational nature of school phobia creates high levels of stress and distress within families and typically may come to have an impact on all members of the household.

13.7 POST TRAUMATIC STRESS DISORDER (PTSD)

PTSD is an anxiety state following a traumatic or catastrophic situation which the child has perceived as life threatening to him or others. Symptoms and experiences associated with post trauma reactions relate to recurrent intrusive thoughts concerning the trauma which leads to increased anxiety. Symptoms associated with avoidance and arousal are developed as a means of distancing oneself from the anxious experiences associated with the trauma.

13.8 PSYCHODYNAMICS OF ANXIETY

Children who experience anxiety states present with patterns of maladaptive behaviours, which result in the child becoming incapacitated to some degree. In particular, there could be an impact on the educational, social and emotional functioning of the child. Anxiety results from dysfunctional ways used by the child of making sense of his world, which leads to a vicious cycle whereby the child would then have increased anxiety due to experiencing the social world in anxiety provoking ways. Consequently, the child could develop and hold irrational expectations, beliefs and thoughts which then produce increased anxiety. The most common defensive response in the face of anxiety is avoidance, in order to prevent an unwanted situation or outcome. The relief from avoiding something unpleasant serves as a positive reward, as such avoidant responses prevent unwanted emotions from being experienced. Although these processes are effective in avoiding increased anxiety, they are maladaptive in that what has been avoided was not by its nature actually producing anxiety stimuli except to the child. The avoidance response engaged in was thus totally unnecessary.

When treating anxiety the process of **exposure** would be essential to all treatment programmes. This would assist children to learn the skills needed in managing anxiety symptoms and reducing anxious arousal. In addition to exposure as a treatment method, **self-instructional training** could also be of benefit. Such training would focus on control and competence in managing the situation causing anxiety as well as relaxation training. **Psychological education** for parents could take the form of providing guidance and/or assistance in learning strategies to reinforce the child's non-anxious or more adaptive behaviour, whilst at the same time ensuring the eliminating of, or not reinforcing, anxious behaviour. Duration of treatments would vary depending on the child and the nature of the anxiety symptoms. Treatment for uncomplicated phobic responses would, for example, require about three sessions, whereas school phobias which are more complex would require at least six sessions. The therapeutic input for school phobia, for example, would involve clarification of the child's problems, discussion of principal concerns with the child, parents and teachers. Development of contingency plans would be needed to ensure maintenance of attending school as well as a degree of 'flooding' techniques where a child is returned as soon as possible and faces the anxious situation while having a support base. For more intense anxiety related problems such as generalised anxiety disorder or separation anxiety, the therapeutic intervention would need to be more skilled. As cognitive behavioural therapy is a more in-depth approach it naturally would require more time to address difficulties associated with complex anxiety states and experiences.

Cognitive behavioural therapy is aimed at teaching anxious children how to monitor and challenge anxiety provoking thoughts about their perceived threatening situation. Methods of self-instruction and relaxation techniques are taught to assist the child reduce arousal levels and to contain their anxieties. Once he is able to control and contain arousal the child is taught to make cognitive changes and offer himself self-reinforcement for consolidating successful coping responses. **Family based treatment** would involve the parents in order to assist in problem solving, reframing and communication skills to assist in reduction of anxiety. In addition to psychotherapeutic means, medication could be indicated for certain conditions and disorders, in particular for disorders such as obsessive compulsive disorder. Medication should, however, always be used in conjunction with cognitive behavioural therapy or psychotherapeutic approaches and along with psycho education for parents.

13.9 CHILDHOOD DEPRESSION

Depression in childhood could range from normal lowering of mood in the form of emotional response such as sadness or unhappiness, to abnormal lowering of mood characterised by more severe depressive conditions. Symptoms of depressed mood could be associated with persistent crying, negative self-evaluation, a lowered activity level, behaviour withdrawal, and negative thoughts and self-destruction could be commonly found with these children. Childhood depression could originate from feelings of loss which may be real or symbolic, such as those involving loss of parents, separation or perception of rejection which could result in lowering of mood. As with adults, cognitive factors and thought processes of children could result in lowering of mood where there is a tendency to interpret events in such a way that it contributes to feelings of self-blame, failure and hopelessness. How the child interprets or perceives a situation would influence the child's mood and its way of relating to the outside world. Depression could also be seen to be a response to a lack of positive reinforcements in the environment caused by events or situations ranging from change in residence to failure to display appropriate social skills, which could result in reinforcement of the behaviour.

A depressed mood presents in different ways depending on the age of the child. In younger children depression is usually reported as feelings of sadness, loneliness, despair and an inability to experience pleasure. Additionally, irritability, anxiety and aggression could coincide with sadness and feelings of loneliness. Depressed adolescents usually have all three components involving depressed mood, irritability and anxiety in their presentation. Depression in children and adolescents could present as an acute or chronic condition. An acute depressive reaction occurs where the depression is preceded by an identifiable precipitating event usually involving a loss or bereavement. A chronic depressive reaction is found in children who display obvious depressive feelings and characteristics which have a gradual onset rather than suddenly becoming observable. In many cases where there are chronic depressive reactions, the background history would reflect frequent separations and losses rather than any one major event or disruptive life experiences. Masked depressive reactions are seen where children's' depression is masked or overshadowed by other clinical features such as disruptive or destructive behaviour, psychosomatic problems, hyperactive behaviour or an eating disorder. With masked depression, the underlying depressed mood is not obvious but could be made to become apparent within the context of clinical interaction or psychological assessment.

Research has noted that children who meet the criteria for other childhood disorders such as anxiety disorder or attention deficit hyperactivity disorder (ADHD) often also meet the criteria for a secondary diagnosis of depression. Anxiety disorders are the most closely linked condition when a diagnosis of depression is made in children and adolescents, then, to a lesser extent, come substance abuse and disruptive behaviour. Family disruption, abuse and neglect are also closely linked with childhood depression, particularly when related to experience of rejection by parents, neglect or lack of interest, hostility or over-controlling behaviours on the part of parents. Having poor relationships with one's parents may set the stage for childhood problems; in particular, a child could experience depression when he feels bad about them, or when he feels unloved, unwanted or insecure as a result of insecure attachments.

Clinical depression goes beyond sadness. It is more than having a bad day or coping with a major loss such as the death of a parent, grandparent, or even a favourite pet. Youths suffering from clinical depression cannot simply 'snap out of it'. Early-onset depression can lead to school failure, alcohol or other drug use, and even suicide.

Signs of early-onset depression include:

(1)   Seriously or vaguely sick and might be less bouncy or spontaneous than usual.

(2)   Tearful or irritable when frustrated.

(3)   Saying negative things about himself and may be self-destructive.

(4)   Persistent sadness and hopelessness.

(5)   Withdrawal from friends and from activities once enjoyed.

(6)   Increased irritability or agitation.

(7)   Missed school or poor school performance.

(8)   Changes in eating and sleeping habits.

(9)   Indecision, lack of concentration, or forgetfulness.

(10) Poor self-esteem or guilt.

(11) Frequent physical complaints, such as headaches and tummy aches.

(12) Lack of enthusiasm, low energy, or low motivation.

(13) Drug and/or alcohol abuse.

(14) Thoughts of death or suicide.

(15) Adolescent may present with academic decline, disruptive behaviour, and problems with friends.

(16) Aggressive behaviour, irritability and talk about suicide.

Factors associated with childhood depression include inconsistent parenting, stressful life experiences, and a negative way of viewing the world. Childhood depression is also associated with a family history of mood disorders and with the existence of other psychiatric conditions. If family members have had childhood or recurrent depression the child is at even higher risk of developing depression. There are different theories on the causes of depression. Some feel that children inherit a predisposition to depression and anxiety but that environmental triggers are necessary to elicit the first episode of major depression.

Many children with depression have one or more other major psychiatric diagnoses. Anxiety disorder, substance abuse, and ADHD are frequently associated with childhood depression. ADHD may be present before the first episode of depression and can complicate the treatment of both conditions. Depression is associated with school and interpersonal problems. It is also correlated with increased incidence of suicidal behaviour, violent thoughts, alcohol use, early pregnancy and drug abuse. Depression can lead to an increased chance of suicide attempts and successful suicides.

Depressed children often have depressed or stressed parents. Can the stress of coping with a depressed child lead to parental rejection or is it the poor parenting that leads to the child's depression? The answer may be different in different cases. A depressed, hyperactive child may be hard to raise. Some parents have more coping skills than others. A child may learn to give up because parents have not modelled good ways of coping with stressful situations.

Other disorders and behaviours commonly coexist with early-onset depression. Children under stress who experience a loss or who have attention, learning, or conduct disorders are at a higher risk for depression. Clinical depression can contribute to eating disorders; while on the other hand, an eating disorder can lead to a state of clinical depression.

Early **diagnosis** and treatment are essential for children with depression. Children who exhibit symptoms of depression should be referred to, and evaluated by, a mental health professional that specialises in treating children and teenagers. Assessment would include psychological testing and clinical interviews with a child and adolescent psychiatrist or psychologist. The diagnostic process should include interviews with parents and the child.

Psychological treatment for depression is not dissimilar to that offered for adults. Antidepressant medication, however, has not been found to be as effective with children as with adults. Cognitive behavioural therapy for children and adolescents would involve self-control training programmes, problem-solving therapy and cognitive reframing, all of which have been found to be effective. The basic principles of cognitive behavioural therapy are related to controlling depressive thoughts, improving social interactions and resolving conflicts. In addition to working with children, parental involvement is indicated as an additional support and reinforcement for assisting the child.

As it is common for depression to be associated with family related problems, family therapy in such cases could also be indicated. This is particularly relevant following bereavement as family therapy in family based work would be beneficial for children and families to deal with their grief. Stress management and relaxation training are also effective and would need to be offered in conjunction with cognitive behaviour therapy techniques and strategies. Group based cognitive behaviour therapy has also been found to be effective, particularly in therapeutic work with adolescents. However, whilst individual circumstances would need to be considered in determining the length of the therapeutic input, it is not uncommon for six to nine group or family therapy sessions to be necessary whilst between twelve and sixteen sessions of individual cognitive behavioural therapy is usually required in the treatment of depression.

A comprehensive treatment plan may include psychotherapy, ongoing evaluations and monitoring, or medication. Generally, with mild to moderate depression, one first tries psychotherapy and then adds an antidepressant if the therapy has not produced enough improvement. If it is a severe depression, or there is serious acting out, one may start medication at the beginning of the treatment. A variety of psychotherapeutic techniques have been shown to be effective. Cognitive-behavioural therapy would be more likely to achieve results quicker. Cognitive therapy helps the child examine and correct negative thought patterns and erroneous negative assumptions about himself. Behaviourally, it encourages the child to use positive coping behaviours instead of giving up or avoiding situations. Family therapy is also indicated and yields positive results and outcome.

CHAPTER 14

ADJUSTMENT DIFFICULTIES

14.1   PARENTAL SEPARATION AND DIVORCE

Separation and divorce involving their parents are common phenomena experienced by children today and should be considered to be features of common childhood experiences. It is found that most pre-school children experience a 2 to 3 year period of adjustment following the divorce of parents. Difficulties associated with readjustment include depression, aggression, acting-out behaviours, problematic peer relationships and non-compliance with advice. After initial distress, the children adjust to the situation, but this could take up to 2 years. Adjustment difficulties in the face of separation and divorce have been found to be greater for boys than is found with girls. Emotional and behavioural problems associated with adjustment are seen in the form of acting out difficulties in school, and withdrawal and disconnection from the family, which is a particular feature with adolescents. Added to this, the child may be faced with feelings of loss, betrayal and concerns for future familial stability. Children in the mid-adolescent years tend to distance themselves from family members to a greater extent in this situation than younger children.

Divorce leads to significant lifestyle changes, both for parents as well as for the children. These lifestyle changes could impact significantly on the emotional well-being of children. As a result of divorce, children and adolescents may be faced with altered residential arrangements, economic change, loneliness associated with social network change and role strain associated with needing to take on new tasks and different roles within the home and family context. It is thus the extent of the changes which impact on the emotional health of children, resulting in mood related difficulties, identity problems, vulnerability and anxiety. Furthermore, any impact upon the parents could have a knock-on effect for the children, as the parents' capacity to cope with their own stresses and strains could compromise their parenting capacity. Parenting styles and approaches tend to change following divorce due to changing family dynamics. A tendency to present as authoritarian or engage in punitive parenting on one hand, whilst engaging in *laissez faire* or neglectful parenting on the other may be the result. Following separation it is not unusual for parenting to be chaotic, oscillating between the two extremes depending on the level of strain or stress experienced at the time by the parent.

Children are more likely to develop difficulties after separation or divorce if there have been previous serious difficulties in the parent/child relationship prior to the separation. This could in particular be related to insecure attachments, inconsistent discipline and where there has been permissive or neglectful parenting before. Furthermore, exposure to chronic family problems, marital discord, and/or domestic violence prior to separation could have an impact on post separation adjustment. Early life stressors experienced by a child such as abuse or bereavement could also have an impact on the child's subsequent capacity to deal with stress following parental separation. On the other hand, positive prognostic indicators are related to having experienced a stable parenting environment before the divorce and separation and the children having had a history of positive physical and psychological adjustment in the past.

It is also the case that ongoing conflict following separation and/or divorce could have a significant impact on the child's emotional, social and psychological functioning. Ongoing parental acrimony and the using of children as weapons in their battle, in particular, could lead to alienation and a source of significant emotional harm.

A comprehensive review of over 200 research reports revealed the following:

(1)   Although short-term distress at the time of separation is common, this usually fades with time and long-term adverse outcomes typically apply only to a minority of children experiencing the separation of their parents.

(2)   However, these children have roughly twice the probability of experiencing specific poor outcomes in the long term compared with those in intact families.

Children of separated families have a higher probability of:

(1)   being in poverty and poor housing;

(2)   being poorer when they are adults;

(3)   behavioural problems;

(4)   performing less well in school;

(5)   needing medical treatment;

(6)   leaving school/home when young;

(7)   becoming sexually active, pregnant, or a parent at an early age;

(8) experiencing depressive symptoms, high levels of smoking and drinking, and drug use during adolescence and adulthood.

Factors affecting outcomes include:

(9) financial hardship can limit educational achievement;

(10) family conflict before, during and after separation can contribute to behavioural problems;

(11) parental ability to recover from distress of separation affects children's ability to adjust;

(12) multiple changes in family structure increase the probability of poor outcomes;

(13) good quality contact with the non-resident parent can improve outcomes.

If recent trends continue, more than a third of new marriages will end within 20 years and four out of ten will ultimately end in divorce. More than one in four children will experience parental divorce by age 16. Divorce rates in England and Wales (but not Scotland or Northern Ireland) are among the highest in Europe, although considerably less than in the United States (where most research has been carried out)

14.2 CHILDREN'S EXPERIENCE OF PARENTAL SEPARATION

Interviews with children around the time of separation have shown that most wish their parents had stayed together and hope they will get back together. They are likely, in the short term, to experience unhappiness, low self-esteem, problems with behaviour and friendships, and loss of contact with a significant part of their extended family. However, good continuing communication and contact between children and both parents is known to be especially important in assisting children to adapt. The immediate distress surrounding parental separation usually fades with time and most children settle into a pattern of normal development. Nevertheless, studies have found that there is a greater probability of poor outcomes for children from separated families than others – and that these can be observed many years after separation, even in adulthood.

Children of separated families:

(1) tend to grow up in households with lower incomes, poorer housing and greater financial hardship than intact families (especially those headed by lone mothers);

(2)   tend to achieve less in socio-economic terms when they become adult than children from intact families;

(3)   are at increased risk of behavioural problems, including bedwetting, withdrawn behaviour, aggression, delinquency and other antisocial behaviour;

(4)   tend to perform less well in school and to gain fewer educational qualifications;

(5)   are more likely to be admitted to hospital following accidents, to have more reported health problems and to visit their family doctor;

(6)   are more likely to leave school and home when young and more likely at an early age to: become sexually active, form a cohabiting partnership; become pregnant; become a parent; and give birth outside marriage;

(7)   tend to report more depressive symptoms and higher levels of smoking, drinking and other drug use during adolescence and adulthood.

Although the differences in outcomes are clear, it cannot be assumed that parental separation is their underlying cause. The complexity of factors that impinge on families before, during and after separation indicates a process, rather than a single event, that merits careful examination.

Research findings for children from **step-families** suggest a number of ways in which they do not fare as well as those from intact families – and, in some instances, not as well as those from lone-parent families. The risk of adverse outcomes for young people in step-families compared with those in lone-parent families appears higher for older children, especially in areas of educational achievement, family relationships and sexual activity, partnership formation and parenthood at a relatively young age. Young children in step-families seem to fare better because it is easier to adapt to a new family structure at an age when they have had a relatively short period of living with either both or just one birth parent.

14.3   PARENTAL DEATH AND PARENTAL SEPARATION

Children from separated families and children who have experienced the death of a parent share the impact of parental loss and the longer-term experience of parental absence (more often of fathers than mothers). Research suggests that bereaved children are adversely affected, but not across the same range of outcomes as children whose parents have separated. In particular, parental death does not carry the same risks of poorer educational attainment, lower socio-economic status and poorer mental health. There is evidence for an impact of bereavement on some behavioural outcomes in childhood and adolescence, including substance use and leaving home at an early age, but these do not appear to persist as disorders in adulthood.

Factors that influence outcome include:

(1) Financial hardship and other socio-economic circumstances, before as well as after separation, play an influential role in limiting children's educational achievements. They appear less important where other outcomes, such as mental health, are concerned.

(2) Family conflict before, during and after separation is stressful for children, who may respond by becoming anxious, aggressive or withdrawn. Conflict appears to be an important influence in a number of adverse outcomes, including behavioural problems.

(3) The ability of parents to recover from the psychological distress associated with their separation is important for children's own ability to adjust. Parental distress is influenced by factors such as social and economic well-being and the presence or absence of conflict. In turn, it affects parent-child relationships and thereby influences outcomes for children.

(4) Multiple changes in family structure – experiencing the breakdown of two or more parental relationships, for example – appear to have an especially detrimental impact on children, either in themselves or because of associated adversity. The likelihood of multiple changes will, inevitably, be greatest for children who are young when their birth parents separate.

(5) Continuing contact with the non-resident parent may benefit children's adjustment following separation, but there is no simple relationship with frequency of contact. It is the quality of contact, rather than quantity that appears important.

Psychological treatment programmes are effective in assisting children to deal with the consequences of parental separation and divorce. The most effective treatment package involves psychological education for the parents, teaching both parents and children problem-solving skills, social skills training for the children and stress management training for both parents and children. Individual counselling would provide a child with a safe forum to express its divorce-related feelings and beliefs, and could serve as a reliable source of information about the experiences of coming to terms with parental separation. Social skills training would assist the children in becoming better equipped in skills to manage psychological and social challenges in the face of the parents' separation.

14.2   CHILDHOOD TRAUMATIC GRIEF (CTG)

A new condition that has been identified since the terrorist attack in New York in September 2001 is childhood traumatic grief, or CTG. CTG refers to an intense stress reaction that may develop in children following the loss of a parent, sibling, or other loved one during a traumatic event. Children with childhood traumatic grief experience the cause of (the loved one's) death as horrifying or terrifying, whether the death was sudden and unexpected (for example, due to homicide, suicide, motor vehicle accident, drug overdose, natural disaster, war, terrorism, and so on) or due to natural causes (cancer, heart attack, and so forth). Even if the manner of death does not appear to others to be sudden, shocking, or frightening, children who perceive the death in this way may develop childhood traumatic grief. In this condition, even happy thoughts and memories of the deceased person remind children of the traumatic way in which the deceased came to die.

CHAPTER 15

MENTAL RETARDATION AND LEARNING DIFFICULTIES

15.1 MENTAL RETARDATION AND ADAPTIVE BEHAVIOUR

Mental retardation is defined as a significant sub-average intellectual functioning which exists concurrently or in addition to deficits in adaptive functioning. Adaptive abilities would be the self-care skills such as the ability to appropriately dress and take care of one's self and ultimately to live independently. A child or adult identified as having mental retardation is significantly sub-average in intellectual functioning and is sometimes incapable of self-care or independent living. In order to identify mental retardation, impairment of both intellectual and adaptive functioning would need to be evident. Intellectual ability is assessed through **cognitive tests**. However a low score on the IQ test is not sufficient for a diagnosis as there need to be deficits in adaptive behaviour. Adaptive behaviour is assessed through **Adaptive Behaviour Scales** which are a measure of independent functioning, language development, responsibility and, for adults, economic, domestic and physical activity.

Criteria for mental retardation are that there is an IQ for the individual of approximately 70 or below in an individually administered IQ test, together with concurrent deficits or impairments in **adaptive functioning** in at least two of the following areas, which include communication, social interpersonal skills, functional academic skills, health, self-care, use of community resources, work, safety, home living, self-direction and leisure. When assessing **competence**, the following areas of adaptive behaviour involving the mentally retarded would include areas of competence such as independent functioning, physical development, language development and numerical skills.

Additionally, the person's economic activity, domestic activity, vocational ability and level of socialisation would need to be assessed. In addition to these areas assessments would need to be made of **behaviours considered unacceptable** by those responsible for the care of individuals, which include:

(1)   violent or destructive behaviour;

(2)   antisocial behaviour and withdrawal;

(3)   inappropriate interpersonal manners;

(4)   self-abusive behaviour, hyperactivity;

(5)   sexually inappropriate behaviour; and

(6)   psychological disturbance.

Cognitive assessments and IQ tests such as the Wechsler Intelligence Scales for Children (WISC) are used in order to assist in the diagnosis of mental retardation. Revised and up-to-date IQ tests use standardised samples that include representative individuals from all types of background. By doing so the test strives to remain fair to all groups. Mental retardation occurs in varying degrees, while normal IQ ranges from Borderline (70 plus) to very superior (130 and above).

The IQ classification is as follows:

Superior	120–129
Above average	110–119
Average	90–109
Below average	80–89
Borderline	70–79
Intellectual deficit	69 and below

The intellectual deficit category includes:

Mild retardation	55–70
Moderate	40–55
Severe	25–40
Profound	less than 25

Mild mental retardation relates to the ability to learn the academic skills of an 11-year-old by the late teens, but the child in question is not able to learn subjects in senior school and needs a programme of special education. Where there is moderate retardation, the child can learn the functional academic skills of a 9-year-old by the late teens but special means of education are necessary. With severe retardation the child can talk and learn to communicate and can be trained in elementary health habits. These children cannot, however, learn functional academic skills, but do profit from habit training. With profound mental retardation the child may have some motor development but does not profit from training and self-help and needs total care. Individuals with mental retardation often have other problems, which include fine motor problems, speech and visual impairment, which are likely to co-exist with the mental retardation. Additionally, some individuals may also have epilepsy and cerebral palsy.

It is widely accepted that unhealthy influences in the pre-natal environment can damage the intellectual ability of a child. When exploring cause, one must consider whether any health problems of the mother could have affected the foetus; in particular those involving poor nutrition, tobacco or alcohol consumption, infections, drug use, radiation and the lack of oxygen could contribute to the sub-normal intelligence of a child. Substances including alcohol regularly cross the placenta during pregnancy and expose the developing foetus to a wide range of harmful effects and could result in substance dependence and subsequent substance withdrawal effects after birth. Thus, many substances (including even small amounts of alcohol) may not be safe for the foetus and it has been suggested that pregnant women should be encouraged to abstain from such substances completely. Social environment could also have an impact on the developing child. In particular, extreme psychological and social deprivation are implicated as factors in the causation of mental retardation. It has been found also that lack of contact with individuals of normal intelligence and limited access to books and verbal stimulation could also have an impact on intellectual development. Lack of educational stimulation or being brought up in a culturally deprived environment where there are limited or virtually no learning opportunities could all hamper intellectual development. Research has also suggested that large family size, poor nutrition, lack of organisation in the home and low expectations for academic achievement can suppress intellectual growth and development.

When considering treatment for mentally retarded children, adjustments need to be made because of the child's level of ability and intellectual limitation in understanding the purposes of treatment. Behavioural training programmes are preferable when teaching retarded children specific skills and more adaptive functioning. Behavioural training programmes emphasise the application of rewards and include social reinforcement to reduce disruptive behaviour, to control aggressive behaviour, and to improve toileting and self-care. Treatment approaches for problems associated with retardation are aimed at assisting in maximising the potential the individual has. However, it is not a condition that has any fundamental cure. The treatment programmes aim to achieve some improvement in behaviour to improve quality of life, but do not change or fundamentally alter the shortfall in intellectual potential.

15.2 LEARNING DISABILITY

The condition of learning disability would include children's specific learning disabilities in one or more of the basic psychological processes and in understanding or in using spoken or written language. These disorders present with difficulty associated with listening, thinking, talking, reading, writing and spelling. Learning problems are expressed independently of sensory functional motor handicaps and basic learning processes. Severe learning disabled children are considered as achieving at an unexpectedly low level given the child's potential, which has given rise to the concept of **below expected age and grade level performance** as a definition of learning disability. The DSM-IV defines learning disabilities as using a combination of IQ score, achievement discrepancy approach and below average grade level approach. The DSM diagnosis includes reading disorder, mathematical disorder and disorder of written expression as well as learning disorders not otherwise specified. In each disorder, specific academic achievements as measured by an individually administered standardised test would be considered below that expected given the person's chronological age, measured intelligence and age appropriate education. In addition, the condition must interfere with academic achievement or activities of daily living. It is not uncommon for children with learning disabilities also to have hyperactivity, perceptual difficulties, disorder of emotionality and coordination, attention problems, impulsivity, language difficulties, or memory deficits along with the specific learning disability.

Treatment approaches for problems associated with learning disabilities are seen to be consistent with the view that these children have difficulties with cognitive processing strategies and, therefore, the approach of getting these children to monitor their own performance by asking themselves questions while performing tasks has been seen to hold promise. Apart from working with children individually, families could be involved in planning and the implementation of services. Additional family support groups are beneficial in assisting families to cope with the learning difficulties and accessing the right support.

CHAPTER 16

ATTENTION DEFICIT HYPERACTIVITY DISORDER

16.1 DIAGNOSIS OF ATTENTION DEFICIT HYPERACTIVITY DISORDER

Where a child has difficulties with inattention, impulsivity and hyperactivity in all situations, it could be suspected that such a child has Attention Deficit Hyperactivity Disorder (ADHD). They could be described as children who are like 'wound-up toys' which are on the go all the time, with no apparent focus to their activity. The essential feature of Attention Deficit Hyperactivity Disorder is a persistent pattern of inattention or hyperactivity-impulsivity that is more frequently displayed and more severe than typically observed in an individual child at a comparable level of development. The **inattention** is seen as the child not being able to listen and failing to complete tasks, particularly with a short attention span, and rapid shift from one activity to another. The child presents as being highly distractible, paying little attention to directions and having difficulty focusing on any particular kind of play or activity. The **impulsivity** is seen in the form of children acting and reacting without thinking, interrupting others, blurting out, running across the road without any inhibitions, and their ability to respond tending to be totally inadequate as a result of this level of distraction. These children experience problems organising school work and have a greater need for supervision, including one to one support at times. The **hyperactivity** aspect of children diagnosed with ADHD is reflected in excessive activity. These children have difficulty playing quietly and are totally unable to shift from free to structured activities, resulting in increased distractibility, which is the feature that gives an impression of the child being like a wound-up clockwork toy.

Social interactions and peer relationships are particularly difficult for these children to achieve as they have difficulty engaging appropriately, involved constantly as they are with rule violations and with aggression and display behaviour, which are perceived as being negative and difficult by their peers. Unfortunately, children with ADHD are prone to experience a degree of social rejection, which in turn increases aggressive acting-out behaviour. Additionally, due to behaviour which is difficult to manage, family relationships are typically under strain with opposition to their parents, being less compliant and parents having greater difficulty maintaining appropriate behaviour management. In school and at home children with ADHD are usually the focus of negative attention, increased punishment and reprimands.

16.2   ASSESSING CHILDREN WITH ADHD

When assessing children with ADHD, information needs to be drawn from behavioural ratings of the child's behaviour made by the parents and teachers, interviews with parents, teachers and the child, as well as direct observation of the child in behaviour performing tasks, in the classroom and/or in the home environment. ADHD is particularly serious as a condition because the core difficulties of inattention, over activity and impulsivity result in a wide range of secondary academic, relationship and social problems. Additional difficulties may lead to poor attainment in school, whilst impulsivity and aggression could lead to greater difficulties in relationships and social involvement.

The DSM-IV diagnostic criteria for ADHD requires a range of symptoms of inattention, hyperactivity and impulsivity that have persisted for at least 6 months, to the degree that it is maladaptive and inconsistent with developmental levels. Some of the hyperactive, impulsive and/or inattentive symptoms would need to have caused impairment before the age of 7, and the impairment would need to be evident in at least two settings such as school and home. There must have also been clear evidence of clinically significant impairment in social, academic and/or occupational functioning for the diagnostic criteria to be met.

Children with a diagnosis of ADHD also present with associated features such as low frustration tolerance, temper outbursts, bossiness, stubbornness and excessive insistence on requests being met. These children may also present with emotional lability, demoralisation, and suffer rejection by their peers. Additionally, poor self esteem and poor academic achievement are common amongst these children. Family conflict and conflict with authority figures is commonly found, with family relationships being characterised by resentment and the individual's symptoms may be disruptive to the extent which leaves people to believe their troublesome behaviour is wilful. The consequent family discord and negative parent/child interactions could in turn result in increased emotional problems for the child. Inadequate self-application to tasks that require sustained effort is often interpreted by others as laziness, with a poor sense of responsibility, or as being oppositional behaviour. However, it needs to be appreciated that these children have fundamental difficulties in these areas and as a consequence are then left behind academically. It is the case that many secondary difficulties evolve owing to the nature of this disorder.

16.3   CAUSES OF ADHD

In exploring the causes of ADHD the research indicates a combination of factors including genetic factors, impairment of brain functioning, neurological features as well as social and environmental causes related to the child's failure to learn adequate cognitive behavioural skills. The current view in the literature suggests that ADHD has a biological predisposition and it is also considered to be a disorder that could be exacerbated by environmental factors. The predisposition is necessary but not sufficient, but there is no single causative environmental factor known to act alone or in combination that is unique or specific to ADHD.

16.4   TREATMENT OF ADHD

When planning treatment for ADHD, a multi-focused approach has been found to be the most effective. The primary approach has routinely been to follow an introductory course of medication, in particular methylphenidate (Ritalin), to take advantage of the effect of this medication to improve focus in the child's behaviour. The medication does assist in enabling the child to sustain attention, decreases impulsivity and improves performance on fine motor tasks. However, there are side effects that can cause concern, particularly those relating to anxiety, insomnia, weight loss, increased blood pressure and heart rate as these medications are stimulant in character. In addition to the use of medication, psychosocial approaches have been found to assist in teaching children the skills necessary to pay attention, to engage in self-control and to reduce or modulate excessive motor activity. Behaviour modification programmes are also taught to parents. This would form part of the psychological education for the parents. The parents need to be taught behaviour management-skills, but also need to gain an understanding of the difficulties inherent in the child with a diagnosis of ADHD.

Assistance at school and in teaching programmes within the school are essential for classroom management programmes to assist the child's ability to benefit from classroom instruction and being better able to make use of educational stimuli in order to fulfil their potential. Individual cognitive behaviour treatment for the child, combined with behaviour management training, has been known to be effective in attempting to instil problem-solving skills in children as well as in generalising what they have learnt outside of the classroom. As medication on its own will not have enduring long term effects, a combination of medication, cognitive therapy and behavioural management strategies for parents could be the most effective management strategy for ADHD.

CHAPTER 17

BEHAVIOURAL DISORDERS

17.1 OPPOSITIONAL DEFIANT DISORDER

Oppositional defiant disorder (ODD) refers to patterns of disturbed and disruptive behaviour related to defiant, negative and hostile behaviour on the part of the child in relation to adults and others in the environment. A distinction is made between ODD and conduct disorder, in the sense that ODD is less pervasive. This disorder tends to be a development precursor of conduct disorder, which does not however imply that ODD is less serious. This disorder reflects significant disturbance of behaviour and has cognitive and affective features which result in specific emotional, social and interpersonal difficulties. Children with these conditions have been found to have limited internalisation of social rules and norms and their hostile approach towards others is based on their interpretation of ambiguous situations as threatening; they respond accordingly with aggressive and negative behaviour. Anger and irritability are strong features of these children's mood and emotional presentation. Social adjustment is significantly disturbed and the main relationship difficulties occur between the child and its parents, as the child's defiance of parental authority and resistance to rules and appropriate behaviour undermines this relationship.

When assessing ODD, exploration of the parent/child relationship would highlight features which could indicate or predict severity and prognosis. The main areas assessed should include the child's characteristics, the parenting practices and the family's organisational problems. Where the child has defiant characteristics and a difficult temperament with impulsivity and aggressiveness, but the family is effective in managing that behaviour, this disorder may not develop or lead to significant impairment of social, academic or occupational functioning in the future. However, all the while there is ineffective monitoring or supervision, or inconsistently applied sanctions as a consequence for violation of rules and lack of reinforcement for positive and adaptive social behaviour, there could be high long-term risks for conduct difficulties in the future.

With regard to the child's characteristics, it has been found that during their school years, children with ODD present with low self-esteem, emotional lability, tend to misuse alcohol and illicit drugs and generally present with a low tolerance for frustration. These children stand out through regularly getting into conflict with their teachers, peers and parents, which in turn, leads to a vicious cycle of increased negativity and oppositional behaviour with authority figures. With regard to organisational problems, children with ODD often have problems associated also with those with Attention Deficit Hyperactivity Disorder, learning disorders and communication disorders. It has been found that children with ODD come from families where at least one parent has a history of mood disorder, ODD, Conduct Disorder or antisocial personality disorder and/or some substance related disorder. These children have also been found to have families where there is serious discord amongst the parents.

For a diagnosis to be made, it needs to be established that there has been a pattern of negative, hostile and defiant behaviour lasting at least 6 months during which the construct of compositionality is the central feature that is evident with four or more of the following also present in the child.

(1) Often loses temper.

(2) Often argues with adults.

(3) Often actively defies or refuses to comply with adults' requests or rules.

(4) Often deliberately annoys people.

(5) Often blames others for his or her mistakes or behaviour.

(6) Often touchy or easily annoyed by others.

(7) Often angry or resentful.

(8) Often spiteful or vindictive.

It would also need to be the case that the disturbance in behaviour has caused clinically significant impairment in social, academic or occupational functioning. The behaviours would not need to have occurred exclusively during the course of psychotic or mood disorder and it would need to be clear that the criteria are not met for conduct disorder.

With regard to management and treatment of children with ODD, it was found in a review of 24 studies by Carr (2000), that behavioural parental training, combined with child-focused problem-solving training, was the most effective intervention for pre-adolescent children with conduct problems and with ODD. To have maximum benefit the behavioural sessions would need to be long-term, involving between 35 and 40 sessions. Additionally, combined programmes such as behavioural programmes and child focused programme skills training were found to be more effective. Group based behavioural parent training programmes which included video modelling were also found to be effective, particularly when used in combination with other approaches. Thus, these behavioural disturbances require a multi-faceted approach to be taken for any level of success to be achieved.

17.2 CONDUCT DISORDER

For a diagnosis of conduct disorder, a high level of defiance on the part of the child needs to be evident. The DSM-IV highlights the essential features of conduct disorders as repetitive and persistent patterns of behaviour in which the basic rights of others or major age appropriate social norms or rules are violated. The behaviours are divided into aggressive and non-aggressive conduct. Aggressive behaviours are related to causing or threatening harm to other people or animals, while non-aggressive conduct is associated with causing property loss or damage, deceitfulness or theft and serious violation of rules. With conduct disorder the disturbance of behaviour would be such that it causes clinically significant impairment in social, academic and/or occupational functioning and these difficulties would need to be present before the age of 18 years. Children with conduct disorders tend to initiate aggressive behaviour and react aggressively to others, and the disorder is particularly associated with bullying behaviour, threatening or intimidating behaviour, frequent fights using weapons and being cruel to humans and other animals. There are two further sub-types of conduct disorder, the first being the **childhood onset type** which is defined by the onset of at least one criterion and is characteristic of conduct disorder prior to the age of 10. **Adolescent onset type** is ascribed to children whose characteristics of conduct disorder occur after the age of 10. Patients with adolescent onset type conduct disorders are less likely to display aggressive behaviour and tend to have more normal peer relationships.

The central psychological or psychodynamic feature of children with conduct disorder involves their having limited empathy or concern for the feelings, wishes and well-being of others. As with children diagnosed with ODD, children with conduct disorder respond aggressively to ambiguous situations and frequently misperceive the intentions of others as being hostile and threatening. These children then consequently respond to these misperceptions and misunderstandings in an aggressive way. They are also found to lack the appropriate feelings of guilt and remorse which are genuine. Other characteristics include extremely low self-esteem, poor frustration tolerance, irritability, lack of impulse control and restlessness. Conflicting relationships with parents and teachers could be related to the defiant behaviour, aggression, bullying and hostility.

The risk or propensity to develop conduct disorder is higher when an aggressive child has in addition cognitive deficits such as limitations in problem solving and has difficulty generating multiple solutions to problems. Aggressive children diagnosed with a conduct disorder typically display cognitive distortions when thinking about social interactions as may happen when they are in an ambiguous situation and also tend to attribute negative motivations to others. This distortion then prompts the aggressive child to retaliate to give rise to another vicious cycle. Family characteristics would also determine the level of risk for the development of conduct disorders in children of the family.

Family patterns where there is parental deviant behaviour, parental rejection, lack of discipline or lack of supervision of children and marital conflict and divorce all serve as high risk factors for conduct disorder. It is not uncommon to find that the parents of children with conduct disorder are very often themselves deviant, displaying maladjustment, anger and/or criminal behaviour. Marital conflict contributes to oppositional behaviour in children and many children with conduct disorders have parents with a personality disorder. Additionally, problems associated with alcoholism, substance abuse, separation from parents and divorce increase the risk of serious behaviour disturbance developing. As its basis, where parents respond negatively and are physically abusive towards children, this could directly contribute to the development of the view by the child that his direct world is a dangerous place in which aggression is an acceptable way to solve problems. Thus poor parenting skills, aggression and negativity produce and promote antisocial behaviour, as do high rates of divorce and conduct disordered behaviour on the part of the parents.

As family conflict and poor parenting skills are viewed to be the core features for conduct disorders, treatment packages need to focus on improving these areas. A combination of behaviour orientated parental training as well as cognitive therapy for the children has been found to be most effective. Parental training needs to address ineffective, punitive and inconsistent parenting practices, and these parents need to be taught skills for management of their children. An action orientated approach which includes a combination of parental training programmes and psychological education is essential. The patient group that is known for its poor success rate is the one which involves the family dropping out before completion of their therapy and treatment. Individual treatment for children would focus on cognitive processing with particular emphasis on teaching children to stop and think, and also encourages reflective problem solving before impulsively engaging in action which may also involve aggressive behaviour. Furthermore, problem solving skills, providing role play to rectify social misconceptions and anger management would also be indicated to assist children to learn impulse control.

Research by Carr (2000) revealed that functional family therapy was highly effective for families where the conduct disorder was of a mild degree. This approach focuses on assisting family members collectively, helping to alter the problematical communication patterns between them and, in the belief that if the lack of supervision and discipline within the families can be altered, the behaviour within the family would improve. The assumption was based on the fact that families showing conduct disorder are characterised by high levels of defensive communication, poor supervision and low levels of supportive communication, compared with families in homes with no conduct disorder. Thus, the initial family assessment would need to focus on identifying the patterns of communication between family members and their beliefs about the solutions.

More serious cases of conduct disorder are, however, found to be better assisted with a multi-systemic therapeutic approach, which not only assists the family, but involves the wider network involved with the child. The focus of the therapeutic input would be to reframe the way of understanding the problem and restructuring the way the child and family interact around the problem. Interventions could focus on the child individually, the family, the school, the peer group and the community, for example facilitating communication between parents and teachers and arranging appropriate educational placements. Interventions with the peer group may involve reducing contact with the deviant peer group and increasing contact with non-deviant peers, thus bringing about structural changes.

In severe cases where parents are unable to manage the behaviour, despite all attempts at intervention, therapeutic foster care may be indicated. The aim is for the child to be temporarily placed with foster parents who have been trained to use behavioural strategies to modify deviant behaviour. Foster carers offering treatment should be carefully selected and trained in the principles of behavioural parental training and an understanding of the distorted cognitions possessed by these children. Within such a treatment foster placement there should be concurrent package of support for the parents, the child, the school, and the wider community. Individual work as well as ongoing support for the foster family would be essential to prevent placement breakdown.

17.3 SUBSTANCE ABUSE

Alcohol and drug abuse in adolescents causes particular concern because it can have negative long-term effects for adolescents who abuse these substances and may consequently also come to have negative effects on their own children. Adolescents' habitual substance use may negatively affect mental and physical health, establish their criminal status and impair educational attainment. It also impacts upon the establishment of autonomy from the family of origin and consequently may adversely affect the development of long-term intimate relationships. Substance abuse includes not only abuse of substances but substance dependency as well. A diagnosis of substance abuse is made where there is a maladaptive pattern of substance abuse leading to clinically significant impairment or distress manifested by impairment within a 12-month period. The impairment is associated with failure to fulfil major obligations at work, school or home, to a level which is physically hazardous; the person may also come to experience legal problems.

Substance dependency is viewed as a maladaptive pattern of abuse leading to clinically significant impairment or distress as evidenced by tolerance. This is where a person requires increased amount of a substance to achieve intoxication, and takes large amounts over a longer period of time than was first intended. Dependency is evident where there is repeated unsuccessful effort to cut down or control substance use. A person is deemed dependent when important, social, occupational, recreational activities are given up or reduced because of the consequences of substance use. Additionally, a person is deemed dependent when substance use is continued despite the knowledge of recurrent physical or psychological problems being caused or exacerbated by misuse of the substance.

Drug use has a significant and overwhelming impact on interpersonal, family and social adjustment, creating conflict and distress. Drug use often occurs in conjunction with other psychological problems including conduct disorder, ADHD, specific learning difficulties, mood disorders, anxiety disorders, schizophrenia and eating disorders. It is not unusual for children who have been abused physically and sexually to resort to alcohol and illicit drug use as a way of coping with the emotional and psychological consequences of the abuse. The relationship between the drug use and co-morbid psychological problems could work in two ways, either the psychological problems coming to precede the drug use and contributing in some way to the development of drug using behaviour or, alternatively, the drug use might have precipitated or maintained the other psychological problems, for example the use of amphetamines leading to anxiety and panic related problems. It could be the case that drug dependency may lead to chronic conduct problems such as those leading to criminal behaviour such as assault and theft.

Treatment for misuse of alcohol and illicit drug use could involve different approaches. With adolescents the most effective treatment approach has been found to be a combination of family therapy and individual treatment methods. Where families cannot be engaged, individual therapy could still, however, be effective. The best outcome, however, appears to involve multi-system family therapy over a longer period of time, for example, over a 9-month period. It is generally held in the literature that at least 4 months of family therapy should be the routine treatment of choice. Therapy would need to assist with improvement of problem solving and to develop effective coping strategies, to address impoverished social skills as well as any deficits in self-regulation. Where there is physical dependency on substances, detoxification and other in-patient methods of treatment should be considered.

CHAPTER 18

EATING DISORDERS

18.1 ANOREXIA NERVOSA

Anorexia nervosa is an eating disorder characterised by intense fear of becoming obese, a distorted self-perception of body-image, and a refusal to maintain minimal body weight and, in females, cessation of menstruation. Patients with anorexia nervosa have a significantly disturbed and insular perception of their size or the shape of their body. In addition, they fail to recognise successful weight loss and have an overwhelming need to control their body through increasing and damaging weight loss. The risk of onset in anorexia is at its highest between the ages of 14 to 18 years, the average age of onset being about 17 years of age. This condition is more common in females than males. With this eating disorder the concern with the control of body weight and shape is paired with an unhealthy pattern of eating particularly related to binge eating and pillaging of food. Thus the main clinical feature is related to distorted perception, in particular distorted body image, and the cognitive processes linked to the preoccupation associated with bingeing and pillaging responses is related to feelings of being out of control and a need to take over control. The psychodynamics of anorexia nervosa appear to involve an internal conflict, torn between remaining dependency and achieving independence. On the one hand, there is an overwhelming wish expressed in internalised needs and feelings to remain dependent owing to the fear of maturity and independence. However, on the other hand, there is also a desire and the need to escape from parental control, with the control of food often seen as a way of controlling parents.

Children and adolescents with eating disorders typically experience low self esteem, low self-efficacy and also strive towards perfectionism. An emotional difficulty associated with anorexia is the fear of fatness, together with the emotional difficulties associated with anxiety and depression. A behavioural component of anorexia is related to restricted eating and the cycle of restricted eating, bingeing and compensatory behaviour, which includes vomiting, the use of diuretics or laxatives or excessive exercise, is in danger of becoming established. While bingeing brings immediate relief it also leads to physical discomfort and a sense of guilt for not adhering to a strict diet. A vicious cycle emerges with the individual feeling worthless, which in turn drives that person towards bingeing, followed by the pillaging which exacerbates the feelings of worthlessness and leads to a negative self-view.

Additional features central to anorexia include impaired interpersonal adjustment, poor school performance and deteriorating family relationships. Physical complications also impact on the emotional and physical well-being with endocrine disorders, amenorrhoea and delayed onset of puberty being well established features. The symptoms of starvation such as reduced metabolic rate, hypothermia and renal dysfunction are significant features. Additionally, erosion of dental enamel may occur due to vomiting and lesions may be found at the back of the hand which is used for initiating vomiting.

For a diagnosis of anorexia nervosa to be made the patient would need to present with refusal to maintain body weight at or above the minimum for the range of the normal weight for the age and height of that individual and is assessed also to experience an intense fear of gaining weight or becoming fat, even though the patient is underweight. The individual also suffers a disturbance in which the perception of one's body weight or shape is distorted. Furthermore, with post-menarche females, amenorrhoea with the absence of at least three consecutive menstrual cycles may become evident.

Associative features of anorexia nervosa include depressive symptoms including a depressed mood, social withdrawal, irritability, insomnia and diminished interest in sex. Such individuals may have a symptomatic presentation that meets the criteria of a major depressive disorder. Obsessive compulsive features both related and unrelated to food are often prominent. Behaviours associated with some form of starvation suggest that obsessions and compulsions are related to food and may cause or exacerbate under-nutrition. Concerns about eating in public, feelings of ineffectiveness, a strong need to control one's environment, inflexible thinking, lack of social spontaneity and overly restrained initiative or expression are common features. A substantial proportion of individuals with anorexia nervosa have personality difficulties that meet the criteria for the diagnosis of at least one personality disorder.

It has been found that persons with anorexia nervosa hold negative views about sexuality, rarely engage in sexual activity and they also may have been found to have low oestrogen levels. It has also been found in research studies that families with an anorexic child are marked by significant emotional enmeshment, where each member lacks a distinct identity. While the child in such a family can feel protected by the group, it also fails to develop a personal sense of autonomy and independence. The symptoms of an anorexic child appear to serve to regulate the family by keeping parental conflict from getting out of control. Patients with anorexia predominantly make use of avoidant response where excessive anxiety is associated with avoidance of food. The food avoidance is then reinforced by the tension that it brings to the individual. Consequently, the child comes to learn that not eating is a successful way of getting attention.

18.2   BULIMIA NERVOSA

Bulimia nervosa is an eating disorder which is characterised by the rapid consumption of large quantities of food in discrete periods of time and the feeling of lack of control over the eating. The essential features of bulimia nervosa are considered to be binge eating and the use of inappropriate compensatory methods to prevent weight gain. Individuals with bulimia tend to be excessively self-evaluating of body shape and weight, and bulimia occurs more often in females and typically later in adolescents. To qualify for a diagnosis, the binge eating and inappropriate compensatory behaviour must occur on average at least twice a week for 3 months. A binge would be defined as eating in a discrete period of time, such as in about 2 hours, an amount of food that is larger than most individuals would eat under similar circumstances, and, therefore, the continual snacking on small amounts of food throughout the day would not be considered to be a binge. The type of food binged on would usually be high calorie food such as ice cream or cake. However, it is the abnormality in the amount of food consumed, rather than a craving for specific food such as carbohydrates, that characterises the condition. Bulimia is also characterised by self-induced vomiting, use of diuretics, fasting and vigorous exercise to prevent weight-gain. A typical feature of bulimia is of a person being ashamed of his eating problems and consequently attempting to conceal his symptoms. Thus, the binge-eating usually occurs in secrecy or as inconspicuously as possible, highlighting a lack of total control. Individuals with bulimia nervosa are typically within the normal weight range, although some may be slightly overweight or underweight. In general, an increase of frequency of depressive symptoms is evident in individuals with bulimia nervosa, whilst an increased frequency of anxiety related symptoms is also associated with anorexia. There are a proportion of individuals with bulimia who have personality features that meet the criteria for one or more of the personality disorders.

18.3   TREATMENT OF ANOREXIA AND BULIMIA

The most effective treatment of anorexia and bulimia involves outpatient family therapy or family based treatment involving concurrent therapy for parents and the individual. Psychological education to inform parents and adolescents about the risks associated with eating disorders, to assist the parents to implement home-based re-feeding programmes in cases with anorexia and, once this has been achieved, to advise about the process whereby the responsibility for maintaining body weight is returned to the adolescent. Additionally, psychodynamic, behavioural, cognitive and family systems may all be effective in the treatment of eating disorders. Hospitalisation, diet modification and force-feeding are approaches which tend to be more prone to relapses and the return of symptoms. Cognitive behavioural treatment for anorexic and bulimic patients is commonly used to assist the adolescent to modify eating patterns and to identify faulty beliefs or expectations. Interpersonal therapy is also useful to assist bulimic and anorexic patients to understand the interpersonal context within which the eating problem occurs. Treatment should then focus on resolving interpersonal difficulties rather than merely altering eating behaviour or eating-related cognitions.

CHAPTER 19

PERVASIVE DEVELOPMENT DISORDERS

19.1   INTRODUCTION

Pervasive development disorders are characterised by a range of severe pervasive impairments in several areas of development. These would include dysfunction in reciprocal social interaction skills, communication skills or the presence of stereotyped behaviour, interests or activity. In order to meet the diagnostic criteria set by the DSM IV, these disorders include these specific features of impairment and would need to be evident within the first year of life. The pervasive impairments are often associated with mental retardation. Pervasive development disorders include autism, Asperger's syndrome and Rhett's disorder. These disorders could be mild, moderate or severe as they are typically seen on a spectrum of severity and complexity.

19.2   AUTISTIC DISORDER

Early infantile autism or autistic disorder would be considered where the presence of abnormal or impaired development in social interaction and communication and restricted repertoire of activities and interests occur. Reciprocal or interactive social interaction is significantly impaired together with the presence of communication difficulties, both on the verbal and non-verbal levels. Diagnostic criteria as set out by the DSM-IV for autistic disorder indicate that for a diagnosis to be made, various qualitative and quantitative signs, symptoms and experiences would need to be present. Qualitative impairment of social interaction would be manifested by marked impairment of multiple non-verbal behaviours such as eye to eye gaze, facial expression, body postures and gestures to regulate social interaction. This would also include failure to develop peer relationships appropriately, the lack of sustained seeking to share enjoyment, and lack of social and emotional reciprocity. Qualitative impairment would take the form of delay in/or total lack of development of spoken language and/or adequate speech. These children would present with marked impairment in the capacity to initiate or sustain a conversation with others and the tendency to use repetitive idiosyncratic language. Further qualitative impairment would involve a lack of varied and/or spontaneous make-believe play or socially imaginative play appropriate to the developmental levels of the child.

An additional diagnostic criterion is related to restricted, repetitive stereotyped patterns of behaviour, interests and activities. It is common for these children to present with a preoccupation with one or more stereotyped interests, specific non-functional routines or rituals and repetitive motor mannerisms. Additionally with autistic children there is a delay or abnormal functioning in social interaction, language as used in social communication and/or symbolic or imaginative play. In children diagnosed with autistic disorder, mental retardation could range from mild to profound and there may also be abnormalities in the development of a variety of skills. Additionally, behaviour and symptoms such as hyperactivity, short-attention span, impulsivity, aggression, self-injurious behaviour and temper tantrums are often evident.

The cause(s) of autism are still not known, however, there are some indications that genetic features and biological factors could contribute to the onset of the autistic disorder. There are also some indications that pre-natal damage or disruptive pre-natal development could contribute to this condition. This disorder is largely cognitive and social, where pathology has occurred at some point between conception and birth. The prognosis and prospect for any significant improvement with autistic children is not good, and while there could be some improvement, most autistic children continue into adulthood remaining severely handicapped and unable to take full care of themselves. Language skills and IQ skills are considered to be the best prognostic indicators for development and progression, in particular early language development and high IQ suggesting a better prognosis. Thus, autistic children who have developed the use of speech have a better outcome and better prognosis for some level of functioning in the community. However, 75% of autistic children fall into the moderate range of mental retardation and 25% of this group develop seizure disorders by the time they reach adulthood. The most effective form of assistance provided to autistic children has been found to be behaviour modification. This approach focuses on teaching and improving levels of learning in the areas of language, self-help and behaviour presentation. Significant help should, however, also be given to parents, particularly in training parents through psychological education to assist in coping with the disruptive and often dangerous behaviour capable of being shown by autistic children. The parents could also assist in language training for their children; however, specialised training for this is usually required. Parental training and support for parents with autistic children are essential as parenting an autistic child is extremely difficult and emotionally taxing to the parent and also makes demands on the family as a whole.

19.3   ASPERGER'S DISORDER

Asperger's disorder is considered to be a syndrome on the autistic spectrum of disorders. The essential feature with these children is considered to be the severe and sustained impairment in social interaction and development of restricted, repetitive patterns of behaviour, interests and activities. These disturbances cause significant impairment of the child's social, occupational and interpersonal functioning. Despite impairment of functioning with children with Asperger's disorder, no impairments are usually evident in cognitive development or with age-appropriate self-help skills. It has also been found that Asperger's disorder is more common in males and in the majority of cases the disorder is lifelong.

The diagnostic criteria for Asperger's disorder include a qualitative deficiency in social interaction, which reflects marked impairment in the use of non-verbal behaviour such as eye to eye contact, facial expression and body postures and gestures. These children fail to develop appropriate peer relationships; they lack spontaneous seeking to share enjoyment, interests or achievement with others. The lack of social or emotional reciprocity is also a hallmark feature of this disorder.

Asperger's children also present with restricted, repetitive and stereotyped patterns of behaviour, interests and activities. These could include preoccupation with one or more stereotyped or restrictive patterns of interest, stereotyped and repetitive mannerisms with persistent preoccupation with parts and objects. The disturbance of behaviour causes clinically significant impairment in social, occupational or other areas of functioning. For such a diagnosis to be made there should be no clinically significant general delay in language or clinically significant delay in cognitive development. Thus, in contrast to autistic disorder, children with Asperger's disorder do not present with mental retardation whatsoever. Rather, they are usually of average to above average ability. Variability of cognitive functioning may be observed often with strengths in verbal ability and weaknesses in non-verbal skills. Motor clumsiness and awkwardness may, however, be present, but this is usually mild, although such difficulties may contribute to rejection by peers and may lead to social isolation. Symptoms of over activity and inattention are frequent in Asperger's disorder and, indeed, many children with this condition receive a diagnosis of ADHD prior to the diagnosis of Asperger's disorder being made.

Asperger's disorder is a continuous and lifelong disorder. In school-aged children the good verbal ability has been found to mask the severity of the child's social dysfunction to some degree and thus misleads carers and teachers to erroneously attribute behaviour difficulties to stubbornness in the child. It is also the case that interests in establishing formal social relationships may increase in adolescence in these patients, as individuals can with assistance learn some way by now of responding more adeptly to their difficulties. The prognosis for Asperger's disorder is significantly better than in autistic disorder. However, specific assistance including both psychological educations of parents and individual work with children is usually necessary.

19.4 RHETT'S DISORDER

The most striking and essential feature of Rhett's disorder is the development of multiple specific deficits following a period of normal functioning after birth. Individuals with apparently normal pre-natal and peri-natal development may display normal psycho-motor development in the first 5 months of life before any deterioration occurs. The head circumference at birth could be within the normal limits. However, between the age of 5 and 48 months, the head growth decelerates and there is a loss of previously acquired purposeful hand skills between the age of 5 and 30 months. Children with Rhett's disorder present as having diminished interest in their social environment in the first few years after the onset of this disorder. Furthermore, although social interaction may often develop later in the course of this condition, Rhett's disorder is typically associated with severe or profound mental retardation. An increased incidence of seizure disorder may also be present in these children. The evolution of this condition suggests that the pattern of developmental regression is highly distinctive and this condition normally would have its onset prior to the age of 4, usually in the first or second year of the child's life. This condition is lifelong and the loss of skills is generally persistent and progressive.

CHAPTER 20

SUMMARY FOR CHILD AND ADOLESCENT DISORDERS

20.1   ASSESSMENT IN CHILD AND FAMILY LAW

The clinical psychologist engaged in family and child litigation is concerned with the identification and treatment of behavioural problems and the emotional functioning of a child within the family context. When working with children or adolescents an understanding of diagnosis and presentation of conditions is important, in particular knowing how certain conditions affect the child's behaviour, its interactions and its relationships. The child and/or adolescent may present with uncommon symptoms and behaviours that could cause the clinical psychologist to suspect that there could be associated with these severe self-harm, sexually harmful behaviours and anxious and distressed reactions. When undertaking medico-legal/forensic assessments, expertise in risk assessments would be important, as would an understanding of how complex behaviour and presentations overlap with other psychological and psychiatric conditions. The aim of the clinical psychologist working with children and adolescents is to minimise the effects of harmful mental disorder and any other factors in the child's environment in order that any future risk to the child and the family could be reduced. The psychologist needs to work within the context of an understanding of child development and be able to systematically promote and alleviate psychological disturbances by making recommendations for treatment and also advise how the family could be assisted in the context of the child's disturbed emotional and behavioural functioning.

In undertaking assessments in the context of child and family law, the effect on a child of separating from primary carers and the parenting they then receive, which has proved to be a key issue in child psychiatry and developmental psychology, needs to be considered. Early separations, inconsistent emotional availability and dysfunctional family experiences could cause a variety of psychiatric disorders in the child that may persist into adult life. These disorders range from anxiety and depression to maladaptive personality functioning. Furthermore, it is known that impaired communication within the family and unsatisfactory patterns of dominance by parental figures play a major role in the origins and causation of psychiatric and psychological disorders. An assessment of not only the child but the family context in which it lives would be important. By identifying the causation of the emotional distress and psychological disturbances it is possible to gain an understanding of the origin of the psychological disturbance presented by the child. This is needed in order to make recommendations for treatment.

Growing up in a disruptive environment could impair a child's development and lead to a lack of a secure sense of self which in turn could lead to anxieties. This may be evident in a child presenting with anxiety disorders and anxiety related symptoms. The disruption in the home environment could also impact on social development, essential for establishing satisfactory peer relationships which are necessary for future appropriate interpersonal functioning. Disturbed interpersonal relationships would thus need to be assessed to give an indication as to what changes and assistance are needed for resolution of the difficulties. Additionally, extreme stresses may give rise to difficulties in reality testing which in turn could lead to a preoccupation with self-annihilation and self-destructive impulses. When undertaking child and family assessments an understanding of these difficulties may help give an indication of and insight into the difficulties the children are experiencing within that context.

It is the case that where children come from families in which both parents have suffered psychiatric illnesses or psychological disturbances that they have a double disadvantage in that they could well inherit the illnesses of one or both of the parents. In addition they could also develop intense vulnerability due to the tempestuous early home environment caused by disturbed parental behaviour. Childhood disturbances and psychological conditions in children need to be understood against the backdrop of parenting influences that a child has experienced. Thus, assessments of children should always be made within the context of the family. Consideration of how parenting and other family experiences influence psychological development and presentation of psychological difficulties in the child would depend on the features of parenting, the nature of the child and the environmental context in which the child grows. All this needs to be taken into account when making an assessment of a child's experiences in order to make appropriate recommendations for treatment and in attempting to resolve the difficulties that the child presents with. Such assessments, which look past the immediate problems of the individual child, could assist in identifying the changes that are needed to reduce the experience of stress and distress which is leading and/or contributing to psychological disturbances and disorders in the child.

20.2   DIAGNOSTIC CONSIDERATIONS IN CHILDHOOD DISORDERS

Children with a history of neglect and/or abuse characteristically present with behavioural difficulties and thus it is not uncommon for these children to be diagnosed with Oppositional Defiant Disorder (ODD) or conduct disorder. Furthermore, their high levels of internalised anxiety, attention seeking behaviour and emotional distraction could and does often cause them to present with a picture similar to children diagnosed with Attention Deficit Hyperactivity Disorder (ADHD). The child's life experiences of abuse and trauma could also cause the child to present with post traumatic stress disorder or depression due to one or more significant losses early in its childhood. To make sense of the child's presenting problems and to gain an understanding of what the core difficulties and diagnoses are, in depth developmental histories need to be taken and explored. As many presenting problems and behaviours have their basis in early parenting disturbances and traumas, it is important to explore the attachment experiences of the child. Attachment is developed in the first years of life and insecure attachments are associated with inconsistent emotional availability of the carers and the child's unmet needs of security. The child's behaviour needs to be understood before diagnoses are made or appropriate interventions set out.

Attachment is the base upon which emotional health, social relationships and a sense of security and belonging develop. The ability to trust and form reciprocal relationships will affect every aspect of the child's future psychological functioning which would include emotional health, a feeling of security and the achievement of satisfactory interpersonal relationships. Without a secure attachment the child will have a fundamental lack of empathy and maladaptive social and interpersonal relationships. Consequently, they could then present similarly to children with diagnoses of ADHD, Asperger's syndrome, ODD and conduct disorder.

Children who have not been adopted by the age of 6 months or so have been found to have attachment problems. Normal attachment usually develops during the child's first two years of life and if an infant's needs are not met consistently in a loving, nurturing way, attachment will not occur normally. Problems with the parent-child relationship or breaks in the consistent caregiver-child relationship could prevent attachment from developing normally. There is a wide range of attachment problems that result in varying degrees of emotional and social impairment which may lead the clinician to misdiagnose. The severity of attachment disorder seems to result from the number of breaks in the bonding cycle and the extent of the child's emotional vulnerability.

A further issue is to try to differentiate between a child who appears attached, and a child who really is making a healthy, secure attachment. Simply because a child presents as having positive interaction giving indications such as snuggles, cuddles, and saying 'I love you', this does not necessarily mean that the child is attached, or even attaching. The key to attachment is the formation of trust, and trust becomes secure only after repeated testing. Thus, it is important to differentiate testing behaviour and emotional and social impairment of children who have insecure attachments from those childen who have autistic spectrum disorders, ADHD or conduct disorders. However, these latter children could also have developed attachment difficulties, and very often do.

Behavioural problems related to insecurity, lack of attachment, and traumatic events in the child's past may surface when the child is placed in alternative care. It is not uncommon for these children to present as manipulative or superficial with features of 'take' and no 'give'. Although these children appear to only give when it is to their own benefit, underlying this could be high levels of internalised anxiety, extremely low self esteem and no sense of values. These children could be suffering from emotional and social impairment with related anger, anxiety and depression-related difficulties which lead to interference with their emotional, social and interpersonal functioning.

PART III

ADULT MENTAL HEALTH

CHAPTER 21

INTRODUCTION

21.1 THE EFFECTS OF MENTAL DISORDERS

The study of adult mental health involves the disciplines of both psychiatry and psychology. The subject of adult mental disorder in respect of the issues arising in family and child law has been considered in a companion to this volume (see Mahendra, 2006). From a psychological point of view sound mental health could be considered to be a state of emotional and psychological well-being in which individuals are able to use their cognitive and emotional capabilities to function appropriately in society and be able to meet the demands of everyday life. Thus, the possession of good mental health may be seen as being an index to a person's overall emotional and psychological state and level of well-being. Mental illness and disorder could therefore adversely affect functioning in areas of economic productivity, the capacity for having healthy relationships and those involving satisfactory social functioning. A person's overall quality of life could be determined by the degree of mental illness suffered as this could have an impact on that person's ability to lead a full and productive life. Mood and anxiety disorders are found to occur most commonly in clinical practice and these types of disorders may constitute forms of mental illness which inhibit activity of all kinds including employment and economic productivity. Furthermore, the feature of suicide, commonly associated with depressive disorders, is a significant cause of death, highlighting the impact mental health and more particularly ill health can come to have on individuals, their families and on the wider society itself. Mental illness and disorder may be viewed as psychological disturbances which may have an adverse impact on a person's capacity to think rationally and logically and impairing also his ability to cope with day-to-day stressors, traumas and losses. Mental disorder usually affects how we view our world, how we relate to others and how we perceive ourselves. Its implications for the issues which usually arise in family and child proceedings are clear.

Good mental health which comes to be experienced in adult life may be seen to be, when looked at from the psychological perspective, a result of all life experiences, beginning with the person having healthy intra-uterine experiences due to the mother's healthy pregnancy, his having received adequate parenting, achieving secure attachments to primary care givers in childhood, having appropriate involvement with various groups of individuals including with his peers and being able to form stable intimate relationships. Sound mental health does not imply the absence of stress or psychological suffering experienced on the part of an individual, rather it reflects the stability the individual possesses to enable him to cope adequately with the ordinary stresses and traumas of life. Experiences are only considered to be dysfunctional, or a person is said to display mental disorder or symptoms of psychological distress, when these become functionally disabling. The known causes of mental illness appear to be very numerous. These causes include a genetic contribution to the disorder, environmental factors, or a combination of these, which may influence one's vulnerability to mental illness and disorder and may also make an impact on one's emotional and psychological well-being. Most significantly, traumatic events throughout one's life, including childhood abuse and neglect, major losses, violence and conflict, could come to threaten one's mental stability. Additionally, it is also the apparently more ordinary stressors such as unemployment, bereavement and relationship problems which could have an impact on an individual's coping capacity, his ability to function satisfactorily and ultimately on his mental health. It is also the case that nutritional deficiencies, infections, and, in some cases, environmental toxins have been implicated in the causation of certain psychological symptoms in association with mental disorder. Substance abuse – involving alcohol and illicit drugs – contribute significantly to the exacerbation and also the occasional precipitation of psychiatric disorders, and also complicate the treatment of these conditions.

When discussing and managing concerns relating to mental health and disorder, a vast and protean subject, consistent and agreed definitions and descriptions are needed. Readers interested in the pitfalls associated with the diagnoses of mental disorder and the steps that have been taken to try to alleviate these problems may find a detailed description available in the companion volume on adult psychiatry. The Diagnostic and Statistical Manual of Mental Disorders – 4th Edition (DSM-IV) is a product of the work which had as its focus the establishing of standardised diagnostic criteria and the creation of a validated descriptive system for those professionals diagnosing and treating mental disorders. This diagnostic system, which brings the influence of American practice, is now more or less universally accepted. It classifies and describes categories of illness. A classification system with rather greater European bias, such as the ICD-10, has a similar basis and these systems of classification may be used alongside one other. Areas of mental disorder of relevance to this work featuring in these classifications include the affective disorders, psychotic disorders, anxiety states, substance abuse, childhood disorders and personality disorders.

There is a vast array of mental disorders which are seen in clinical practice. In this book only those mental disorders of psychological interest in family and child proceedings are discussed in any detail.

Affective disorders involve often cyclical patterns of significant underlying mood disturbance and may include major depressive episodes that may be precipitated by stressful life events, but which may also have a genetic basis contributing to the patient's predisposition to experiencing stressful situations and reacting adversely to them. Psychotic disorders are characterised by particular and characteristic symptoms such as hallucinations, delusions and bizarre behaviours as well as symptoms such as the paucity or disorder of speech, a poverty of ideas, the blunting of the affect, impairment of expression and a loss of insight which all conspire to lead to functional deterioration. Anxiety disorders are considered to be amongst the most debilitating psychiatric disorders in the general population and these disorders lead to both psychological distress as well as increased utilisation of healthcare provision. Disorders due to substance abuse, involving the excessive consumption of alcohol and the use of illicit drugs, are common within all segments of society and can lead to major problems in school and work situations and may be associated, apart from the relationship they have with physical illness, also with accidents, violence and crime. Childhood disorders include pervasive developmental disorders, childhood abuse and neglect, and mood and anxiety disorders. Personality disorders have their origins in late adolescence and are characterised by pervasive and persistent maladaptive patterns of behaviour that are deeply ingrained and which are not attributable to other psychiatric disorders.

CHAPTER 22

STRESS RELATED DISORDERS

22.1 INTRODUCTION

Stress is a person's response to environmental demands or pressures. The part played by stress in causing difficulties for parents, spouses and partners is not difficult to imagine. The impact of stress on an individual depends not only on the severity of stress experienced but also on that individual's pre-existing vulnerabilities, in other words his capacity for responding to the stress. The impact stress makes needs to be assessed against a person's habitual functioning in an environment where all situations, both positive and negative, require adjustments which, in some cases, may be experienced by that person as being excessively stressful. However, the extent to which any stress impacts on an individual depends on a variety of factors, in particular the severity of stress, the unique characteristics possessed by the person experiencing the stress and the nature of the stressful situation itself. The impact of the stressors experienced will be in proportion to the levels of frustration and conflict that arise in and the pressures that come to be put on an individual. Frustration is experienced when strivings are blocked or obstacles impede progress towards a desired goal. Conflicts are viewed as two or more incompatible needs or motives experienced by a person who is then placed in a position of needing to make a choice between them. The choice may involve that between a positive and negative goal or even between two desirable positive goals. Being placed in a situation of pressure to choose between specific goals elicits conflict in the individual and consequently may result in his experiencing high levels of stress. The severity of the stress depends upon the degree of disruption that occurs, which depends partly on the characteristic of the stressor and partly on the individual's available resources to cope, the personal and situational factors involved and the relationship between all these. Additionally, when facing stress, pressure or conflicts, there are two options facing an individual; either to meet the demands of a stressor or to protect one's self from psychological damage through withdrawal or avoidance and making use of defensive patterns and reactions in the process of doing so. A reaction to stress could take the form of **damage repair mechanisms** such as crying, repetitive talking or mourning in the face of stress or distress. Alternatively, one can make use of **self-defence mechanisms** which tend to be maladaptive. These include responses such as denial and repression in order to relieve tension or anxiety or to protect oneself from hurt and devaluation.

The symptoms of stress can be either physical or psychological. Stress-related physical illnesses, such as irritable bowel syndrome, heart attacks, arthritis, and chronic headaches, result from long-term over stimulation of a part of the nervous system that regulates the heart rate, blood pressure, and digestive system. Stress-related emotional illness results from inadequate or inappropriate responses to major changes in one's life situation, such as marriage, completing one's education, becoming a parent, losing a job, or retirement. In such cases the term adjustment disorder is used to describe this phenomenon. In the workplace, stress-related illness often takes the form of 'burnout' – a loss of interest in or ability to perform one's job due to long-term high stress levels.

Treatment for stress and stress-related conditions could include one or more of the following treatment regimes: medication, stress management programs, behavioural approaches, cognitive therapy and/or alternative treatments such as physical exercise, yoga, aromatherapy, nutrition-based treatments, acupuncture or homeopathy.

22.2 ADJUSTMENT DISORDERS

Initially, adjustment disorders were termed a transient mental disturbance which was seen as being provoked by overwhelming stress. This reaction has now become known as an adjustment disorder, which is similar in many ways to acute stress disorder and post traumatic stress disorder (PTSD) as they all require an external event to have occurred before such a diagnosis can be made. To meet the criteria of this diagnosis there needs to have been a stressful life event or life change in the individual and the duration of symptoms should begin within a month and not exceed 6 months except where there is a secondary depressive reaction. Adjustment disorder describes patterns of psychological and/or behavioural disturbances in response to this stress, which could be in the form of one or more of the common stressors and which may arise in the context of family life. However, the stress experienced usually proves to be beyond that which one would normally experience in terms of the resulting impairment of social and occupational functioning. The individual's reactions should not be seen as an over reaction to stress but rather as a pattern of behaviour which typically would be expected to resolve after the impact of the stressor has subsided. For a diagnosis of adjustment disorder to be made the clinical significance of the reaction should be marked either by distress that is in excess of what one would have expected given the nature of the stressor or result in significant impairment in different areas of functioning. The stressor may be a single event or involve multiple situations inducing stress.

There are various sub-types of adjustment disorders. The first of these is related to depressed mood where there is a predominant manifestation of depression-related symptoms such as tearfulness, lowering of mood and feelings of hopelessness. Where adjustment disorder is related to anxiety, on the other hand, there could be a manifestation of symptoms associated with nervousness, worry, fears of separation and a general sense of apprehension. An adjustment disorder could also present as a sub-type where there is mixed anxiety and depressive symptoms. With this sub-type there is disturbance of behaviour to the extent that there may be a violation of the rights of others by the behaviour of the individual afflicted or violation of age-appropriate social norms or rules by that individual. There could also be a sub-type associated with mixed disturbance of emotions and behaviour. With persons suffering with an adjustment disorder one would expect to see subjective distress in the individuals when they function in important areas of their life. The adjustment disorder could also be associated with suicide attempts, excessive substance use or misuse and somatic complaints and symptoms.

An adjustment disorder is a debilitating reaction, usually lasting less than 6 months, to a stressful event or situation. It is not the same thing as PTSD, which usually occurs in reaction to a life-threatening event and can be longer lasting. An adjustment disorder usually begins within 3 months of a stressful event, and ends within 6 months after the stressor stops. There are many different sub-types of adjustment disorders, including adjustment disorder with: depression, anxiety, mixed anxiety and depression conduct disturbances, mixed disturbance of emotions and conduct; it could also be unspecified.

An adjustment disorder occurs when a person cannot cope with a stressful event and develops emotional or behavioural symptoms. The stressful event can be of any kind; it may also be one isolated incident, or a string of problems that wears the person down. The stress may range from a car accident or illness to a divorce, or even a certain time of year such as Christmas.

Psychotherapy or counselling is the treatment of choice for adjustment disorders. It is usually a short-term treatment that focuses on resolving the immediate problem. The therapeutic interventions would need to focus on assisting the patient to develop coping skills, understand how the stressor has affected their lives and develop alternative social or recreational activities. Family or couples therapy may be helpful in some cases. Medication is not usually used to treat adjustment disorders, although on occasion a few days or weeks of treatment with a mildly sedating drug can help to control anxiety or sleeping problems. Self-help groups and social support could also help assist a quicker recovery.

22.3   ACUTE STRESS DISORDER

The essential features of acute stress disorder are related to the development of characteristic anxiety, dissociative and other symptoms that occur within a month after exposure to an extremely traumatic stressor. This condition is different to an adjustment disorder in that in the former condition the stress is common whilst for acute stress disorder (and also for PTSD) the stressor would usually be an uncommon one to experience. Following the experience of the extreme stressor, where there is a reduction of stress symptoms within a 3-month period, this suggests that the reaction to the acute stress was a normative response following the trauma. However, for a diagnosis of PTSD the high level of acute stress will continue and not remit within a few months.

For a diagnosis of acute stress disorder to be made, the individual will need to present with at least three dissociative symptoms which would include the symptom of re-experiencing the threatening stimulus, avoidance and the symptoms associated with increased arousal. Some level of disturbance and impairment in general functioning and/or in the general satisfaction associated with life experiences would also need to be evident. The major difference between acute stress disorder and PTSD is the emphasis that is placed on the acute dissociation which is experienced with acute stress disorder. Such dissociation is associated with the subjective sense of numbing or detachment, reduced awareness of the person's surroundings and the symptom of derealisation (feeling the world is unreal). Additionally, it could be found that the sufferer experiences the feature of depersonalisation (feeling one is unreal) with or without accompanying dissociative amnesia. Research studies have found that people who develop acute stress disorder are at high risk for the later development of PTSD. However, this need not invariably be the case and many other individuals who develop PTSD would not have initially met the criteria for an acute stress disorder.

It is often found that the experiences involving an acute stress disorder could be related to feelings of despair and hopelessness. In such cases these experiences could develop to the extent that an additional diagnosis of depressive disorder could also be made. Where the acute stress symptoms persist beyond a month, the criteria for a diagnosis of PTSD could also be met. The severity, duration and proximity of the individual's exposure to the trauma or traumatic event are the most important factor in determining the likelihood of the development of acute stress disorder. Certain variables such as the level of social support available, the family history involved, childhood experiences of the individual and any pre-existing mental disorder suffered may influence the development and progression of this disorder.

22.4   POST TRAUMATIC STRESS DISORDER

The essential features of a PTSD involve the development of characteristic symptoms following exposure to an extreme traumatic stressor. This could involve direct personal experience of the event that involves actual threat of death or serious injury. This diagnosis would also be valid where the individual's integrity has been threatened or the event has involved death, injury or the learning about unexpected or violent death involving an intimate of the individual's. The person's response to the event must involve intense fear, helplessness or horror. PTSD occurs when the stress or trauma is uncommon, for example due to catastrophic situations, extreme abuse including serious cases of domestic violence or very serious road traffic accidents. Symptoms would normally occur immediately after or soon after the trauma and are usually dramatic, including the recurrent sense that one is re-experiencing or reliving the actual traumatic event along with a general lack of responsiveness to the present environment and a variety of other psychological disturbances.

Anyone who has experienced or witnessed any life-threatening or highly traumatic event may be vulnerable to PTSD. Witnesses to or victims of violent crime, such as rape, domestic violence, kidnapping, armed robbery or assault, could be susceptible to PTSD. Symptoms vary but often involve reliving the ordeal in the form of flashbacks, distressing memories, nightmares or frightening thoughts, especially when exposed to something reminiscent of the trauma. Emotional numbness, feeling detached from other people, sleep disturbances, depression, anxiety, guilt, irritability or angry outbursts are not unusual among PTSD sufferers. Symptoms typically begin within a few hours or days of the traumatic event, and PTSD is diagnosed when symptoms last more than 1 month.

The symptoms involved with re-experiencing the event could be associated with having upsetting thoughts or images about the traumatic event that come into the person's mind when he does not want them there, having bad dreams or nightmares about the traumatic event and/or reliving the traumatic event, and acting or feeling as if it was happening all over again. Additionally, it is found that the individual suffering from this condition feels emotionally upset when reminded of the traumatic event (for example, feeling scared, angry, sad, guilty, etc) and also may experience physical symptoms when he is reminded of the traumatic event in some way (for example, by breaking out in a sweat, feeling the heart beating fast).

Avoidant symptoms would involve the person trying not to think about, talk about, or have feelings about the traumatic event, trying to avoid activities, people or places that remind the person of the traumatic event and not being able to remember later some important aspect of the traumatic event. Furthermore, the person could come to have much less interest or participate much less frequently in activities that had previously been important and pleasurable to him, feels distant or cut off from people around him and also feels emotionally numb (for example, being unable to cry or unable to have loving feelings).

Arousal symptoms are also associated with having trouble falling or staying asleep, feeling irritable or having fits of anger and/or having trouble concentrating (for example, drifting in and out of conversations, losing track of the plot of a story or situation on television, forgetting what has been read). Arousal symptoms involving being overly alert (for example, checking to see who is around one, being uncomfortable with one's back to a door, etc) and being jumpy or easily startled (for example, when someone walks up behind one) are also common.

Acute PTSD begins within 6 months of the stressor while chronic PTSD is long-lasting and could last for 6 months or more. Delayed PTSD could begin after 6 months following the stressor.

When assessing PTSD, particularly in a forensic setting, such evaluations need to be conducted with particular care and sensitivity owing to the potential for dissimulation or exaggeration of symptoms because of the opportunity that a diagnosis of PTSD could give for secondary gain, either in terms of avoiding criminal prosecution or being rewarded with a possibly greater award of compensation. The basis of any assessment would be information derived from a variety of sources which include independent informants, other reports which have been written, General Practitioner notes, psychometric measurements and a clinical interview. In making a diagnosis within a forensic setting, it is essential to explore psychiatric disorders and symptoms to make sure the diagnostic criteria associated with re-experiencing symptoms, avoidant symptoms, hyper-arousal and functional impairment are all carefully assessed and explored. Assessing victims of sexual assault or abuse also demands of an examiner that he has an understanding of the psychodynamic factors involved in these difficulties which need to be taken into account when making an appropriate assessment. It should be noted that acute stress reactions and symptoms of PTSD are common in the short-term following rape or abuse, but tend to resolve spontaneously in the majority of victims.

With regard to treatment of PTSD, medication is useful for symptom relief that makes it possible to participate in psychotherapy. In particular medication can reduce the anxiety, depression and insomnia often experienced with PTSD. The mainstream treatment would involve cognitive-behavioural therapy, group therapy or exposure therapy. A new psychotherapeutic technique, eye movement desensitization and reprocessing (EMDR), has been shown to help people with PTSD and certain other anxiety disorders. During the EMDR therapy session, the patient recalls the traumatic event, including any thoughts, feelings and memories the event evokes. In most cases the therapist's fingers are held about 18 inches from the patient's face and moved back and forth quickly. The patient's eyes track the finger movements while concentrating on the traumatic memory. When the therapy works, the painful feelings associated with the trauma transform into more peaceful emotions.

CHAPTER 23

ANXIETY BASED DISORDERS

23.1 INTRODUCTION

Perhaps the commonest condition met with in clinical psychological and psychiatric practice is the group of disorders making up the anxiety states. Anxiety based disorders, previously classified among the neuroses, have at their base neurotic behaviour which is maladaptive. Anxiety states are to be distinguished from psychotic disorders in that the former do not involve gross distortions of reality or marked personality disorganisation; rather they involve typically anxious, ineffective, unhappy and often guilt-ridden individuals who are caught up in various conflicts and are prone to experiencing high levels of stress and anxiety. Anxiety is an extremely unpleasant emotional experience as it increases in intensity without obvious cause and is described as one of the most painful of the emotions. Anxiety is indistinguishable from fear in terms of the feelings experienced, but the difference lies in saying that what one is afraid of is easily identifiable but this is not so with anxiety. A person experiencing anxiety has the feelings of dread and apprehension but is unable to make sense of his or her experiences as the stimuli provoking such responses are not easily identifiable. Anxiety is best described as an irrational response to a harmless stimulus and normal situations which results in escape behaviour as if the individual were faced with truly dangerous and life threatening situations. These responses are based on the person's natural instinctual response of fight or flight, which is an instinctive built-in fear response pattern found in animals. In the case of anxiety, the built-in fear response or natural instinctive survival mechanism appears to have been learned or acquired as a response to a stimulus that is in itself non-threatening. This reflects the fact that the person has been conditioned to fear a harmless stimulus and, as such, this type of fear-like state comes to be called anxiety. Once the anxiety response is established, the individual will learn to avoid the stimulus that had provoked the processes of anxiety, albeit the behaviour is usually recognised by the individual as being irrational. The individual's own behaviour and thoughts may then evoke even greater responses of anxiety which that person then attempts to deal with through increased avoidance behaviour, thereby often ratcheting up the feelings of anxiety.

In order to understand anxiety disorders, it is not only the anxiety experienced by the person that must be studied but also that individual's efforts to defend against the anxiety. This makes up the essential experiences and responses in the features that are presented and is reflected in the clinical picture. The person's response to his anxieties may be seen in the form of avoidance, which is most evident in phobic disorders, or in the attempts made to control anxiety through activity, as is seen with obsessive compulsive disorder, or being overwhelmed by free-floating anxiety which presents as the clinical picture of a generalised anxiety disorder.

23.2   GENERALISED ANXIETY DISORDER

It is normal to feel worried or anxious before taking a big test, after losing one's job and during other stressful times in your life. But when intense feelings of anxiety, apprehension or dread emerge in the face of ordinary problems or routine situations and those feelings continue for 6 months or longer, a diagnosis of generalised anxiety disorder (GAD) would be made. GAD is characterised by chronic diffused anxiety and apprehensiveness which may be punctuated by episodes of more acutely debilitating anxiety referred to as acute anxiety or panic attacks. In GAD, excessive worry is accompanied by restlessness or feeling keyed up or edgy, becoming fatigued easily, having difficulty concentrating, irritability, muscle tension and/or sleep disturbance. Additional symptoms include trembling, lightheadedness, breathlessness, headaches, having a constant lump in their throat. The severity of GAD symptoms ranges from mild to severe. People with mild GAD can function fairly normally and do not tend to avoid situations as people with panic disorder often do. People with moderate to severe GAD feel intensely keyed up for all or most of the time. They startle easily and are unable to relax and enjoy themselves. It is not unusual for people with severe GAD to become clinically depressed.

The treatment of choice would be a combination of anti-anxiety medication and cognitive behavioural therapy. Relaxation techniques and exercise are also recommended to reduce or relieve symptoms.

23.3   PANIC ATTACKS

Panic disorder is associated with persistent raised levels of anxiety punctuated by episodes of intense fear accompanied by physical symptoms that strike often and without warning, even during sleep. Panic attacks tend to be brief, usually lasting a few minutes, although in rare instances, they can persist for an hour or more. Panic disorder has been found to occur twice as often in women as in men. Panic attack includes four or more of the following symptoms: palpitations, sweating, trembling/shaking, shortness of breath, chest pain or discomfort, nausea or abdominal distress, feeling dizzy, lightheaded, feelings out of touch with reality, fear of losing control, fear of dying, numbness or tingling sensations and/or hot flushes. Recurring episodes can cause considerable disability and require therapeutic assistance. Without treatment, people with panic disorder may develop a generalisation of their anxiety and develop a fear of supermarkets, public transport or other places or situations in which they have experienced previous panic attacks.

Panic disorder is best helped by cognitive-behavioural psychotherapy, medication or a combination of both. Improvement is usually seen within 6 to 8 weeks. Cognitive-behavioural psychotherapy operates on the theory that panic attacks are learned responses to something the patient is afraid of. Thus a process of unlearning together with relaxation techniques, such as slow, controlled breathing, to refocus attention when panic begins to rise is undertaken. The therapist may also offer reassurance by pointing out, for example, that a slightly elevated heart rate cannot cause a heart attack.

23.4   OBSESSIVE COMPULSIVE DISORDER

Obsessive compulsive disorder (OCD) is an anxiety disorder where the person would experience obsessions which are persistent, unpleasant and unwelcome mental images, ideas or fears, often with a violent theme. An obsession is an impulsive thought, experienced as irresistible, where individuals feel compelled to think about something that they do not want to think about. They would also experience disturbing thoughts or impulses that may conflict with moral or religious beliefs. They experience these thoughts as being persistent, irrational and as interfering with everyday behaviour and functioning. Often, the person may come to believe the only way to get relief from these obsessions is to carry out rituals, which are uncontrollable urges to count, touch or reorganise everything in sight. Such a compulsion is the impulsive urge to carry out some action against the individual's will. Alternatively, rituals may be undertaken such as washing hands until they are raw to relieve an excessive fear of germs, or repeatedly checking, for example, if the door is locked or the stove is turned off because the individual is convinced that disaster will strike unless he does so. Anyone can develop OCD at any age; about one-third of adults with OCD experiencing their first symptoms as children. Children with OCD seldom realise that their obsessive thoughts and ritualistic behaviours are unusual. Adults with OCD generally recognise that their obsessions or compulsions are unreasonable or extreme.

Obsessive compulsive disorder is highly debilitating and maladaptive as it involves irrational and exaggerated behaviour in the face of stressors and severely reduces the flexibility of behaviour and the capacity the individual possesses for self-direction and autonomous action. These patients come to feel controlled by their thoughts and/or actions.

Prognosis is good if the sufferer commits to work within the therapeutic situation. Cognitive behavioural therapy and other behavioural therapies are the most effective treatment for OCD. A form of behavioural therapy known as 'exposure and response prevention' exposes the person to the situation that triggers the compulsion and then helps that person to avoid engaging in his usual ritual.

23.5   A PHOBIA

A phobia is a persistent fear of some object or situation that, looked at rationally, should not be presenting any actual dangers to the person or where any actual dangers inherent in the object or situation are experienced out of all proportion to their actual or potential seriousness. With phobic disorder the fears reach a level of intensity such that it may come to interfere significantly with an individual's everyday activities. However, by means of withdrawal and avoidance it is possible for the person suffering from these conditions to be able to function in certain areas which have no connection with the phobic object or situation.

The focus of a person's fear dictates the extent to which the disorder affects normal functioning. Most individuals with specific phobias experience mild-to-moderate symptoms when they encounter the feared object. When symptoms are severe enough to disrupt normal life, an evaluation by a medical professional is indicated.

One such phobia is a social phobia which is an overwhelming and disabling fear of disapproval in social settings. The patient experiences a persistent, irrational fear of certain social situations, and becomes overwhelmed by their anxiety to the extent that they will do almost anything to avoid the object of their fear.

When avoidance is impossible and individuals with social phobia are forced into a social situation they may experience blushing, sweating, trembling, rapid heartbeat, muscle tension, nausea or other stomach discomfort, lightheadedness and other symptoms of anxiety.

Most patients with specific phobias tend to recover without medication, although anti-anxiety drugs have been found to help. By taking the edge off the physical symptoms of fear, medication may help a patient confront a phobic situation and ultimately conquer his fear. Anxiety management and behavioural therapies are effective in reducing or eliminating the phobia.

23.6   ASSESSMENT AND MANAGEMENT OF ANXIETY STATES

When psychologically assessing anxiety states an in-depth clinical interview and psychometric assessment is carried out, exploring current experiences, the nature of the symptoms and the duration of these symptoms. A number of self-report psychometric questionnaires are used including the Beck Anxiety Inventory (BAI), General Health Questionnaire (GHQ) and Hospital Anxiety and Depression Index (HADI), which assist in the screening of symptoms and in assessing severity of current symptoms concerning anxiety. Areas assessed would relate to physiological symptoms as well as the cognitive experience of anxiety. Management and treatment of anxiety states involve approaches on various levels. The best results for long-term effectiveness are usually to be achieved through psychotherapy followed by medication and self-help. Where medication is used without psychotherapeutic support, the patient may be helped with medication when rapid relief from symptoms is required but this relief would need to be followed up through behaviour modification to provide a more sustained response and for long-term effectiveness. Psychological treatment would need to focus on improving problem-solving abilities and encouraging self help with support and information. Cognitive behavioural therapy is nowadays the treatment of choice for effective and long lasting responses. It is essential that this form of psychotherapy is delivered by appropriately trained professionals, and the optimum duration of therapy is usually 16–20 sessions, initially on a weekly basis, thereafter on a twice monthly basis. Relaxation therapy and bio-feedback could be used as part of the cognitive behaviour therapy but is not usually a replacement for it.

Cognitive behaviour therapy focuses on changing the way the patient thinks about his anxiety and helps him to attempt to learn to gain control of experiences by reducing anxiety symptoms. Therapeutic strategies which are particularly helpful include distraction techniques which, by reducing anxiety symptoms, help to shift the focus of the mind away from distressing thoughts, focusing its attention instead onto something else in the immediate surroundings. As this engages demanding mental activity it will assist in shifting and replacing anxious thoughts as a coping mechanism and by neutralising or reducing anxiety symptoms. The use of neutralising as a strategy reduces the impact on anxiety provoking thoughts which are used in rehearsed cognitions. Additionally, giving reassuring responses and helping to reframe distorted or negative thought processes are effective cognitive strategies. For example, by getting the individual to learn to say 'My heart is going fast because I am anxious, not because I'm having a heart attack' is a productive treatment approach. Managing or confronting thought processes involves changing hitherto maladaptive thoughts and beliefs. These maladaptive beliefs might have become internalised and are then held by the individual to be fact despite evidence to the contrary. The cognitive distortion and irrational thought process come to result in the person viewing things in illogical ways such as by over generalising from a single incident. By confronting the distorted thought patterns and challenging the existing beliefs, one helps to shift the illogical way of thinking that the individual has. Should the individual engage with conviction in cognitive behavioural therapy and related psychological treatment, the prognosis for uncomplicated anxiety states is usually good.

CHAPTER 24

AFFECTIVE DISORDERS

24.1 INTRODUCTION

Affective disorders are so named because they involve changes in *affect* which refers to emotion or mood. The changes in affect or mood could involve extremes of affect which could lead to moods of elation or severe depression coming to dominate the clinical picture. Lowered mood and depression of mild intensity are part of the fabric of our lives and a feature of our normal human experiences. Sadness, discouragement, pessimism and a sense of hopelessness about being able to improve matters, are familiar themes to most people. Most people are prone to repeated cycles of mood changes throughout their lives which is very often related to experiences that affect most people at various times. Most people suffering from normal, that is non-pathological, depression, would not need to seek specialist help from mental health professionals, as normal depression is almost always the result of more or less obvious stressors in a person's life. One such situation is the grief and the grieving process following loss, not only through the death of a loved one and ensuing bereavement but also due to separation or divorce, financial loss, the break up of a relationship, retirement or being absent from home for the first time. The situation of grief and the grieving process involves lowered mood and the loss of interest. However, there is usually a gradual regaining of previous interest and recovery. The level of sadness is expected to abate and the person would normally be able to emotionally move on into a more productive engagement with his daily life. Some people, however, do become stuck in this process and will then require further assistance. Individuals may also develop more serious psychological responses due to the grieving process as becomes evident with pathological and complicated bereavement.

In **mild or moderate affective disorders**, the severity of the condition is usually seen to depend on the number of dysfunctions experienced and the degree of impairment experienced in each of these areas. Furthermore, the type of symptoms experienced and the duration of these would determine the diagnosis and description of a depressive illness. As a general description, depressive disorders are characterised by profound and persistent feelings of sadness, despair and/or loss of interest in things that were once pleasurable. Disturbance in sleep, appetite and in cognitive functions are a common accompaniment and are features associated with these experiences.

From the psychological point of view, there are two main categories of depressive disorders, major depressive disorder and dysthymic disorder. **Major depressive disorders** are characterised by a moderate to severe episode of depressive illness lasting 2 or more weeks. Individuals experiencing this disorder may have, among other symptoms, trouble sleeping, have a loss of interest in activity that they previously undertook without difficulty and which might have given them pleasure, experience changes in their weight, have difficulty concentrating, feel worthless and may have a preoccupation with death or suicide.

While major depressive episodes may be acute, **dysthymic disorders** are characterised by ongoing depression that lasts 2 or more years. A mild to moderate depression of dysthymic disorder may rise and fall in intensity, alternating with some periods of normal non-depressed mood, for up to 2 months in duration. This can also occur in bipolar disorder which is an affective mental illness that is characterised by radical emotional changes and mood swings from manic highs to depressive lows. The majority of those suffering from bipolar illness experience an alternation between episodes of manic and depressive illness. An understanding of the constellation of symptoms displayed is needed in diagnosing depression disorders.

24.2   CAUSES OF DEPRESSION

In exploring the causes of depression, one must appreciate that there are usually no clearly identifiable causative factors for any particular type of depression. While it is known, in the current state of knowledge, that there may be some levels of imbalance of certain neurotransmitters, which are the chemicals in the brain that transmit messages between nerve cells, external factors or environmental influences such as one's upbringing may also play a significant role. For example, individuals who have been abused and/or neglected throughout their childhood and adolescence have been shown to have patterns of low self esteem, negative thinking and varying degrees of depression. Furthermore, external stressors and significant life changes such as physical disorders, death of a loved one, divorce, loss of employment and similar life events can result in adjustment disorders where a depressed mood could be a key symptom. It is clear that the brain is the focus of all mood changes, whether these be pathological or not, and that the effects of environmental changes also come to be mediated by the brain.

24.3 ASSESSMENT OF DEPRESSION

In assessing clients suffering from depression, a clear understanding of the types of depression, clinical presentations and the diagnostic criteria is essential. An in-depth clinical interview needs to be undertaken, which could be assisted by using self-reporting or self-rating questionnaires such as the Beck Depression Inventory–Second Edition (BDI-II) or similar self-rating scales for depression. For a diagnosis of major depressive episodes to be made, the person would need to experience some or most of the following symptoms which include irritability, significant change in weight, insomnia or hypersomnia, psychomotor agitation or retardation, fatigue or loss of energy, feelings of worthlessness or inappropriate guilt, diminished ability to work or to concentrate or indecisiveness and recurrent thoughts of death, and suicidal thoughts and/or suicide attempts. It is not uncommon for dysthymic disorder to occur in the presence of other psychiatric and physical disorders. To meet the diagnostic criteria these symptoms would need to have been experienced on a daily basis for a period of 2 or more years, with features of under or overeating, insomnia, hypersomnia, low energy or fatigue, low self esteem, poor concentration or having trouble making decisions and possessing feelings of hopelessness. Thus, the distinctions between these different types of depression need to be well understood.

When approaching the understanding of depression from a *psychodynamic* or *psychological* framework, central to mood disorders is the concept of loss and guilt, together with a deep seated sense of insecurity and impaired self image. These dynamics can be traced to early life experiences, for example a child who grows up in an atmosphere of parent rejection, double standards, eco-centric mothers and inadequate parenting develops a self-image which is characterised by uncertainty, anxiousness and depression. When this person is confronted with requirements, demands, frustrations or challenges in later life, his self-confidence will fail him due to the intrinsic experience of insecurity. The dramatic experience will have a great effect on a child who has grown up in an emotionally impoverished situation. Furthermore helplessness and dependency is central to a depressive person which leads to aggression. The mere fact that he or she becomes aggressive against those who the person is dependent upon makes them feel more guilty, increasing feelings of frustration, negativity and directing negative feelings inward. From the psychodynamic perspective, aggression turned inward or suppressed presents clinically as depression.

The impact that depression has on a person depends upon the person's perceptions based on their life experiences. From this perspective, having experienced loss in the past, the depressed individual will perceive his world as if further losses were probable and thus selectively focus on negative features in his environment. Hence, as a result, a pattern of engaging in depressive thoughts and cognitions and reinforcing unrewarding behaviour patterns lead to an entrenched depressed mood and negativity. Negative thoughts about the self and their world are reflected in negative cognitions. Depressed persons would describe themselves in negative terms, value themselves as worthless and be critical of their achievements and situation in life. With negative self-evaluation and low self-esteem goes guilt about lack of achievement or letting others down. Guilt is associated with the belief that a person should be punished, hence directing negative feelings inwards in a form of self punishment, resulting in suicidal thoughts and feelings. It is possible that patients who have extreme negative thoughts about their self and their world could also develop delusional thoughts and beliefs.

Due to losses, guilt and negativity the individual is left with lowered mood associated with feelings of sadness, loneliness, loss of pleasure, despair and desperation. Their behaviour could be characterised by reduced or ineffective activity levels and failure to engage in activities. As a consequence of this passivity, lack of motivation and negativity, relationships deteriorate leaving the depressed person in a vicious cycle of becoming increasing lonely, isolated and unable to make contact with others. Self-destructive behaviour, suicidal thoughts and feelings and suicide gestures, which may serve as a cry for help or avoidance of emotional pain, are commonly found in depressed individuals.

In making an assessment, the level of disturbed mood and the extent of the sadness, pessimism, emotionally lability and the sense of worthlessness experienced by the individual needs to be determined. Further, the nature of the negative cognitions particularly relating to pessimism, self-dislike, self-criticism, punishment feelings and indecisiveness is assessed. This would give an indication as to whether the depression is within the clinical range, and its severity could have implications for treatment and management of the condition.

In addition to assessing the symptoms and clinical presentation, the **risk and precipitating factors** would also need to be assessed. Family history of depression, childhood adversity, parent/child relationships, loss of a parent in childhood are all features which could increase or precipitate depression. Major life stressors particularly relating to separation, divorce, bereavement and injury could be seen as precipitating factors. Low levels of sunlight are also a feature which has an impact on mood and, as a consequence, depressive experiences. Absence of a confiding relationship, an unsupportive marriage, an inadequate personal network and high levels of environmental stress are also features that would need to be considered when making an assessment of depression.

24.4   SELF-HARM OR SUICIDAL RISK

Self-harm and suicidal behaviour are specific features associated with the affective disorders although they may occasionally be found also with other mental disorders. Self-harm is also known as self-injury or self-mutilation and along with suicidal gestures or para suicidal behaviour is considered a cry for help or attention seeking and/or manipulative behaviour. These behaviours are used by individuals as strategies to deal with overwhelming feelings or emotions they have come to experience, with many incidents of self-harm and suicidal gestures functioning as survival strategies and even, perversely, as forms of life saving acts to cope with difficult life experiences. Self-harming behaviour could become addictive in nature leading to the frequency and severity of the behaviour increasing with the passing of time, whereas with true suicidal attempts, if dealt with appropriately with a satisfactory response to the causes leading to the attempt which may well also involve dealing with the presence of clinical depressive illness, these behaviours may subside with time and need not recur.

The assessment of risk with patients who are presenting with depression or following attempted suicide or threatening self-harm involve evaluating the degree to which the risk of protective factors are present and the impact that they have had on the person. This process involves clinical interview, psychometric assessment, clinical judgment and an understanding of the risk factors. **Risk factors** may involve several elements. If there has been a communication of intent prior to an act, this is of serious import. If an individual has suicide intentions or suicide thoughts and there is evidence of planning for the suicidal act, the risk factors are then particularly high. Furthermore, if the individual making the threats has the availability, knowledge or a clearly set out plan for self-harm, this poses a higher risk in comparison with no planning or no availability of lethal methods available to the individual. Precipitating factors which pose a risk for completed suicide would be loss of family member, status or situation, severe personal injury, threat of prosecution or conflict with a partner.

Suicidal self-harm is greater when there is a history of self-harm and previous suicide attempts or suicide gestures. Individuals not in stable relationships have a higher risk of suicide than highly educated married persons. Early life experiences would also suggest possible risk, for example, where there are early life losses, abuse, family history of suicide and a family history of depression. Additionally, drug and alcohol abuse or being exposed to domestic violence suggests a higher risk of suicide. It has been found that a significant number of males who attempt suicide in prisons have a history of sexual and physical abuse in their formative years.

When assessing suicide, positive early family experiences, positive attachment experiences and stable home environments are viewed as *protective factors*. Where an individual is assessed to have effective coping mechanisms in the face of emotional pain and complex and challenging life experiences, this may reflect lower risk of suicide or self harm. All the while the person is equipped with functional coping mechanisms and the ability to resolve interpersonal conflicts and is able to go through appropriate grief and mourning process following losses, the risk may be reduced as these are seen as protective factors.

The most effective **psychological treatment for suicide behaviour** has been found to be intense dialectical behaviour therapy (DBT), problem-solving therapy and cognitive behavioural therapy (CBT). DBT involves not only individual psychotherapy, but group-based problem-solving skill training systemic intervention, mediation and training. Problem-solving approaches in therapy are particularly effective to reduce suicide risk and the therapeutic approach is to assist the client and family members to implement step-by-step solutions to cope with challenging or difficult situations. Role play and rehearsal of play may be effective.

24.5 VARIANTS OF DEPRESSIVE DISORDERS

24.5.1 Manic illness

Manic illness is usually taken to involve a pathological elevation of mood but it is not strictly correct to consider the manic state to be a true polar opposite of the depressed state. The pathology probably also involves the centres in the brain regulating mood and, as with depressive illness, environmental and personal factors, including genetic predisposition, play a significant part, the brain undeniably playing its usual mediating role. The central feature of mania (or the milder version, hypomania) is an elevation of mood which may take the form of elation but equally commonly presents with hostility, irritability and aggression. There is considerable over activity on the part of the patient who may be seen to be garrulous, grandiose and, as is said, manically full of energy. It is a psychotic condition and therefore may also display hallucinations, delusions and speech disorder. There is usually a loss of insight and of a sense of reality. Treatment is essentially through the administration of anti-psychotic drugs although upon recovery there may be scope for some supportive psychotherapy. Prophylaxis is important especially where the condition of bipolar disorder exists and modern drugs such as lithium and sodium valproate play a significant role in preventing bouts of depressive and manic illness or, where the illness does break through despite the prophylaxis, in diminishing the intensity of the ensuing illness.

24.5.2 Major depression

Mood disorders are mental disorders characterised by periods of depression, sometimes alternating with periods of elevated mood. Major depression refers to a single severe period of depression, marked by negative or hopeless thoughts and physical symptoms such as fatigue. In major depressive disorder, some patients have isolated episodes of depression. In between these episodes, the patient does not feel depressed nor has other symptoms associated with depression. Other patients have more frequent episodes. Bipolar depression or bipolar disorder (sometimes called manic depression) refers to a condition in which patients experience the two extremes in mood. They alternate between depression (the 'low' mood) and mania or hypomania (the 'high' mood). These patients can go from depression to a frenzied, abnormal elevation in mood. Mania and hypomania are similar, but mania is usually more severe and debilitating to the patient.

24.5.3   Dysthymia

Dysthymia is a recurrent or lengthy depression that may last a lifetime. It is similar to major depressive disorder but dysthymia is chronic, long-lasting, persistent, and mild. Patients may have symptoms that are not as severe as in major depression but the symptoms last for many years, giving the impression that a mild form of the depression is always present.

Mood disorders could run in families and also be associated with imbalances in certain neurotransmitters including serotonin. Major life stressors could provoke the symptoms of depression in susceptible individuals. The symptoms of major depression may include: loss of appetite, a change in sleep patterns, feelings of worthlessness, hopelessness, inappropriate guilt and or fatigue. In addition, symptoms such as intense feelings of sadness or grief, disturbed thinking, difficulty in concentrating or making decisions would make up the diagnostic criteria.

24.5.4   Seasonal affective disorder (SAD)

Seasonal affective disorder (SAD) is a form of depression most often associated with the lack of daylight in extreme northern and southern latitudes from the late autumn to the early spring. It is considered that the hormone melatonin plays a role in this disorder, as melatonin is associated with the 'internal body clock'. The body produces more melatonin at night than during the day, which means there is more melatonin in the body during winter, when the days are shorter. Some researchers believe that excessive melatonin release during winter in people with SAD may account for their feelings of drowsiness or depression. The symptoms of SAD are similar to those of other forms of depression. These include feeling sad, irritable, or tired and needing increased sleep.

The treatment of choice for seasonal affective disorder is light therapy, exposing the patient to bright artificial light to compensate for the gloominess of winter. Light therapy uses a device called a light box, which contains a set of fluorescent or incandescent lights in front of a reflector. The patient needs to sit for about 30 minutes in front of the light box.

Recently, researchers have begun testing whether people who do not completely respond to light therapy could benefit from tiny doses of the hormone melatonin to reset the body's internal clock. Early results look promising, but the potential benefits must be confirmed in larger studies before this type of treatment becomes widely accepted. Additionally, medication is also prescribed and cognitive behavioural therapy explores how the patient's view of the world may be affecting mood and outlook.

24.5.5   Bipolar disorder

Bipolar disorder, also known as manic depression, is a mental illness that features extreme changes in mood. An individual's mood alternates between manic highs and depression. These mood changes can last for days, weeks, months or even years.

This condition usually starts in late adolescence, although bipolar disorder can also affect children. It is a disorder which necessitates treatment, without which a patient's life could be severely affected, damaging relationships with family and friends and hurting their professional careers. In its classic form it involves recurrent episodes of severe mania and depression. Bipolar disorder is considered to be a spectrum disorder which means that the person is always at a particular level of the condition. Different levels include: severe depression, moderate depression, mild low mood, normal or balanced mood, hypomania and severe mania. Most patients with the condition do respond well to treatment that includes a combination of medication and psychotherapy. Bipolar disorder could be a chronic recurrent illness for most patients and those untreated or poorly treated have a suicide rate of 15 to 25%.

24.6   TREATMENT OF AFFECTIVE DISORDERS

Treatment of affective disorders involving depression primarily takes the form of using antidepressant drugs in conjunction with psychological treatment. Psychotherapeutic approaches involve a focus on personal or interpersonal issues underlying the depression. Antidepressant medication provides fairly rapid relief for the symptoms of the disorder and this clinical improvement may help to put the patient into a position in which he is more receptive to psychological approaches. However, research and clinical practice strongly suggest that both of these approaches used correctly and concurrently form powerful and effective tools for the treatment of the depressed patient and are superior to any one treatment approach alone.

Psychotherapy with a patient would explore an individual's life experiences and situation to help the individual gain insight into the contributing causes of the current depressive illness. The therapist helps the patient to gain a greater level of self-awareness of his or her thinking patterns and how they came into being. There are several different approaches or types of psychotherapy, but all have a common goal of attempting to help the patient develop problem-solving and coping skills.

Cognitive behavioural therapy (CBT) assumes that the patient's faulty and negatively distorted thinking is causing the current depression, and thus this approach focuses on changing thought patterns and perceptions as its primary aim. The therapist would also help the patient to identify negatively distorted thought patterns and the emotions and behaviours that accompany them. The goal of CBT is to assist the client to monitor mood changes to changes in activating events. Initially the clients would be assisted to reactivate themselves by using behavioural strategies such as time management, establishing routines and structures and making behavioural changes on a day-to-day basis. The client is assisted to understand the thought process, thought catching or identifying negative thoughts, which is essential before any negative or unhelpful thoughts can be changed in any way. An understanding of how thoughts impact on mood and emotions is essential. It is the understanding of thought/mood links which enables patients to recognise activating events on their mood and depression levels. Through CBT the client is equipped with skills to take control of thought processes, and thereby able to control and manage his mood to improve general mood and functioning.

Psycho-education is a useful part of a treatment package for depression as it could assist the client or patient to understand what depression is and make sense of his or her experiences. The client needs to understand that depression is a complex condition involving changes in mood, thinking behaviour, relationships and biological functioning including attitudes. The client also needs to gain an insight into his or her vulnerability to depression, to recognise the influence of stressful life events or small stressors which have contributed to current experiences. By having this awareness the client will be better able to manage external events and reduce the impact of depression. An understanding of how past experiences have impacted on the client's current day-to-day functioning and the development of the depression could assist in the coping process. The guidance and education enhances the understanding that overcoming depression involves learning how to control and change patterns of thinking and to keep the number of stressors in the client's life to manageable proportions.

Antidepressant medication to address symptoms relating to sleep, appetite, energy levels and the mood itself is important. Where medication has proved to be ineffective electroconvulsive therapy (ECT) is sometimes used which is known to positively influence the neurotransmitters in the brain, as does the medication.

A holistic approach related to good nutrition, exercise and a full engagement in life will further improve mental health. **Alternative therapies** may help in the treatment of mood disorders. These include acupuncture, homoeopathy, aromatherapy and light therapy. The herb St. John's Wort has been found to be effective in treating some types of depression and many patients view it as a safe alternative to conventional antidepressants with fewer side effects.

CHAPTER 25

PERSONALITY DISORDERS

25.1 INTRODUCTION

It is fair to say that in family and child proceedings problems due to personality disorders cause more concern and confusion than those due to formal mental illness. Personality disorders are not responses to actual distress, as in adjustment disorders or post traumatic disorders, or forms of defences against anxiety, as in the case of anxiety states. Personality disorders, rather, stem from immature and distorted personality development. This development leads to an individual engaging in persistently maladaptive ways of perceiving, thinking and relating to the world around him. Whilst it is the case that these maladaptive approaches to the world could cause significant impairment of functioning, there are times when they could also cause subjective distress to the individual. It does, however, need to be understood that individuals with personality disorders are usually acting out patterns of behaviour rather than experiencing intra-psychic disturbances. Individuals with personality disorders behave in ways that are contrary to prevailing social attitudes or the expectations of others and do not seem able to suppress or defend against such behaviour which, had it not been undertaken, could have resulted in these individuals experiencing internalised anxiety. Their acting out behaviour could be seen as a means by which overwhelming anxiety is kept at bay. Nevertheless, the price they pay for keeping anxiety at bay by means of their acting out behaviour is the disruption they often bring to their roles as spouse, partner or parent; hence the interest of the family courts in these individuals.

25.2 FEATURES OF PERSONALITY DISORDERS

The central features of personality disorders are the patterns of disruptive personal and interpersonal relationships in the course of which the individual demonstrates problems which are generally of long-standing and which are marked also by behaviour that is considered troublesome to others. The difficulties do not consist of discrete episodes of maladaptive or pathological behaviour, but are, rather, persistent patterns of recurring problems which reflect difficulties which may be said to be stable in their instability as far as these patients are concerned. Thus, the features of a personality disorder are consistent over time with no apparent learning from experience on the part of the patient from his previous difficulties. The reason for this is the fact that the patterns of behaviour are highly resistant to change which, of course, has implications for prognosis and therapeutic intervention, not to mention the problems that arise and are identified in the course of family and child proceedings. It would also explain the feature of dysfunctional and deteriorated relationships which is the hallmark of personality disorders. Individuals with personality disorders are rigid, not adaptable and tend to respond inappropriately to problems, to the point where relationships with family, friends and colleagues are adversely affected. The maladaptive responses usually begin in adolescence or early adult life and do not change over time, but could vary in severity. Although the features or symptoms do not cause distress, most individuals with personality disorders are, in fact, distressed about their lives and have significant problems within relationships and in social situations. Many individuals with personality disorders could also have depressed mood, anxiety, and be prone to such conditions as substance abuse and eating disorders. It is thus a feature of personality disorders that, as these individuals are usually unaware that their thoughts or behaviour patterns are inappropriate; they do not seek help on their own account. Instead, they are usually referred by friends or family members, or by way of the criminal justice system, because their behaviour is causing difficulty for others. In cases involving family and child proceedings professionals are early apprised of their impaired functioning as spouse, partner or parent – due to their behaviour per se as well as misconduct flowing from misuse of alcohol and illicit substances and related criminal behaviour – and psychological assessment may be commissioned in the course of the proceedings.

25.3 CLASSIFICATION AND DIAGNOSIS

The whole idea behind diagnostic classification of personality disorders was to describe basic traits of each particular type of personality presentation. The *Diagnostic Statistical Manual (DSM IV)* (American Psychiatric Association, 1994) has personality disorder as part of its classification, based on the concept of personality traits. The central feature of personality disorders is regarded as enduring patterns of perceiving, relating to and thinking about the environment. Traits only constitute a personality disorder when they are inflexible and maladaptive with significant functional impairment and/or subjective distress. All these areas are encompassed in the diagnostic criteria for each personality disorder and particular types of disorder as described above have their typical features. On the whole, children under the age of 18 are not diagnosed as having personality disorders, the reasons being that although personality disorders have their origins in the patterns of thoughts, behaviours and emotions from early childhood and adolescence, significant developmental changes do occur in adolescence. Thus what may present as disturbed maladaptive behaviour could very well change, and as a result of diagnosing a personality disorder the adolescent may well receive inappropriate treatment, or be inaccurately labelled, with enduring implications as to discrimination against them and/or undermining their self-esteem. Generally research suggests about 10% of the population have problems which would be of sufficient complexity and severity to be diagnosed as having a personality disorder.

Although personality disorders are diagnosed in adult life, one has to look at the development of the child particularly during its formative years in order to gain an understanding of the child's life experiences, parenting it has received and any abusive or neglecting experiences it has had. Central to the child's developing personality are attachment patterns which, if insecure and dysfunctional, could be viewed as risk factors for later problems. It should, however, be noted that the effect of attachment patterns on adult behaviour depends on a variety of developmental experiences associated with developmental arrest, such as experience of rejection, problematical mother/child relationship, security during the formative years and the problems faced during adolescence.

A child coming through developmental phases, having enjoyed a secure base and appropriate attachment experiences, would enter adult life with an intact self-concept and a very clear idea of its primary attachment figures and significant others. It would also have control over its emotions and impulses, have emotional containment and show no evidence of emotional dysregulation. Furthermore, it would have a sound grasp of social values and norms and able to contain its impulses to live by these, including effective management of its aggressive and libidinal impulses. In other words, the individual would present as being emotionally contained, be well able to create his own internalised stability and security, and have the ability to engage in meaningful personal relationships. On the other hand, where a person presents with distortions in interpersonal relationships, lack of impulse and emotional control, rage and lack of trust in relationships, this could reflect problematical development during its formative years leading to the distortions and the consequent maladaptive behaviour.

It would be simplistic to state that lack of appropriate attachment and some form of developmental arrest is at the root of personality problems; the situation is far more complex. An understanding of the impact of neglect, abuse, trauma and stress on the developing child, would be essential when making an assessment. There is no single cause for the development of personality disorders and thus an appreciation that biological, social and psychological factors are at play to influence personality development is necessary. Research has shown that a vulnerability to stress is a central feature related to the development and/or maintenance of personality disorders. Research by Perry (2002) found that infants raised in environments lacking in individual attention, cognitive stimulation, emotional affection and other enrichments, had consistently shown lower intelligence and a greater tendency to display autistic spectrum disorders. It is widely viewed by researchers and clinicians that childhood neglect does lead to significant emotional, psychological and physiological changes in a child. Perry (2002) had also found that associated with childhood neglect was a lack of sensory input in infancy, being associated with decreased brain size and decreased metabolic activity in orbital frontal gyri. The research by Perry (2002) which found that a global set of abnormalities matched by functional abnormalities in cognitive, emotional, behavioural, and social function-ing, highlights the effects of neglect having long-term consequences and the situation is probably irretrievable. This highlights that neglect not only causes significant emotional harm, but significant neurological harm with permanent enduring consequences. Johnson et al (1999) has demonstrated in his work and writings that neglect during childhood has also been associated with diagnosis of antisocial, avoidant, borderline, dependent narcissistic, paranoid and schizoid personality disorders. He also found that there were clear associations between a history of physical abuse with antisocial, borderline, passive aggressive and psychopathic personality disorders, whereas sexual abuse was associated with borderline, histrionic and depressive personality disorders. It should, however, be noted that trauma alone is not a necessary or sufficient cause of personality disorders, as other factors including temperament and multiple distressing life experiences could also impact on the development of personality disorders.

Childhood abuse and neglect has as a consequence high levels of stress and trauma. Post traumatic stress disorder occurs when any individual has been overwhelmed by terror and helplessness. Individuals abused in childhood have been placed in terrifying situations where they could have felt helpless. It is not unusual to find in clinical settings that where individuals present with personality disorders, they could also be observed to be suffering from post traumatic stress disorder.

Work by Paris (1996) found a high degree of psychological and social dysfunction in families of individuals who develop personality disorders, particularly in the presence of depression and alcohol related problems and the parents themselves having personality disorders. A high incidence of poverty, unemployment, family breakdown and the witnessing of domestic violence has been found to be associated in the background history of adults presenting with personality disorders. Research has also shown that the highest risk factor for the development of antisocial personality was antisocial behaviour in the father and parental alcoholism. Individuals who go on to develop antisocial personalities develop within family structures where there has been a chronic failure to discipline or supervise the children.

A dysfunctional cycle emerges wherein families where there are maladaptive family interactions such as abuse or neglect would invariably have problems with the quality of the parent child relationships. This correlates with research and clinical practice which reflect that adults with personality disorder have been emotionally neglected during childhood with frequent reports of problems of poor bonding with parents, lack of affection, lack of discipline and a lack of autonomy.

As personality disorders have their origins in disturbed and dysfunctional early life experiences, it has led some to conclude that resistance to change is a fundamental attribute to the personality and the possibility of changing adult personality is limited. This has serious implications for future prognosis. It has been found that problems associated particularly with borderline and antisocial personality disorders diminish steadily over time, even without treatment, which is linked to the fact that individuals tend to become less impulsive as they get older. For the rest, clinical experience and research has found that whilst there are therapeutic approaches which bring about some change in personality, the prognosis remains poor.

Personality disorders, studied from the psychological point of view, may be grouped into three clusters. Cluster A involves personality disorders which involve odd or eccentric behaviour. Cluster B is the group related to dramatic or erratic behaviour, while Cluster C is characterised by anxious or inhibited behaviour.

25.4   CLUSTER A

Cluster A includes paranoid, schizoid or schizoid type of personality disorders.

A paranoid personality is characterised by being paranoid, distrustful and suspicious of others. They suspect, a belief based on little or no evidence, that others are out to harm them and usually find hostile or malicious motives behind other people's actions. Thus, individuals with a paranoid personality may take actions that they feel are justified or retaliate accordingly, behaviours that others may find baffling. As these behaviours often lead to rejection by others, this then tends to vindicate their original feelings of having been targeted in an unjust way. Their approach to others is often characterised by being cold and distant in relationships.

A schizoid personality describes individuals who are introverted, withdrawn and solitary. They are also emotionally cold and distant and are most often absorbed in their own thoughts and feelings. It is also characteristic that these personalities are fearful of closeness and intimacy with others. They talk little, are given to daydreaming, fantasising and preferring theoretical speculation to engaging in practical action.

A schizoid type personality, like those of a paranoid and schizoid personality, involves an individual who is socially and emotionally detached. However, an individual with schizoid type personality may also display oddities of thinking, perceiving and communicating which are similar to those shown by patients suffering from schizophrenia. Some individuals with schizoid type personality show signs of magical thinking in the course of which they come to believe their thoughts and actions can control something or someone.

25.5   CLUSTER B

Cluster B includes histrionic, narcissistic, antisocial and borderline personality disorders. Individuals with these disorders tend to be dramatic, emotional and erratic, with impulsive behaviour, and engage in antisocial activities and aggressive behaviours which would be more likely to bring them into contact with the mental health services or the criminal justice system.

People with **histrionic personalities** conspicuously seek attention, are dramatic and excessively emotional, with an over concern with their appearance. Their largely expressive nature results in easily established, but often superficial and transient, relationships. The expression of emotions is characterised by exaggerated, childish and contrived responses aimed to evoke sympathy or attention from others. Individuals with histrionic personalities are prone to sexually provocative behaviour or to sexualising non-sexual relationships; however they often do not really seek sexual relationship. Rather, their seductive behaviour often masks their wish to be dependent and to be protected.

Individuals with a **narcissistic personality** have a sense of superiority and need for admiration, which is found in conjunction with a lack of empathy. They tend to behave with exaggeration, filled with their own value, importance and grandiosity, are extremely sensitive to failure, criticism or being confronted by a failure, and with a primary focus on fulfilling a high opinion they have of themselves. When this need of theirs is frustrated they may become easily enraged or severely depressed. Homicidal and suicidal behaviour involving individuals who have not previously shown any tendency to violence is sometimes reported in these cases. Because they believe themselves to be superior in their relationships with other people, they expect to be admired and often suspect that they are envied by them. They believe they are entitled to have their needs met without delay so that they come to exploit others whose needs or beliefs they deem to be less important. This behaviour is usually offensive to others who come to view them as self-centred, arrogant and selfish. This personality disorder typically occurs in people with high achievements, although those with little to show by way of conventional achievement are not excluded from their ranks.

Individuals with **antisocial personality disorder** often show a callous disregard for the rights and feelings of others. Dishonesty and deceit permeate their relationships, and it is often the case that they exploit others for material gain or personal gratification. Individuals with an antisocial personality act out their conflicts impulsively and irresponsibly, they have poor frustration tolerance and tend to be hostile or violent. These personalities have difficulty anticipating the negative consequences of their antisocial behaviours and, despite the problems or harm they cause others, do not usually feel or experience remorse or guilt. Furthermore, they are prone to alcohol and drug addiction, sexual deviation, promiscuity and imprisonment following serious criminal behaviour. They are likely to fail at their jobs and move from one area to another. It is not uncommon for the families of these personalities also to have a history of antisocial behaviour, substance abuse, divorce and physical abuse.

Individuals with a **borderline personality** are unstable in their self-image, mood, behaviour and interpersonal relationships. Their thought processes are more disturbed than those of individuals suffering with antisocial personality disorder and their aggression may often be turned against themselves. They are angrier, more impulsive and more confused about their identity than are people with histrionic personality disorder. This personality disorder has as its central feature immaturity and instability. Borderline personality disorder becomes evident in early adulthood but becomes less common in older age groups, there usually being amelioration with the approach of middle age. Individuals with borderline personality disorders often report being neglected or abused as children and in consequence they feel empty, angry and deserving of nurturing. They are far more dramatic and intense in interpersonal relationships than normal individuals and when they feel abandoned by a person whom they have come to believe cared for them they characteristically express inappropriate and intense anger. Individuals with borderline personality disorders make use of splitting as a defence mechanism and tend to see events and relationships as being black and white, good or evil, but almost never neutral. Individuals with borderline personality disorders often feel abandoned, alone and could experience the sense of not actually existing. They may become desperately impulsive, engaging in reckless promiscuity, substance abuse and self-mutilation. This is the personality type most commonly treated by therapists for the primary reason that they relentlessly seek someone to care for them.

25.6 CLUSTER C

Cluster C includes avoidant, dependent, compulsive and passive aggressive personality disorders. In this cluster of disorders, unlike the others, there is often anxiety and fearfulness experienced by the sufferer making it difficult in some cases to distinguish these from anxiety based disorders.

People with **avoidant personality** are extremely sensitive to rejection and they fear starting relationships or involving themselves with anything new. They have a strong desire for affection and acceptance but avoid intimate relationships and social situations for fear of disappointment and criticism. Unlike those with a schizoid personality, they are openly distressed by their isolation and inability to relate comfortably to others. Avoidant personality is similar in some respects to generalised social phobia.

Individuals with a **dependent personality** generally tend to surrender major decision making and the taking on of responsibilities to others and permit the needs of those they depend on to supersede their own. They lack self-confidence and feel intensely insecure about their ability to take care of themselves. They often protest that they cannot make decisions and do not know what to do or how to do it. These behaviours are due partly to a reluctance to express their own views for fear of offending the people they need and partly due to the belief that others may not be capable of helping them.

Individuals with **obsessive compulsive personality** are preoccupied with order, neatness and control. They are reliable, dependable, orderly and methodical, but their inflexibility makes them unable to adapt to change. Because they are cautious and weigh up all aspects of a problem, they often have difficulty making decisions. They take their responsibilities seriously, but because they cannot tolerate mistakes or imperfections, and have difficulty delegating, they often have trouble completing tasks. Unlike patients with the corresponding mental disorder, obsessive compulsive disorder, these personalities do not suffer from repeated unwanted obsessions or ritualistic behaviour. People with an obsessive compulsive personality are often high achievers especially in the sciences and other intellectually demanding fields that require order and attention to detail. However, their responsibilities make them so anxious that they can rarely enjoy their success. They are uncomfortable with their feelings, with relationships and with situations in which they lack control and must rely on others which tends to make events and situations unacceptably unpredictable for them.

25.7   OTHER PERSONALITY DISORDERS

In addition to these clusters, there are also other personality disorders, in particular passive aggressive or negativistic personality, cyclothymic personalities and the depressive personality. Individuals with a **passive aggressive personality** behave in ways that appear inept or passive. However, these behaviours are actually ways used by them to avoid responsibility or to control or punish others. Individuals with a passive aggressive personality often procrastinate, perform tasks inefficiently or claim to suffer from some implausible disability. Individuals with a **cyclothymic personality** alternate between high spirited buoyancy and pessimism, each mood lasting weeks or longer, the mood changes occurring regularly without any identifiable external cause. Many gifted and creative people belong to this personality type. The depressed personality is characterised by chronic moroseness, worry and self-consciousness, with a generally pessimistic outlook on life which impairs their initiative and disheartens others. To them any satisfaction gained seems undeserved and even sinful and they may unconsciously believe their suffering is a 'badge of merit' and that they need to earn the love and admiration of others.

25.8 ASSESSMENT OF PERSONALITY DISORDER

From a clinical point of view interview-based assessments are essential to diagnosing personality disorders. Self-report instruments do have validity in the broad assessment of personality traits, but it always needs to be kept in mind that self-report instruments and reporting during clinical interview tend to yield a level of distortion particularly in forensic settings. It has been found that interview and self-report methods perform equally well in assessment of personality disorder characteristics. Structured interviews for the purpose of personality disorders are recommended such as the International Personality Disorders Examination (IPDE) or the Structured Clinical Interview the DSM-IV (SCID II). Information obtained through interview should not necessarily be taken at face value. The response of clients to interview pressure may be limited due to poor insight and inter-personality functioning, particularly in forensic settings where there may be a desire to mislead the interviewer about the presence of characteristics which may be perceived as negative. Attempts should be made to confirm important claims made by the client being assessed, particularly related to criminal records, educational records, general practitioner notes and employment records. The British Psychological Society (BPS) recommends the use of instruments designed for structured assessment of personality traits and disorders but these should be carefully selected for their relevance to the treatment and management needs of individual clients. A combination of self-report instruments and semi-structured instruments is recommended as good practice in personality disorder assessment. Furthermore, only instruments that have a good history of application in clinical settings and have been established and well-documented psychometric property should be considered for use in assessments of personality disorders (BPS 2006).

25.9 FORENSIC ASSESSMENTS OF PERSONALITY DISORDERS

In his work related to forensic issues, Harte (2001) makes the point that personality disorders are unlikely to result in major impairments of thoughts and speech or involve obvious irrational perceptions and beliefs about the external world. Thus, a diagnosis of personality disorder is not thought to be sufficient to make a person incompetent to stand trial or not clinically responsible with respect to any criminal act. Furthermore, in the legal setting, symptoms of personality disorder should be assessed using methods that integrate information obtained from a number of different sources, for example the family, employment and education, in addition to information obtained directly from the client during clinical interview. Thus, assessment based only on interview and written self-reports should not be relied upon.

In order to make a diagnosis and assessment of personality disorders, a detailed history of a person's past and current functioning, in particular in areas such as repetition of maladaptive thoughts and behaviour patterns, is required to be taken. Furthermore, the person's immature and maladaptive mechanisms which interfere with daily functioning are usually explored. Interviews with family members are important to gauge the person's general functioning and ability to relate interpersonally. Background history as well as psychometric assessments and tests are useful in gaining an understanding of underlying functioning, needs and feelings and defensive structures. The occupational history and a record of convictions and details of the criminal behaviour (eg from pre-sentence reports) that led to these convictions may yield valuable information.

In assessing personality disorders, an in-depth exploration of the *coping mechanisms* and the nature of the individual's coping are particularly important. Certain personality disorders involve the predominant use of particular defence mechanisms. Some of these are now considered briefly.

Projection, which is attributing one's own feelings towards others, is common in most personality disorders, particularly borderline, antisocial and narcissistic personalities, especially when these individuals are under acute stress. Borderline personality disorders typically involve **splitting** in which the individual perceives his world in black and white or engages in inanimate thinking to divide people into groups of idealised beings seen as all good or vilified as all bad. This defence mechanism allows a person to avoid the discomfort of having both loving and hateful feelings for the same person, as well as experiencing feelings of uncertainty and helplessness.

Acting out as a coping mechanism is particularly associated with antisocial and borderline personality disorders. Acting out behaviour is a direct behavioural expression of an unconscious wish or impulse that enables a person to avoid thinking about painful situations or experiencing a painful emotion such as excessive anxiety. The effect of this mechanism could lead the person into acting in ways that are often irresponsible, reckless or foolish, and may include acts involving delinquent, promiscuous and substance abusing behaviours.

Personality disordered individuals also tend to *turn aggression towards themselves*, particularly by expressing anger feelings that they have towards others by hurting themselves through self-harm or through passive aggressive responses. People with avoidant or schizoid personality types make use of **fantasy**, which is imagining relationships in a private belief system to resolve conflict and to escape from painful realities such as loneliness. Making use of fantasy is associated with eccentricity, inhibitions in respect of interpersonal intimacy and the avoidance of involvement with the outside world.

Dependent, histrionic and borderline personality disordered individuals make use of **hypochondria**, using health complaints to gain attention. This provides the person with nurture and attention from others as well as being an outlet for the passive expression of anger towards others.

When looking to treat personality disorders, relief of anxiety, depression and other distressing symptoms, where present, would be the first goal of treatment, and medication could help in these areas. Medication does not, of course, affect the personality traits themselves, and any change or alteration of personality traits can only be achieved through long-term psychological treatment. There is no short-term treatment for personality disorders, and although some changes may be accomplished faster than others, the attempted achievement of behavioural and interpersonal changes makes it a *long-term reconstructive process*. It has to be said that the psychological treatment of personality disorders is a daunting process in even the most promising of cases and the prognosis most often remains guarded. It is not often appreciated that the forms of therapy most likely to produce satisfactory results in these cases – formal psychotherapy – make considerable demands on the patient who needs to have the resources of intelligence and the capacity to approach his difficulties with the requisite 'psychological mindedness' if he is to show positive change. There is also the consideration that the patient needs to be able to avoid excessively emotionally upsetting situations (something these patients often find themselves embroiled in) in the course of treatment if they are to derive benefit from therapy. For all these reasons and given the timescales normally envisaged especially in childcare proceedings, positive change in behaviour of a fundamental nature and of a degree to satisfy a court is not usually expected in cases with personality disorder where they are involved in family and child proceedings.

25.10   PSYCHOLOGICAL TREATMENT AND INTERVENTION

It is generally considered that there is no standard treatment for individual personality disorders in the UK nor has any one treatment been shown to be particularly superior above the others. However various approaches are more widely used, in particular cognitive behavioural therapy (CBT). This approach is concerned with dysfunctional, emotional and social reactions through education and behavioural skills. Training procedures such as cognitive restructuring, relaxation training, social skill training, self-control methods and problem-solving techniques are used. The aim is to provide personal strategies for coping with problematic situations because the focus is on problem behaviours as they occur in specific contexts. Cognitive therapy used specifically for personality disorders should take the form of structured individual treatments that are problem focused and are less intensive in terms of time than is employed in psychodynamic, psychotherapeutic or dialectic behaviour therapy. The first stage of the therapy would need to be arrived at through a formulation to understand the difficulties the individual is currently experiencing. The basis of these cognitive strategies is the modification of maladaptive core beliefs about the individual's self and others, behaviour strategies used in particular to reduce self-harm and other maladaptive behaviours as well as to help the person develop better ways of coping with his difficulties.

Dialectical behaviour therapy (DBT) is widely used in the treatment of borderline personality disorders. DBT integrates CBT with dialectical philosophical principals with treatment particularly targeting parasuicidal behaviours and emotional dysregulation. Skills training and problem-solving techniques applied with DBT are primarily used in group treatment to improve the person's interpersonal conflict resolution, distress tolerance and emotional regulation. The dialectical strategies of DBT focus on teaching patients a more balanced pattern of thinking and behaviour, looking to reduce suicidal behaviours or other self-defeating behaviours such as substance abuse and aggression.

DBT involves both individual therapy and group psycho-educational component. In the group component people are taught self-management skills, distress tolerant skills and how to deal with personal situations more effectively. In accompanying individual therapy sessions, the therapist first focuses on behaviour and supportive techniques to reduce maladaptive behaviour and to reduce self-harm before moving to apply other directive and supportive techniques to other problem areas, including behaviour which interferes with ongoing working therapy.

Cognitive analytical therapy is an integrative short-term therapy drawn on concepts from psychoanalysis, cognitive research and development psychology. It has at its centre object relation theory and in emphasising actual childhood experiences, rather than unconscious fantasies. The focus would also be on assisting the client to control interpersonal actions and self-management.

Psychodynamic psychotherapy associated with partial hospitalisation, has been found to be more effective than standard psychiatric care in the treatment of men and women with a diagnosis of borderline personality disorder. Partial hospitalisation includes both individual and group therapy lasting for at least 18 months. Therapeutic communities vary where clients are involved with the day-to-day running of communities and would be crucially involved in supporting each others' treatment, and in confronting each other's self-destructive, antisocial and inappropriate behaviour. Community discussions and debate aimed at understanding causes of destructive behaviour including destructive staff and staff to patient interactions commonly experienced in this client group is a consistent feature. Mood processes affecting the interpersonal and social functioning of the community are of key importance to regulate. The term therapeutic community therefore refers to the culture in which treatment is delivered and the principles underlying it rather than a specific package of treatment.

CHAPTER 26

PSYCHOSIS

26.1 INTRODUCTION

Psychosis is a form of mental illness typically characterised by radical changes in personality, impaired functioning, and a distorted sense of objective reality. Psychotic features may appear as a symptom of a number of mental disorders, including mood and personality disorders. These are, however, the defining features of schizophrenia, schizophreniform disorder, schizoaffective disorder, delusional disorder, and the psychotic disorders. Psychotic disorders would include brief psychotic disorder, shared psychotic disorder and a psychotic disorder due either to a general medical condition or which is substance-induced. Patients suffering from psychosis have impaired reality testing; that is, they are unable to distinguish personal subjective experience from the reality of the external world.

Psychosis is characterised by distinctive symptoms such as delusions which are distorted thoughts and belief systems which in schizophrenia are bizarre and not in any way similar to occurrences in real life. Delusions occurring in delusional disorder are more plausible, and could have a kernel of truth, but are still basically untrue. In some cases, delusions may be accompanied by feelings of paranoia. Hallucinations are distorted perceptions of patients who see, hear, smell, taste, or feel things that are not there, the most common of these being auditory or visual phenomena. Psychotic patients present with disordered speech and may tend to ramble on and be incoherent with nonsensical speech patterns. Behaviour could also be disturbed with catatonic features in which the patient remains rigid and immobile or presents with disorganised behaviour by engaging in excessive motor activity which is inappropriate for the situation, or unpredictable.

The psychosis in **schizophrenia** appears to be related to abnormalities in the structure and the chemistry of the brain, and there are also strong genetic links. It is also known that high levels of stress could trigger the underlying predisposition towards this disorder. Trauma and stress have been seen to precipitate a brief psychotic disorder which is deemed to be a psychosis of less than a month's duration. Major life-changing events could stimulate brief psychotic disorder in patients with no prior history of mental illness. **Delusional disorders**, on the other hand, are not necessarily associated with traumas but tend to develop in individuals who are isolated from others in their society by language difficulties and cultural differences.

Substance-induced psychotic disorder presents with psychosis which could be a side effect of the use, abuse, and withdrawal from certain drugs, be they recreational drugs or certain prescription medications. Toxic substances such as carbon monoxide could also cause substance-induced psychotic disorder. Shared psychotic disorder, also known as *folie a deux* or psychosis by association, is a delusional disorder involving two people with close emotional ties.

Psychotic symptoms and behaviours are usually considered to be psychiatric emergencies, and patients showing signs of psychosis are frequently admitted to hospital. A person diagnosed as psychotic can be compulsorily detained against his or her will when he or she is violent, threatening to commit suicide, or threatening to harm another person.

Treatment of psychosis is firstly carried out by a psychiatrist with the appropriate course of medication. Once the patient is stabilised a psychologist may become involved and offer psychosocial therapy to address any underlying difficulties. Treatment of shared psychotic disorder involves separating the affected persons from one another as well as using antipsychotic medication and psychotherapy.

While the prognosis for psychosis associated with brief psychotic disorder is quite good, it used to be less so for schizophrenia. It is found that the longer and more severe a psychotic episode, the poorer is the prognosis.

26.2 SCHIZOPHRENIA

Schizophrenia is a psychotic disorder marked by severely impaired and disturbed thinking, emotions and behaviours. The course of schizophrenia in adults can be divided into three phases or stages. In the first, acute, phase there is an overt loss of contact with reality (psychotic episode) and this requires intervention and treatment. The second, stabilisation, phase is where the psychotic symptoms are brought under control, but the patient is at risk of relapse if treatment is interrupted. The third stage is the maintenance phase where relative stability is achieved over the long term with antipsychotic medications.

For psychological purposes there may be said to be five subtypes of schizophrenia.

The central feature of **paranoid schizophrenia** is the combination of delusions and auditory hallucinations, but the patient may maintain cognitive functions and normal emotions. The delusions of paranoid schizophrenics usually involve thoughts of being persecuted or harmed by others or involve grandiosity where the patient has exaggerated opinions of his own importance. Delusions of jealousy or excessive religiosity are also found. Paranoid schizophrenics function at a higher level than other subtypes, but are at risk of suicidal or violent behaviour under the influence of their delusions.

The central feature of **disorganised schizophrenia** is marked by disorganised speech, thinking, and behaviour on the patient's part, coupled with flat or inappropriate affect. The patient may act in silly ways or withdraw socially to an extreme extent.

Catatonic schizophrenia is characterised by disturbances of movement that may include rigidity, stupor, agitation, bizarre posturing, and repetitive imitations of the movements or speech of other people. This type is now uncommon, but where found they would be at risk of malnutrition, exhaustion, or self-injury.

Patients in the **undifferentiated schizophrenic** subtype are characterised by having many of the symptoms of schizophrenia, but do not meet the specific criteria for the paranoid, disorganized, or catatonic subtypes.

The **residual type schizophrenia** category involves patients who have had at least one acute schizophrenic episode but thereafter do not present definite psychotic symptoms, such as delusions and hallucinations. They rather present with symptoms such as withdrawal from others.

The risk of schizophrenia among first-degree biological relatives is 10 times greater than that observed in the general population. Most patients are diagnosed in their late teens or early twenties, but the symptoms of schizophrenia can emerge at any age in the life cycle. Schizophrenia is rarely diagnosed in pre-adolescent children, although patients as young as 5 or 6 have been reported.

The diagnosis of schizophrenia is based on a set of symptoms rather than a single symptom. These symptoms include delusions, somatic hallucinations, hearing voices commenting on the patient's behaviour, thought insertion or thought withdrawal. Somatic hallucinations refer to sensations or perceptions concerning bodily organs that have no known medical cause or reason, such as the notion that one's brain is radioactive. Thought insertion and/or withdrawal refer to delusions that an outside force has the power to put thoughts into one's mind or remove them.

The symptoms may be divided into two categories, positive and negative symptoms. The positive symptoms of schizophrenia are those that represent an excessive or distorted version of normal functions. **Positive symptoms** include disorganised thought processes (reflected mainly in speech) and disorganised or catatonic behaviour. Disorganised thought is reflected in looseness of associations where a patient rambles on from topic to topic in a disconnected way, or makes a 'word salad', in which the patient's speech is so incoherent that it makes no grammatical or linguistic sense. Disorganised behaviour has the effect that the patient has difficulty with any type of purposeful or goal-oriented behaviour, including personal self-care or preparing meals. Other forms of disorganised behaviour may include dressing in odd or inappropriate ways, inappropriate sexual behaviour, agitated shouting and cursing or swearing.

Negative symptoms are related to the lack or absence of behaviours, such as the lack of emotional response (affective flattening), poverty of speech, and absence of volition or will.

For a **diagnosis of schizophrenia**, the patient must meet a set of specified criteria:

(1)   the patient must have two (or more) of the following symptoms during a 1-month period: delusions; hallucinations; disorganised speech; disorganised or catatonic behaviour; negative symptoms;

(2)   there is a decline in social, interpersonal, or occupational functioning, including self-care;

(3)   the disturbed behaviour must last for at least 6 months;

(4)   mood disorders, substance abuse disorders, medical conditions, and developmental disorders should have been ruled out.

The **treatment** of schizophrenia depends in part on the patient's stage or phase of illness. The primary form of treatment of schizophrenia is **antipsychotic medication** which helps to control almost all the positive symptoms although they have less effect on the negative symptoms such as disorganised behaviour. Most patients with schizophrenia are kept long term on antipsychotic medication to minimise the possibility of relapse.

Many schizophrenic patients could benefit from **psychotherapy** once their acute symptoms have been brought under control by antipsychotic medication. Behaviour therapy is helpful in assisting patients to acquire skills for daily living and social interaction. Family therapy is often recommended for the families of schizophrenic patients, to relieve the feelings of guilt that they may have, as well as to help them understand the patient's disorder. The family's attitude and behaviours toward the patient are key factors in minimising relapses and family therapy can often strengthen the family's ability to cope with the stresses caused by the schizophrenic patient's illness. Family therapy which focuses on communication skills and problem-solving strategies could be particularly helpful. Many families benefit from support groups for relations of schizophrenic patients.

26.3   SCHIZOAFFECTIVE DISORDER

Schizoaffective disorder is a mental illness that shares the psychotic symptoms of schizophrenia and the mood disturbances of depression or bipolar disorder. The current definition of schizoaffective disorder in the American Psychiatric Association's *Diagnostic and Statistical Manual of Mental Disorders IV* (*DSM-IV*) is that these are disorders where mood symptoms are sufficiently severe to warrant a diagnosis of depression or other full-blown mood disorder and where mood symptoms overlap at some period of the illness with psychotic symptoms that satisfy the diagnosis of schizophrenia (eg hallucinations, delusions, or thought process disorder). Symptoms of schizoaffective disorder vary from patient to patient. Delusions, hallucinations, and evidence of disturbances in thinking could present as they are observed in full-blown schizophrenia and/or there could be mood fluctuations such as those observed in major depression or bipolar disorder. For a diagnosis of schizoaffective disorder to be made, mania, psychotic depression, schizophrenia and medical and neurological disorders that mimic psychotic/affective disorders need to be ruled out.

The main treatment of choice would be antipsychotic medication used to treat schizophrenia and the antidepressant drugs and mood stabilisers used in depression and bipolar disorder. Certain forms of psychotherapy for both patients and family members can be useful, particularly to assist the patient to create structure in his or her life, learn appropriate problem-solving strategies and to reduce stress. This approach and psychological education may assist the patient to improve their ability to function in the day-to-day world, thereby reducing the risk of recurrence.

26.4   PARANOIA

Paranoia is an unfounded or exaggerated distrust of others, sometimes reaching delusional proportions. Paranoid individuals constantly suspect the motives of those around them, and believe that certain individuals, or people in general, are 'out to get them'. Paranoid perceptions and behaviour may appear as features of a number of mental illnesses, including depression and dementia, but are most prominent in three types of psychological disorders: paranoid schizophrenia, delusional disorder (persecutory type), and paranoid personality disorder (PPD).

Individuals with paranoid schizophrenia and persecutory delusional disorder experience what is known as **persecutory delusions**: an irrational, false, yet unshakeable, belief that someone is plotting against them in a plot or plan to harm an individual.

Persons with paranoid personality disorder tend to be self-centred, self-important, defensive, and emotionally distant. Their paranoia manifests itself in constant suspicions rather than full-blown delusions. The disorder often impedes social and personal relationships and career advancement.

Patients with paranoid symptoms should undergo a thorough psychiatric assessment in order to rule out possible organic causes (such as dementia) or environmental causes (such as extreme stress). If a psychological cause is suspected, a clinical psychologist will need to conduct a clinical interview and may administer one of several clinical inventories, or tests, to evaluate mental status.

Paranoia that is symptomatic of paranoid schizophrenia, delusional disorder, or paranoid personality disorder should be treated first with antipsychotic medication, then with cognitive therapy or psychotherapy to help the patient cope with his paranoia and/or persecutory delusions.

26.5   DELUSIONAL DISORDER

A delusion is an unshakeable belief in something untrue. These irrational beliefs defy normal reasoning, and remain firm even when overwhelming proof is presented to dispute them. Delusions are often accompanied by hallucinations and/or feelings of paranoia, which act to strengthen confidence in the delusion. They are also the major feature of delusional disorder. Individuals with delusional disorder suffer from long-term, complex delusions that fall into one of six categories: persecutory, grandiose, jealousy, erotomanic, somatic, or mixed. There are also delusional disorders such as dementia that clearly have organic or physical causes.

Persecutory delusions: Individuals with persecutory delusional disorder are plagued by feelings of paranoia and an irrational yet unshakeable belief that someone is plotting against them, or out to harm them.

Grandiose delusions: Individuals with grandiose delusional disorder have an inflated sense of self-worth. Their delusions centre on their own importance, such as believing that they have done or created something of extreme value or have a 'special mission'.

Delusions of jealousy: Jealous delusions are unjustified and irrational beliefs that an individual's spouse or significant other has been unfaithful.

Erotomanic delusions: Individuals with erotomanic delusional disorder believe that another person, often a stranger, is in love with them. The object of their affection is typically of a higher social status, sometimes a celebrity. This type of delusional disorder may lead to stalking or other potentially dangerous behaviour.

Somatic delusions: Somatic delusions involve the belief that something is physically wrong with the individual. The delusion may involve a medical condition or illness or a perceived deformity. This condition differs from hypochondriasis in that the deformity is perceived as a fixed condition not a temporary illness.

Mixed delusions are those characterised by two or more of persecutory, grandiose, jealousy, erotomanic, or somatic themes.

Delusions that are symptomatic of delusional disorder should be primarily treated with antipsychotic drugs, while cognitive therapy could be of assistance to address distorted cognitions.

CHAPTER 27

SUBSTANCE RELATED DISORDERS

27.1 INTRODUCTION

Substance abuse and dependence refer to any continued pathological use of a medication, non-medically indicated drug (called drugs of abuse) or toxin. Substance abuse is any pattern of substance use that results in repeated adverse social consequences related to drug-taking – for example, interpersonal conflicts, failure to meet work, family, or school obligations, or legal problems. Substance dependence, commonly known as addiction, is characterised by physiological and behavioural symptoms related to substance use. These symptoms include the need for increasing amounts of the substance to maintain desired effects, withdrawal if drug-taking ceases, and a great deal of time spent in activities related to substance use.

The term substance, when discussed in the context of substance abuse and dependence, refers to medications, drugs of abuse, and toxins. These substances have an intoxicating effect, desired by the user, which can have either stimulating (speeding up) or depressive/sedating (slowing down) effects on the body. Substance dependence and/or abuse can involve any of the following 10 classes of substances:

(1)   alcohol;

(2)   amphetamines (including 'crystal meth', some medications used in the treatment of attention deficit disorder (ADD) and amphetamine-like substances found in appetite suppressants);

(3)   cannabis (including marijuana and hashish);

(4)   cocaine (including 'crack');

(5)   hallucinogens (including LSD, mescaline, and 'Ecstasy');

(6)   inhalants (including compounds found in gasoline, glue, and paint thinners);

(7)   nicotine (substance dependence only);

(8)   opioids (including morphine, heroin, codeine, methadone);

(9)   phencyclidine (including PCP, angel dust, ketamine);

(10) sedative, hypnotic, and anxiolytic (anti-anxiety) substances (including benzodiazepines such as valium, barbiturates, prescription sleeping medications, and most prescription anti-anxiety medications).

27.2   CAUSES

It is known that substance use may be a way to relieve the symptoms of a psychological disorder. In these cases unless the underlying pathology is treated, attempts to permanently stop substance dependence are ineffective. Psychopathologies that are associated with substance dependence include antisocial personality disorder, bipolar disorder, depression, anxiety disorder, and schizophrenia.

Substance dependence is also related to social environment. Drug-taking is essentially a socially learned behaviour. Local social norms determine the likelihood that a person is exposed to the substance and whether continued use is reinforced. External penalties, such as legal or social sanctions, may reduce the likelihood of substance use.

27.3   SYMPTOMS

The DSM-IV-TR identifies seven criteria (symptoms), at least three of which must be met during a given 12-month period, for the diagnosis of **substance dependence**:

(1)   Tolerance, as defined either by the need for increasing amounts of the substance to obtain the desired effect or by experiencing less effect with extended use of the same amount of the substance.

(2)   Withdrawal, as exhibited either by experiencing unpleasant mental, physiological, and emotional changes when drug-taking ceases or by using the substance as a way to relieve or prevent withdrawal symptoms.

(3)   Longer duration of taking substance or use in greater quantities than was originally intended.

(4)   Persistent desire or repeated unsuccessful efforts to stop or lessen substance use.

(5)   A relatively large amount of time spent in securing and using the substance, or in recovering from the effects of the substance.

(6) Important work and social activities reduced because of substance use.

(7) Continued substance use despite negative physical and psychological effects of use.

Symptoms of **substance abuse**, as specified by DSM-IV-TR, include one or more of the following occurring during a given 12-month period:

(1) Substance use resulting in a recurrent failure to fulfil work, school, or home obligations (work absences, substance-related school suspensions, neglect of children).

(2) Substance use in physically hazardous situations such as driving or operating machinery.

(3) Substance use resulting in legal problems such as drug-related arrests.

(4) Continued substance use despite negative social and relationship consequences of use.

In addition to the general symptoms, there are other physical signs and symptoms of substance abuse that are related to specific drug classes.

(5) Signs and symptoms of alcohol intoxication include such physical signs as slurred speech, lack of coordination, unsteady gait, memory impairment, and stupor, as well as behaviour changes shortly after alcohol ingestion, including inappropriate aggressive behaviour, mood volatility, and impaired functioning.

(6) Amphetamine users may exhibit rapid heartbeat, elevated or depressed blood pressure, dilated (enlarged) pupils, weight loss, as well as excessively high energy, inability to sleep, confusion, and occasional paranoid psychotic behavior.

(7) Cannabis users may exhibit red eyes with dilated pupils, increased appetite, dry mouth, and rapid pulse; they may also be sluggish and slow to react.

(8) Cocaine users may exhibit rapid heart rate, elevated or depressed blood pressure, dilated pupils, weight loss, in addition to wide variations in their energy level, severe mood disturbances, psychosis, and paranoia.

(9) Users of hallucinogens may exhibit anxiety or depression, paranoia, and unusual behaviour in response to hallucinations (imagined sights, voices, sounds, or smells that appear real). Signs include

dilated pupils, rapid heart rate, tremors, lack of coordination, and sweating. Flashbacks, or the re-experiencing of a hallucination long after stopping substance use, are also a symptom of hallucinogen use.

(10) Users of inhalants experience dizziness, spastic eye movements, lack of coordination, slurred speech, and slowed reflexes. Associated behaviours may include belligerence, tendency toward violence, apathy, and impaired judgment.

(11) Opioid drug users exhibit slurred speech, drowsiness, impaired memory, and constricted (small) pupils. They may appear slowed in their physical movements.

(12) Users of sedative or hypnotic drugs show slurred speech, unsteady gait, inattentiveness, and impaired memory. They may display inappropriate behaviour, mood volatility, and impaired functioning.

Overdosing on a substance is a frequent complication of substance abuse. Drug overdose can be purposeful (with suicide as a goal), or due to carelessness. Substances with depressive effects may dangerously slow the breathing and heart rate, drop the body temperature, and result in a general unresponsiveness. Substances with stimulatory effects may dangerously increase the heart rate and blood pressure, produce abnormal heart rhythms, increase body temperature, induce seizures, and cause erratic behaviour. The interview would also explore a history of psychiatric treatments and outcomes and include a social history.

27.4 DIAGNOSIS AND TREATMENT

One of the most difficult aspects of diagnosis involves overcoming the patient's denial. Denial is a psychological state during which a person is unable to acknowledge the (usually negative) circumstances of a situation. In this case, denial leads a person to underestimate the degree of substance use and of the problems associated with substance use. To get an objective assessment substance use can be detected through laboratory testing of his or her blood, urine, or hair. Laboratory testing, however, may be limited by the sensitivity and specificity of the testing method and by the time elapsed since the person last used the drug.

The main focus or goals for treatment would involve interventions to assist the patient to abstain from or reduce the use and effects of the substance, for the patient to reduce the frequency and severity of relapses; and for the patient to develop the psychological and emotional skills necessary to restore and maintain personal, occupational, and social functioning.

The first stage of treatment is detoxification, which is the process of weaning the patient from regular substance use. Thereafter the treatment could commence with an assessment together with the formulation of a treatment plan and, after that, psychiatric management. The treatment approach would need to include helping the patient adhere to the treatment plan through therapy and the development of skills and social interactions that reinforce a drug-free lifestyle. Patients typically undergo psychosocial therapy and, in some cases, pharmacological treatment. Psychosocial therapeutic modalities include cognitive behavioural therapy, behavioural therapy, individual psychodynamic or interpersonal therapy, group therapy, family therapy, and self-help groups. Pharmacological treatment may include medication that eases withdrawal symptoms, reduces craving, interacts negatively with substances of abuse to discourage drug-taking, or treats associated psychiatric disorders.

27.5 RECOVERY AND RELAPSE

Recovery from substance use is notoriously difficult, even with exceptional treatment resources. Although relapse rates are difficult to accurately obtain, the literature suggests that 90% of alcohol dependent users experience at least one relapse within the 4 years after treatment. Relapse rates for heroin and nicotine users are believed to be similar. Certain pharmacological treatments, however, have been shown to reduce relapse rates.

Relapses are most likely to occur within the first 12 months of having discontinued substance use. Triggers for relapses can include any number of life stresses (problems in a job or in a marriage, loss of a relationship, death of a loved one, financial stresses), in addition to seemingly mundane exposure to a place or an acquaintance associated with previous substance use.

The development of adaptive life skills and ongoing drug-free social support are believed to be two important factors in avoiding relapse. The effect of the support group Alcoholics Anonymous has been intensively studied, and a 1996 meta-analysis noted that long-term sobriety appears to be positively related to Alcoholics Anonymous attendance and involvement. Support for family members in addition to support for the individual in recovery is also important. As substance dependence has a serious impact on family functioning, and because family members may inadvertently maintain behaviours that initially led to the substance dependence, ongoing therapy and support for family members should be provided.

CHAPTER 28

IMPULSE CONTROL DISORDERS

28.1   INTRODUCTION

Impulse control disorders are characterised by an inability to resist the impulse to perform an action that is harmful to one's self or others. This is a relatively new class of personality disorder, and the most common of these are intermittent explosive disorder, kleptomania, pyromania, compulsive gambling disorder, and trichotillomania.

The central features of these disorders are the individual's inability to stop impulses that may cause harm to themselves or others. These persons would often feel anxiety or tension in considering these behaviours. This anxiety or tension is relieved or diminished once the action is performed.

28.2   TYPES OF IMPULSE CONTROL DISORDERS

Intermittent explosive disorder is more common among men, and involves aggressive outbursts that lead to assaults on others or destruction of property. These outbursts are unprovoked or seem to be out of proportion to the event that precedes them. It involves severe acts of assault or destruction of property.

Kleptomania is more common among women, and involves the theft of objects that are seemingly worthless, are unnecessary and of little monetary value. The act of stealing relieves tension and is seen by the individual to be rewarding. The actual stealing is not preplanned, and the concept of punishment for the crime does not occur to these individuals, although they are aware that what they are doing is wrong. The act of stealing is not an expression of anger or vengeance. There is increased tension experienced by these individuals before the act is committed, and this is resolved or relieved once the object is stolen.

Pyromania is more common among men, and involves setting fires in order to feel pleasure and relieve tension. It is classified by the deliberate setting of fires more than once. The individual will exhibit a fascination with and attraction to fire and any objects associated with it. Before the fire is set, there is tension, with a feeling of relief once the fire is set. Acts of true pyromania are not done for monetary gain, to express anger, to conceal criminal behaviour, or in response to a hallucination.

Pathological gambling occurs in roughly 1–3% of the population, and involves excessive gambling despite heavy monetary losses or monetary insufficiency. These losses actually act as a motivating factor in continuing gambling in order to recoup some of what was lost. This disorder typically begins in youth, and affected individuals are often competitive, easily bored, restless, and generous. For a diagnosis of pathological gambling, five or more of the following symptoms must be present:

(1)   a preoccupation with gambling;

(2)   a need to gamble with more money to achieve the thrill of winning;

(3)   repeated attempts to control or stop gambling;

(4)   irritability or restlessness due to repeated attempts at control;

(5)   gambling as an escape from stress;

(6)   lying to cover up gambling;

(7)   conducting illegal activities, such as embezzling or fraud, to finance gambling;

(8)   losing a job or personal relationship owing to gambling;

(9)   borrowing money to fund gambling.

Trichotillomania involves pulling hair from one's own scalp, face, or body, and is more common in women. It often begins in childhood, and is often associated with major depression or attention-deficit hyperactivity disorder. There is an increased sense of tension before pulling the hair, which is relieved once it is pulled out. Recurrent pulling out of one's hair does often result in noticeable hair loss. Affected individuals can undergo significant distress and impaired social, occupational, and functional behaviour.

28.3   DIAGNOSIS AND TREATMENT

A diagnosis of any of these impulse control disorders can be made only after other medical and psychiatric disorders that may cause the same symptoms have been ruled out. A combination of psychological counselling and medication are the preferred treatments for the impulse control disorders. For kleptomania, pyromania, and trichotillomania, behaviour modification and cognitive behavioural therapy is usually the treatment of choice. For pathological gambling, treatment usually involves an adaptation of the model set forth by Alcoholics Anonymous. Individuals are counselled with the goal of eventual response to appropriate social limits. In the case of intermittent explosive disorder, anger management and medication may be used in extreme cases of aggression.

28.4 INTERMITTENT EXPLOSIVE DISORDER (IED)

Intermittent explosive disorder (IED) is a mental disturbance that is characterised by specific episodes of violent and aggressive behaviour that may involve harm to others or destruction of property.

A person must meet certain specific criteria to be diagnosed with IED:

(1) There must be several separate episodes of failure to restrain aggressive impulses that result in serious assaults against others or property destruction.

(2) The degree of aggression expressed must be out of proportion to any provocation or other stressor prior to the incidents.

(3) The behaviour cannot be accounted for by another mental disorder, substance abuse, medication side effects, or such general medical conditions as epilepsy or head injuries.

In many cases individuals diagnosed with IED do in fact have a dual psychiatric diagnosis. IED is frequently associated with mood and anxiety disorders, substance abuse and eating disorders, and narcissistic, paranoid, and antisocial personality disorders. Individuals diagnosed with IED sometimes describe strong impulses to act aggressively prior to the specific incidents reported to the doctor and/or the police. They may experience racing thoughts or a heightened energy level during the aggressive episode, with fatigue and depression developing shortly afterward. Many people diagnosed with IED appear to have general problems with anger or other impulsive behaviours between explosive episodes. Some are able to control aggressive impulses without acting on them while others act out in less destructive ways, such as screaming at someone rather than attacking them physically.

From a cognitive behavioural perspective, IED results from rigid beliefs and a tendency to misinterpret other people's behaviour in accordance with these beliefs. Most individuals diagnosed with IED believe that other people are basically hostile and untrustworthy, that physical force is the only way to obtain respect from others, and that life in general is a battlefield. Certain errors in thinking are associated with IED, in particular personalising, where the person interprets others' behaviour as being directed specifically against him. Selective perception occurs where the person notices only those features of situations or interactions that fit his negative view of the world rather than taking in all available information. Another error of thinking or distorted cognition is related to misinterpreting the motives of others where the person tends to see neutral or even friendly behaviour as either malicious or manipulative. These areas could be addressed in cognitive behavioural therapy.

CHAPTER 29

FACTITIOUS DISORDERS

29.1   INTRODUCTION

Factitious disorders are a group of mental disturbances in which patients intentionally act as being physically or mentally ill without obvious benefit accruing to themselves. The name factitious comes from a Latin word that means artificial. These disorders are different from malingering, which is defined as pretending illness when the 'patient' has a clear motive, such as financial gain. Patients with factitious disorders produce or exaggerate the symptoms of a physical or mental illness by a variety of methods, including contaminating urine samples with blood, taking hallucinogens, injecting themselves with bacteria to produce infections, and other similar behaviours.

29.2   TYPES OF FACTITIOUS DISORDERS

Munchausen syndrome refers to patients whose factitious symptoms are dramatised and exaggerated. Many persons with Munchausen syndrome go so far as to undergo major surgery repeatedly, and, to avoid detection, at several locations. Many have been employed in hospitals or in health care professions. The syndrome's onset is in early adulthood. It has been suggested that Munchausen patients are motivated by a desire to be cared for, have a need for attention, dependency, an ambivalence toward doctors, or a need to suffer. Many Munchausen patients are very familiar with medical terminology and symptoms.

Munchausen syndrome by proxy is the name given to factitious disorders in children produced by parents or other caregivers. In Munchausen syndrome by proxy (MSBP), an individual, typically a mother, intentionally causes or fabricates illness in a child or other person under her care. The parent may falsify the child's medical history or tamper with laboratory tests in order to make the child appear sick.

Individuals with Munchausen by proxy syndrome use their child (or another dependent person) to fulfill their need to step into the patient role. The disorder most commonly victimises children from birth to 8 years old. Parents with MSBP may only exaggerate or fabricate their child's symptoms, or they may deliberately induce symptoms through various methods, including poisoning, suffocation, starvation, or infecting the child's bloodstream.

Common Munchausen by proxy symptoms include apnoea (cessation of breathing), fever, vomiting, and diarrhoea. In both Munchausen and MSBP syndromes, the suspected illness does not respond to a normal course of treatment. The parents may push for invasive diagnostic procedures and display an extraordinary depth of knowledge of medical procedures.

Ganser's syndrome is an unusual dissociative reaction to extreme stress in which the patient gives absurd or silly answers to simple questions. It has sometimes been labelled as psychiatric malingering, but is more often classified as a factitious disorder.

29.3   CAUSES AND SYMPTOMS OF FACTITIOUS DISORDERS

From a psychological and psychodynamic point of view these disorders could be attributed to a variety of situations or conditions. These include child abuse, the wish to repeat a satisfying childhood relationship with a doctor or male authority figures, underlying personality disorder and/or the desire to deceive or challenge authority figures. Patients with factitious disorders fundamentally wish to assume the role of patient, be cared for and elicit secondary emotional gain.

Clinical features of a factitious disorder would include:

(1)   the person having a dramatic but inconsistent medical history;

(2)   extensive knowledge of medicine and/or hospitals;

(3)   negative test results followed by further symptom development;

(4)   eagerness to undergo operations and procedures; and

(5)   the fact that symptoms occur only when the patient is not being observed.

29.4   DIAGNOSIS OF FACTITIOUS DISORDERS

The diagnosis of factitious disorders is usually based on the exclusion of bona fide medical or psychiatric conditions, together with a combination of the typical clinical features in some cases. The diagnosis is made on the basis of records from other hospitals. Because Munchausen sufferers often go from doctor to doctor, gaining admission into many hospitals along the way, diagnosis can be difficult. Their caregivers may also notice that symptoms such as high fever occur only when the patient is left unattended. Occasionally, unprescribed medication used to induce symptoms is found with the patient's belongings. When the patient is confronted, he often reacts with outrage and denial.

29.5 MALINGERING

Malingering could be understood as the act of intentionally feigning or exaggerating physical or psychological symptoms for personal gain. People may feign physical or psychological illness for any number of reasons. Faked illness can get them out of work, military duty, or criminal prosecution. It can also help them obtain financial compensation through insurance claims, lawsuits, or workers' compensation. Feigned symptoms may also be a way of getting the doctor to prescribe certain drugs.

People who malinger are different from people who invent symptoms for sympathy (factitious diseases). Patients who malinger clearly have something tangible to gain. People with factitious diseases appear to have a need to play the 'sick' role. They may feign illness for attention or sympathy.

Malingering may take the form of complaints of chronic whiplash pain from road traffic accidents. Whiplash claims are controversial. Although some individuals clearly do suffer from whiplash injury, others may be exaggerating the pain for insurance claims or for compensation. Some intriguing scientific studies have shown that chronic whiplash pain after road traffic accidents is almost nonexistent in Lithuania and Greece. In these countries, the legal systems do not encourage personal injury lawsuits or financial settlements. The psychological symptoms experienced by survivors of disaster, in particular post-traumatic stress disorder and the anxiety states, are also faked by malingerers.

Malingering may be suspected:

(1) when a patient is referred for examination by a lawyer;

(2) when the onset of illness coincides with a large financial incentive, such as a new disability policy;

(3) when objective medical tests do not confirm the patient's complaints;

(4) when the patient does not co-operate with the diagnostic work-up or prescribed treatment;

(5) when the patient has antisocial attitudes and behaviours (antisocial personality).

Treatment of malingering

Patients who are purposefully faking symptoms for gain usually do not wish to be cured. Often, the malingering patient fails to report any improvement with treatment and the psychologist and medical professionals may try many treatments without success.

CHAPTER 30

SUMMARY OF ADULT DISORDERS

30.1 Accounts have been given above of the psychological aspects of adult mental disorders that are relevant to the work undertaken by a clinical psychologist who has been commissioned to give opinions on the spouses, partners, parents and other carers of children who may be involved in family and child care proceedings. Perhaps the most important rule for the psychologist – and the psychiatrist in his own field – is for him to realise that no mental disorder, by itself, necessarily stands in the way of a spouse, partner, parent or carer being able to fulfil his or her duties to an adequate degree. Perhaps the single most confusing issue to participants in this field is the realisation that an individual could be suffering from a mental disorder or other psychological difficulties, even to a severe degree, and yet is able to function satisfactorily in the relevant areas. This should be a self-evident truth, for there are millions suffering from mental disorders or psychological difficulties who are able to perform adequately their duties as spouse, partner, parent or carer. Conversely, individuals with no mental disorder or psychological disturbance afflicting them may fall down in these tasks and duties. Failure to appreciate this point has led to injustice and even tragedy (one notes how uncommon mental disorder is in those who have been investigated following the systematic abuse of children, their own as well as those of others). There is no alternative to the express determination of suspected impairment where the functions of individuals participating as spouses, partners, parents or carers are concerned. In undertaking family assessments in the field of child and family law, information about the parents (or other relevant persons), including the state of their mental health, history of substance abuse and other difficulties, their intellectual ability and any risk of future physical and sexually abusive behaviour directed against the children they could pose, may be required. An assessment needs to be made of the individual adults concerned to determine the presence of any diagnosable disorder and, thereafter, to make recommendations for treatment and give a prognosis. The assessment as to the extent to which mental health or psychological difficulties may impair the parent's ability to care, say, for a child needs to be determined. The abilities of the parents evaluated would include cognitive capacity and to what extent this could impair parental capacity and the ability to make changes where needed. The ability of the parents in various areas including their cognitive functioning should be assessed and it is important to consider if any shortfall is significant enough to be capable of impairing parental capacity. Furthermore, an evaluation of any risk of future abusive behaviour, and of relapsing into alcohol or drug abuse, is required, particularly in cases where a parent has previously injured a child physically or emotionally. The assessments of the emotional and psychological functioning of an adult may assist in providing a prognosis about the future risk that the parent may pose to children in his or her care.

It is important also for the clinical psychologist engaged in these assessments to have an understanding and knowledge of adult psychiatric disorders and psychological disturbances and to attempt to make an assessment of how these conditions could have an impact on the family functioning and the parenting these individuals provide. It is usually difficult to try to assist the parties and the court in gaining an understanding of the causes of a child's difficulties without a full assessment also being undertaken of the emotional and psychological functioning of the parents or those caring for it. Assessments of the parents or carers may provide an insight into and an understanding of the extent to which a child's needs are currently being met, the nature of care that has been given and the kind of assistance and therapy the child may require, as a result of previous inadequacy of care. Such an assessment may also assist in making recommendations as to the level of contact with family members that is feasible if a child is to be placed away from the family.

Thus, in order to inform the parties and the court, a full psychological assessment of a parent's functioning is required which needs to describe that parent's strengths and difficulties. The assessment will also need to highlight the parent's capacity to fulfil the child's future needs, what help may be required to enable him or her to do this and to advise as to whether the timescale required for sufficient positive change to be achieved on the part of the parent meets the child's needs as envisaged in these proceedings.

From what has been said above it becomes clear that when a parent is suffering from a psychiatric condition or disorder, such as a clinical depression, bi-polar disorder or a personality disorder, it is essential to determine in specific terms to what extent, if any, the disorder may be affecting the parenting, whether the condition, even if treated and brought under control and stabilised, could still continue to impact adversely upon the parenting and on the day-to-day functioning of the individual. It also needs to be assessed whether parenting may be permanently interfered with as a result of any disorder or disturbance, and whether this could have an impact on the provision of good enough parenting and interfere with giving priority to the basic needs of the child or children of any parent or carer who is affected by such a disorder.

APPENDIX 1

SOME SPECIMEN INSTRUCTIONS

CASE 1

Ann is the child of Belle Cash and David Earl. They had been married when she was born. Ann was on the Child Protection Register when she was very young. The relationship between husband and wife was said to be violent and volatile by Mrs Cash. This is not accepted by Mr Earl.

When the parties separated Mrs Cash was involved in another relationship which the local authority believes was also violent. Mr Earl had regular contact with Ann until Mrs Cash moved away from the area without notifying Mr Earl. Mrs Cash then met and married Mr Cash. Mrs Cash then left him and lived with a Mr Ford. It was around the time of this relationship ending that George was conceived. Mr Ford was violent towards Mrs Cash and their relationship ended.

Mr and Mrs Cash were reconciled when Mrs Cash left Mr Ford. George was born some eight months later. The local authority has raised the issue of paternity testing for George but this was refused by Mr and Mrs Cash.

There are medical notes for Ann dealing with various injuries that she has sustained over the years. There are also papers dealing with Ann's educational needs, her emotional needs and attachments with adults she comes into contact with, whether she knows them well or not.

Mr Cash has a history of alcohol abuse. Mr Cash also suffers with epilepsy and is aware of the impact alcohol has on that condition. Mrs Cash has a history of alcohol abuse and admits to having a temper. She has attended anger management counselling in the past. During the course of their relationship there have been incidents of domestic violence and arguments which the children have witnessed.

There have also been incidents where the risk to George has been deemed by the local authority as being unacceptable.

It is the local authority's view that Ann is consistently saying she does not wish to return home to Mr and Mrs Cash and is only seeking contact with them if it remains supervised.

The Guardian has asked for play therapy to be organised for Ann. The local authority is not seeking to put this in place as they are currently undertaking one to one work with Ann and feel that additional work would be too much for her. The local authority is also seeking a parenting assessment of Mr and Mrs Cash and a risk assessment has been undertaken in respect of Mr Earl jointly with the Probation. Services

You are instructed to consider the following issues.

(1) To give a detailed account of the relationships between:
 (a) the brother and sister;
 (b) each of the children with Mrs Cash;
 (c) each of the children with Mr Cash;
 (d) each of the children with their mother and Mr Cash;
 (e) each of the children with any other important adults in their lives.

(2) Please consider what further work could/should be undertaken with this family to ensure the children remain with/return to their mother (and Mr Cash), if appropriate.

(3) Please consider whether either Mr Cash or Mrs Cash would be able to offer 'good enough' parenting to each of the children on his or her own?

(4) Is either of the parents of these children able to recognise the Local Authority's concerns and does he or she have any insight into the difficulties the Local Authority has highlighted?

(5) Is Mrs Cash able to learn empathy towards Ann, and, if so, what timescale would be involved?

(6) Are George's emotional needs being met in the family home? What impact, if any, is there on George's emotional or other development if he remains in the family?

(7) If it is within your area of expertise to do so, please consider whether there is any merit in the concern of the local authority that Mrs Cash could be suffering from a personality disorder and, if not, whether you are able to identify any other reason for what is perceived by the local authority to be erratic behaviour. If you reach any conclusions in this regard, could you please set them out and comment on the prognosis, indicating any therapeutic work or medication that might be needed to assist her specifically in this regard.

(8) Is Mr Earl able to, with or without his partner, offer good enough parenting to Ann, both now and in the future?

(9) Please consider what further work could/should be undertaken with Mr Earl and his partner to ensure Ann could live with them, if this is appropriate.

(10) Please consider what contact the children should have with their mother, Mr Cash, Mr Earl (and his partner) and each other, if the children live separately from any of these persons.

(11) Please advise as to the impact and likely future impact of the mother's relationship with Mr Cash on her care of the children, in particular as to whether, and if so to what extent, he is able to mitigate or compensate (if necessary) for the consequences of any deficits in the mother's parenting abilities. This exercise should be carried out in relation to Ann and George separately and then together.

(12) Please provide an assessment of the relationship between Mr Earl and his partner Miss Henry.

(13) Please advise as to the impact and likely future impact of the mother's relationship with Mr Earl in relation to Ann, in particular as to their past relationship and any issues potentially arising in the risk assessment of Mr Earl.

(14) Please comment on your assessment of Ann and what, if any, other support or intervention she may require whether it be in relation to her educational, emotional or other needs.

(15) What weight, if any, should be placed on the wishes and feelings Ann is expressing to her family members and the professionals involved in these proceedings?

(16) Please comment generally on the timescales involved in relation to any further work you feel is necessary with either of the children or the adults you have assessed, and their ability to change.

(17) Please comment on your assessment of George and what, if any, other support or intervention he may require whether it be in relation to his educational, emotional or other needs.

(18) Please raise any other issues that you feel are relevant to these proceedings relating to any aspect of the assessment you have undertaken, and which you feel able to comment upon.

CASE 2

A local authority has instituted care proceedings in relation to Isla, aged 2. Her mother is Kate Leonard, aged 16, and her father is Michael

Norman aged 35. Mr Norman is a party to these proceedings and also has parental responsibility for Isla. Miss Leonard and Mr Norman live separately.

At present Miss Leonard and Mr Norman say that they are not in a relationship although Mr Norman has indicated to the Children's Guardian that when she turns 18 years of age it is their intention to resume their relationship and for them to care for Isla together. It is not clear whether this position is shared by Miss Leonard. The local authority believes that both parents continue to be in contact with each other.

The Social Services Department received a referral on account of Miss Leonard's behavioural difficulties when she was aged 14. Subsequently, there were ongoing referrals from the Emergency Duty Team and the Domestic Violence Unit relating to the conflict between Miss Leonard and her parents. There were also concerns that she was having a sexual relationship with a neighbour, Mr Norman, who was many years her senior.

Miss Leonard's name was placed on the Child Protection Register under the category of emotional abuse. The unborn baby was registered under the category of neglect and this registration continues to date.

Following Isla's birth, she and her mother lived with Isla's maternal grandparents, Jane and Ken Leonard until Miss Leonard was asked to leave the family home.

During the period that Miss Leonard and Isla lived with Mr and Mrs Leonard there was ongoing conflict between Miss Leonard and her parents. Isla was exposed to this conflict. Mrs Leonard appeared to be responsible for much of the care given to Isla. There were also concerns that Miss Leonard was failing to give priority to Isla's needs.

A referral was made to the Family Resource Centre to conduct an assessment of Miss Leonard's ability to care for Isla. Miss Leonard's attendance at the Family Resource Centre was poor in that she attended a total of 9 out of 21 sessions. Although some positive aspects of Miss Leonard's parenting were noted, there were also areas of concern.

Miss Leonard and Isla were accommodated and placed in foster care together. That placement broke down. The foster carer had noted that Miss Leonard was not giving priority to her child's needs. She also appeared to be having a continuing relationship with Mr Norman and allowing him to have access to Isla in defiance of agreements made with the Social Services. Miss Leonard and Isla were then placed at a residential unit for the purposes of a parenting assessment. There were then indicators of some positive aspects of Miss Leonard's physical care of Isla although there were also areas of concern including her ongoing contact/relationship with Mr Norman, lack of supervision of Isla, etc.

This placement, however, had to be terminated on account of mounting concerns. Isla was then removed from her mother's care and placed separately in foster care.

In the meantime, the proposal for contact between Miss Leonard and Isla was that contact will be supervised. Contact will also be offered to Mr Norman and the maternal grandparents.

It should be noted that Mrs Leonard has made an application for a residence order and wishes to be considered as a primary carer for Isla. The local authority will be carrying out a kinship assessment of Mr and Mrs Leonard by an independent social worker.

Your instructions are as follows.

In respect of the parents

(1)   Please provide an assessment of the Cognitive Functioning of each parent.

(2)   Please undertake an assessment of each parent's learning capacity. To what extent, if any, in your opinion, is this in any way restricted by the parent's level of functioning?

(3)   If it is your opinion that either parent has a learning disability, what is the impact of such on the parent's ability to meet Isla's needs in the short-term, medium-term and long-term?

(4)   Please provide a psychological profile in respect of Kate Leonard and Michael Norman.

(5)   Please comment on the relationship between Miss Leonard and Mr Norman.

(6)   Please comment on the relationship between each parent and Isla including:
   (i)   The ability of each parent to recognise, understand and act upon Isla's emotional, social and physical needs.
   (ii)   The ability of each parent to provide appropriate stimulation to Isla and to recognise and act upon situations which may be harmful to Isla.
   (iii) Each parent's ability to set age appropriate boundaries for Isla in the future and to meet Isla's growing needs.
   (iv)   Each parent's ability to see his or her own needs as being separate from those of Isla.

(7) Please comment on any particular strength evident in each parent's parenting.

(8) Comment on whether the parents are able to meet Isla's needs on a pro-active or a re-active level.

(9) Please comment on Miss Leonard and Mr Norman's capacity to care for Isla together in the future and/or separately.

(10) What is Miss Leonard's ability to understand and keep Isla safe from identified risks?

(11) What is Miss Leonard's ability to identify and act upon Isla's needs at present and Isla's growing needs and future needs (from basic care to emotional stimulation)?

(12) What support would Miss Leonard need to ensure that Isla is parented safely and appropriately? Please consider this in context of the fact that Miss Leonard is a very young mother with a volatile relationship with her own mother and with limited ability to access support from her immediate family members.

(13) Please assess Mr Norman in respect of the nature of his relationship with Miss Leonard and, given the age difference between the two, to what extent, if any, Mr Norman poses a risk to Isla in the future.

(14) Please assess each parent's ability to co-operate with Social Services, agencies and other professionals and to listen to advice and act upon it.

(15) Assess Miss Leonard's relationship with her parents and siblings and, if that relationship is a volatile relationship, to what extent, if at all, does it impact on her ability to care for Isla in the future.

In respect of Isla

(16) Please undertake a developmental assessment of Isla.

(17) Please assess and comment on the attachment between each parent, Mr and Mrs Leonard and Isla.

In respect of Mr and Mrs Leonard

(18) Please provide an assessment of the cognitive functioning of Mr and Mrs Leonard.

(19) Please undertake an assessment of Mr and Mrs Leonard's learning capacity. To what extent, if any, in your opinion, is this in any way restricted by their level of functioning?

(20) If it is your opinion that either Mr or Mrs Leonard have a learning disability, what is the impact of such on their ability to meet Isla's needs in the short-term, medium-term and long-term?

(21) Please assess the relationship of Mr and Mrs Leonard with Miss Leonard.

(22) Please provide an assessment of Mr and Mrs Leonard's insight to the domestic conflict between Miss Leonard and Mr Norman and what insight they have as to the effect of such on Isla and their ability to protect Isla from domestic conflict should Isla be placed with them in the long-term.

(23) Please assess Mr and Mrs Leonard's ability to managing conflicting needs of their own children and Isla's needs. Do they have the capacity and ability to adequately meet the growing needs, to include teenage years, of their own children and those of Isla's?

(24) Given the conflict between Miss Leonard, Mr Norman and Mr and Mrs Leonard, in your opinion, what is the impact/risks to Isla if Isla were to be placed with Mr and Mrs Leonard in the long-term?

(25) Please assess the relationship of Mr and Mrs Leonard with Mr Norman.

(26) Please comment upon the attachment between Mr and Mrs Leonard and Isla including:
  (i)   The ability of Mr and Mrs Leonard to recognise, understand and act upon and meet Isla's physical, emotional and social needs.
  (ii) The ability of Mr and Mrs Leonard to provide age appropriate stimulation to Isla and to recognise and act upon situations which may be harmful to Isla.
  (iii) Mr and Mrs Leonard's ability to meet Isla's growing needs.

Future planning

(27) What are your views in relation to future contact between Isla and her parents, together or separately, in the event, Isla is:
  (i)   Placed with Mr and Mrs Leonard.
  (ii) Placed outside the family.

(28) If Isla is placed with Mr and Mrs Leonard in the long-term against the wishes of Miss Leonard and/or Mr Norman, would Mr and Mrs Leonard be able to protect Isla?

(29) How would Mr and Mrs Leonard be able to manage any proposals for contact between Isla, Miss Leonard and/or Mr Norman if Isla were to be placed with them?

(30) What support would they require and from what agencies to ensure that contact is appropriately managed?

CASE 3

Miss Otto and Mr Pedro were in a relationship from 1985 until March 2004. Mr Pedro is the father of all of the children. He left Miss Otto and began a relationship with his current partner, Miss Quinsee. Miss Otto suffered a breakdown, and all four children were placed with their father for a week following this. Since that time the children have been in a shared-care arrangement, whereby they spend half of the week with their mother and the other half of the week with their father. Ron Pedro, the eldest child, divides his time between his mother, his father and his grandmother. Mr Pedro lives with his new partner and her baby.

At the last hearing the parents admitted that the children have, on occasion, suffered neglect because their needs have not always been consistently given priority by the parents. The children have also been exposed to the risk of physical harm as a direct result of a well-documented history of domestic violence, inappropriate boundaries and poor supervision. Mr Pedro has anger-management difficulties, for which he has in the past refused to seek assistance, and Miss Otto is vulnerable because she may have moderate learning difficulties (which she denies) and has a diagnosis of depression.

Currently the position is that following the hearing the magistrates made an interim care order in respect of the three younger children in favour of the local authority. The magistrates did not approve the care plan, and the order was then appealed by the legal representatives of the Guardian. A stay of the order was obtained in the county court on the same day, pending an appeal of the magistrates' decision.

The position of Miss Otto is that she wishes to care for all of her children on a full-time basis. If this should not be possible then she wishes to share the care of the three younger children with Mr Pedro. Mr Pedro wishes to have sole care of all four children, and currently this is being supported by the local authority depending upon the outcome of the expert assessments.

Issues to be addressed

(1)   Does Miss Otto have learning difficulties?

(2)   If so, how do her learning difficulties or any mental health issues affect her ability to parent her children?

(3)   What, if any, treatment would you recommend she receive?

(4)   If applicable, what are the timescales for such treatment, and is it within the children's timescales?

(5)   To what extent does Mr Pedro have difficulty managing his anger?

(6)   How do his anger management difficulties or any mental health issues affect his ability to parent his children?

(7)   What, if any, treatment would you recommend he receive?

(8)   If applicable, what are the timescales for such treatment, and is it within the children's timescales?

(9)   In relation to Miss Quinsee, what does she anticipate her role as being in providing parenting to the children, currently and in the future?

(10) What is the nature and quality of attachment the siblings have to one another?

(11) Three of the children appear to have concerning and challenging behaviour. What, if any, support or treatment do you believe the children would need to address their individual issues?

(12) With regard to the issue of placement, do you believe a shared-care arrangement is meeting the needs of the children currently, and would it do so in the future?

(13) With regard to the issue of placement, would you suggest that all of the children are placed together?

(14) If you believe a shared-care arrangement is not appropriate for any reason, please provide an opinion as to which placement would best be able to meet the children's needs.

(15) What treatment, if any, would be available to the parents to assist them in working together to manage contact between the children and both parents to enable them to meet their children's needs.

CASE 4

The background to the current application is that the parties began cohabiting in May 1996 and separated in February 1999. Miss Samuels applied for a residence order and for an order defining Mr Thomas's contact with the children. Mr Thomas then saw the children at a Contact Centre having previously last seen them several months before.

Thereafter Miss Unwin of CAFCASS recommended further contact at the Contact Centre for two months with a view to contact then being unsupervised.

A residence order was made subsequently in favour of Miss Samuels and an order for defined contact in favour of Mr Thomas by consent.

Subsequently, Mr Thomas had been having overnight staying contact with the children for a period of time when Miss Samuels applied to the court to vary contact following incidents of domestic violence and the court made findings of fact concerning findings that Mr Thomas had been violent towards Miss Samuels. A further CAFCASS Report was then ordered and the latest CAFCASS Report recommends that a psychological assessment in relation to Mr Thomas be carried out.

Issues to be addressed

(1) To complete a psychological assessment of Mr Thomas to include a psychological profile.

(2) To complete a risk assessment regarding contact with the children.

(3) What action Mr Thomas needs to take, if any, to minimise any risk to the children together with your recommendations as to what intervention could help change Mr Thomas's behaviour if change is needed?

(4) If change is required, please comment on Mr Thomas's capacity to make such a change and as to whether and if so to what extent he may require help and/or support in order to effect the necessary change.

(5) If he is capable of such a change, what would be the time scale required to effect sufficient change to enable the children to safely resume contact with Mr Thomas at the Contact Centre?

(6) Please set out your recommendations regarding the future of contact.

CASE 5

Mr and Mrs Vernon have two children, Wendy and Xenia. The parties separated in 1997 after several years of marriage. Mrs Vernon says she left Mr Vernon because of prolonged emotional and sexual abuse. She speaks of feeling undermined by Mr Vernon in dealing with the care of their children. Mr Vernon denies all allegations his former spouse made against him. Those allegations have never formed the basis of any fact finding hearing and indeed, there has never been any contested hearing between the parents in all the litigation there has been.

When the parties separated, Mrs Vernon petitioned for divorce. She also applied for a no contact order and a residence order in relation to both children in her favour. Mr Vernon contested both applications. There were a series of Section 7 reports completed by Social Services. Many of the reports were undertaken by different social workers.

Mr Zeeman had known both parents in Wales and maintained a friendship with Mrs Vernon and the children once she moved to London. He later moved in with the family.

Issues relating to Mr Zeeman, Mrs Vernon's new partner, began to surface when he moved into the family home. Over the years allegations have been made by Mr Vernon and also by Mrs Vernon's parents. Matters have also been raised with the junior school that each child has attended. A Case Conference was convened and both girls were registered on the Child Protection Register. The girls were both later de-registered. Wendy then left her mother's care and chose to live with her grandparents. She remains there to this day.

Matters finally came to a head owing to recent events. Xenia made a serious allegation against Mr Zeeman at school. Social Services and the police intervened. Mrs Vernon was called to the school where she was advised as to the content of what Xenia had said. As a result of that meeting, Mrs Vernon supported an absence of Mr Zeeman from the home so matters could be investigated by the police and Social Services.

Mr Zeeman was staying with friends. The family was in a period of limbo, not knowing what was happening and when matters would be resolved one way or the other.

Some months ago the Social Worker conducted an unannounced visit with the police to Mrs Vernon's home and found Mr Zeeman at the property. Xenia was removed under the terms of a police protection order and placed in her grandparents' care. Xenia has remained with her grandparents ever since and had supervised contact with her mother, initially once a week but increasing to twice a week. The Guardian has recommended that during periods of school holidays contact should be increased.

It is accepted by Mrs Vernon that contact should remain supervised, to offer her protection as well as Xenia

At the recent Hearing Mrs Vernon indicated to Social Services and the Guardian her intention to separate from Mr Zeeman. This decision was conveyed to Mr Zeeman within days. Arrangements were completed by Mrs Vernon and Mr Zeeman during the course of the following weeks leading to their physical separation. Mrs Vernon does not know where Mr Zeeman is living now.

Issues to be addressed

(1)   Mrs Vernon's appreciation of the need to place Xenia's needs above her own, historically and currently into the future.

(2)   Mrs Vernon's insight into the need for change.

(3)   Mrs Vernon's capacity to change and ability to sustain change and her resilience to any inappropriate influences others may try to exert.

(4)   Mrs Vernon's capacity to provide adequate care for Xenia on her own.

(5)   An assessment of any other guidance, support or therapy that Mrs Vernon may need to support and sustain change, indicating when these should begin and, if appropriate, after what period it is likely to become clear that sufficient and sustained change has occurred.

(6)   Any other matter as may arise during the course of your assessment that you feel able to comment upon given your field of expertise.

CASE 6

The parties met and had cohabited for several years when the mother changed the locks of the family home, excluding the father and, having packed up his possessions, in effect 'threw him out'. Angela is their only child. Since the separation the parties have not come to any terms in relation to contact. There was an unfortunate series of events some months ago when the father, endeavouring to cause contact, attempted to make telephone calls and leave voicemail messages. The police were involved and he was cautioned.

Issues to be addressed

(1)   What are Angela's express wishes, feelings and views about her father and the prospect of any form of contact with him, exploring the whole range of possible contact orders, to include both indirect and direct forms of contact?

(2)   In your opinion, are those feelings and views those of Angela herself? If they are not, please comment on the potential source of such feelings and views.

(3)   Has the conflict between her parents contributed to Angela's feelings towards her father and if so, to what extent?

(4)   Is it possible for contact to be re-established between Angela and her father and, if so, how should this be approached in order to ensure the best possible chance of a successful outcome?

(5)   Are you able to identify any therapeutic needs that Angela has which both can and should be addressed in her own best interests? If so, which organisations/agencies would be best placed to commence this work? If such therapeutic needs were addressed, would this assist in the process of re-establishing contact between Angela and her father and what are the likely timescales?

(6)   Are there any behaviour/attitudes/mind-sets held by either of the parents that are at present having a damaging impact upon Angela and, if so, are these capable of change and, if so, what steps/work can be recommended and undertaken with the parents to achieve this and what are the likely timescales?

(7)   Do you have any recommendations to make as to any additional expert evidence that may assist?

(8)   Please advise on the capacity of each parent to understand Angela's needs and welfare and how their behaviour can potentially impact upon this.

(9)   Dependent upon the outcome of your assessment, are there any steps you would recommend that either parent, or Angela, or indeed the family as a whole, should undertake including counselling and/or therapeutic work that may assist in re-establishing contact and the likely timescales for this?

APPENDIX 2

PSYCHOMETRIC TESTS AND QUESTIONNAIRES

QUESTIONNAIRES

The Adult Personality Scales (Revised) (EPQ-R)

The EPQ-R attempts to measure the major dimensions of personality as they have emerged from self-rating. The Adult EPQ-R is a 106 question rating scale specifically addressing introversion/extroversion and emotionality or stability/instability scale. In addition the EPQ-R addresses underlying disposition or personality traits which are present in various degrees in all persons.

The Beck Anxiety Inventory (BAI: Beck Epsom Brown and Steer 1998)

This self report questionnaire is a 21-item scale which measures the severity of anxiety in adults and adolescents. This Inventory was included to assess current emotional state and specifically to measure symptoms of anxiety which could be shared with those of depression such as those mentioned in the Beck Depression Inventory.

The Revised Beck Depression Inventory, 2nd edition (BDI-II) (BDI: Beck Rush Shaw and Emery, 1979)

This is the revised self report questionnaire which is a short form instrument designed to assess the severity of depression in adults and adolescents. This instrument specifically assesses the intensity of depression as well as detecting possible depression.

The Parenting Stress Index/Short Form (PSI/SF)

Measures stress in the parent-child system. It was designed to target families most in need of follow-up services, extent of parental stress and dysfunctional parent-child interaction. Areas of stressors assessed are:

(a) parent characteristics,

(b)   child characteristics, and

(c)   situation/demographic life stress.

As the Parenting Stress Index (PSI) has been shown to have strong psychometric properties at 120 items, the length of the PSI can be burdensome especially when more than one construct is being studied and other questionnaires must be administered. Therefore, use is made of the **Parent Stress Index/Short Form (PSI/SF)** developed by Abidin (1995). This questionnaire assists in the understanding of behaviours which the children may engage in that may make parental management of children more difficult, the levels of distress parents feel about their parenting role, usually in light of other personal stresses that relate to parenting, as well as the parental beliefs associated with their children not reinforcing them as a parent or meeting their expectations.

The Post Traumatic Stress Diagnostic Scale (PDS)

This psychometric assessment is a self-report instrument designed to aid in the diagnosis of post traumatic stress disorder based on the DSM IV criteria. This assessment questionnaire should give an indication of the severity of post traumatic stress disorder symptoms.

The Symptom Checklist 90-R (SCL-90-R)

In order to gain some understanding of the client's emotional health, the **SCL-90-R** provides a measure of mental health. This self report questionnaire highlights the presence of psychological distress and psychological symptom patterns. Each item represents a problem or complaint people sometimes have. The SCL-90-R generates mental health scores in a variety of areas including anxiety, depression, somatization, phobic anxiety, obsessive-compulsive, interpersonal sensitivity, hostility, paranoid ideation, and psychoticism, as well as three general mental health scales.

Trauma Symptom Inventory (TSI)

The TSI is a hundred-item self report questionnaire which highlights the presence of post traumatic stress and other psychological sequelae of traumatic events. It is intended for use in the evaluation of acute and chronic traumatic symptomatology, including but not limited to, the effects of rape, spouse abuse, physical assault, combat, major accidents, and natural disasters, as well as the lasting sequelae of childhood abuse and other early traumatic events. The various scales of the TSI assess a wide range of psychological impacts. These not only include symptoms typically associated with post traumatic stress disorder (PTSD) and acute stress disorder (ASD), but also those intra-and interpersonal difficulties often associated with more chronic psychological trauma. The TSI contains three validity scales.

The Asperger Syndrome Diagnostic Scale (ASDS)

The Asperger Syndrome Diagnostic Scale (ASDS) is a standardised test designed to aid in the identification of individuals aged 5 to 18 who manifest the characteristics of Asperger Syndrome (AS). The ASDS provides norm-referenced information that can assist in the diagnosis of AS.

Beck Youth Inventories of Emotional & Social Impairment (BYI) (Beck J, Beck A and Jolly J, 2001)

The BYI are five self-reporting measures that assess a child's experience of depression, anxiety, anger, disruptive behaviour and self-concept. This questionnaire is used to assist in the understanding of the child's or adolescent's current emotional functioning and to assess if he or she is experiencing any levels of emotional and social impairment.

The Beck Depression Inventory for Youth is designed to identify symptoms of depression in children. It includes items that reflect children's negative thoughts about themselves, their lives and their future; feelings of sadness; and physiological indications of depression.

The Beck Anxiety Inventory for Youth reflects children's fears, worry and physiological symptoms associated with anxiety. The Beck Anxiety reflects children's fears, worrying and physiological symptoms associated with anxiety.

Anger Inventory for Youth includes perceptions of mistreatment, negative thoughts about others, feelings of anger, and physiological arousal.

The Beck Disruptive Inventory for Youth reflects behaviour and attitudes associated with conduct disorder and oppositional defiant disorder are included in this inventory.

The Beck Self-Concept Inventory for Youth includes self-perceptions such as competence, potency, and positive self-worth.

The Trauma Symptom Check List for Children (TSCC) (Briere, J, 1996)

This questionnaire is a self-report measure of post traumatic distress and related psychological symptomatology. It is intended for use in the evaluation of children who have experienced traumatic events, including childhood physical and sexual abuse, victimisation by peers, major losses, the witnessing of violence done to others and natural disasters. This assessment consists of 54 items that yield two validity scales (under-response and hyper-response); six clinical scales (anxiety, depression, anger, post-traumatic stress, dissociation, and sexual concerns); and eight critical scales.

ABILITY AND PERFORMANCE TESTS

The Wechsler Pre-school and Primary Scale of Intelligence – revised WPPSI-RUK

The Wechsler pre-school and primary scale of intelligence revised is an individually administered clinical instrument for assessing the intelligence of children aged from 3½ to 7 years, 3 months. The WPPSI-R provides standardised measures of a variety of abilities thought to reflect difference aspects of intelligence. This assessment measures intelligence by probing the individual ability using various tasks.

The Wechsler Intelligence Scale for Children, 3rd edition UK (WISC-III UK)

The WISC-III UK is an individually administered clinical instrument for assessing the intellectual ability of children aged from 6 years through to 16 years 11 months. The WISC-III UK consists of several sub-tests, each measuring a different pattern of intelligence. The performance on these various measures is summarised in three composite scores, verbal, performance and full scale IQ which provides estimates of intellectual ability.

The Wechsler Adult Intelligence Scale – III (British Adaptation) (WAIS-III)

The (WAIS-III) is an individually administered clinical instrument for assessing the intellectual ability of an adult. The WAIS-III is used to assess verbal, performance and full scale IQ. It endeavours to measure intellectual potential and ability to function effectively in a relatively impersonal or unfamiliar situation which draws upon previous experience and problem-solving abilities. In general the WAIS-III assesses general intellectual ability and specifically provides an indication of **verbal abilities** such as comprehension, ability to use verbal skills, reasoning and problem-solving situations and a capacity to learn verbal material. The **performance scale** specifically focuses on the individual's perceptual organisation, including non-verbal reasoning skills, ability to employ visual images in thinking and the ability to process visual material. During the assessment the individual is not required to read or write in order to complete this assessment. In order to assess cognitive and intellectual functioning, the individual needs to draw from the cognitive capacity, ability to concentrate on tasks, neurological status and previous exposure to previous educational and social experiences.

The Wechsler Memory Scale, 3rd edition (UK Adaptation) (WMS-III UK)

This technique is an individually administered battery of learning, memory and working memory measures. Dysfunction of memory and attention is commonly reported in individuals diagnosed with a wide range of neurological, psychiatric, and developmental disorders. The WMS-III UK provides a detailed assessment of clinically relevant aspects of memory functioning, allowing the clinician to estimate the level and pattern of memory functioning.

PROJECTIVE TECHNIQUES

Projective techniques such as the Roberts Apperception Test for Children (RATC) and the Thematic Apperception Test (TAT) are methods of revealing to the trained interpreter some of the dominant drives, emotions, sentiments, complexes and conflicts of a personality. Special value resides in the power to expose the underlying inhibited tendencies of the subject or patient who is not willing to admit to or cannot admit to them because he is unconscious of them.

The Thematic Apperception Test (TAT: Murray 1943)

This assessment takes the form of a projective technique. It is a method of revealing dominant drives, emotions, sentiments and conflicts of a personality. The specific value of the projective test results in an ability to expose the underlying inhibited tendencies of a person to which they are not willing to admit or cannot admit being unconscious of them.

Family Relationships Test (Children's version) (Bene-Antony – Revised Edition, 1985)

The Family Relations Test attempts to help children to express emotional attitudes of which they are aware, but which they might find difficult to verbalise. The test responses are expected to reflect the conscious feelings of the child towards his family, including his more or less private ones. His 'deeper' emotions can only be inferred from the test results. The child's test feelings are accepted at face value and give them a behavioural connotation. The child's perception might have more to do with wishes and projections than with external reality, but, it is his 'psychic reality' that is concerned, and it is this segment of reality that is explored by the test. The test attempts to measure feelings which cannot be operationally defined, and for which there are no adequate criteria available. There is probably a continuum of freedom of expression between the repressed feelings, the suppressed feelings maintained privately, the feelings expressed to familiar persons and the feelings expressed to strangers. The test responses are expected to reflect conscious feelings of the child towards his family, including his more or less private ones. His 'deeper' emotions can only be inferred from the test results.

The Roberts Apperception Test (RAT)

These assessments take the form of **projective techniques,** which are methods of revealing dominant drives, emotions, sentiments and conflicts of a personality. The specific value of these techniques resides in an ability to expose underlying inhibited tendencies of a child which it may not be willing to admit or be unable to admit because it is unconscious of them.

INDEX

References are to paragraph numbers.